Your Rights at Work

". . . Covers every topic of practical importance on the legal rights of employees. . . . Full of excellent questions and issues for employees as well as employers."

DAVID W. EWING
former Managing Editor, *Harvard Business Review*

"Authoritative, essential, thorough, and unique. It's a book that fills an important need. Really, really good and helpful."

MELVIN A. BELLI

". . . A valuable work on an important subject."

RAY MARSHALL
former Secretary of Labor

". . . An excellent guide for employees and prospective employees in an area which is changing fast. It will also be of great interest to people in personnel, to supervisors and to all who are interested in people in the workplace."

D. QUINN MILLS
Albert J. Weatherhead Professor of Business Administration
Harvard Business School

Your Rights at Work

DARIEN A. McWHIRTER

WILEY

John Wiley & Sons
New York • Chichester • Brisbane • Toronto • Singapore

Library of Congress Cataloging in Publication Data
McWhirter, Darien.
    Your rights at work / by Darien McWhirter.
        p.   cm.
    Bibliography: p.
    ISBN 0-471-50029-1.   ISBN 0-471-50028-3 (pbk.)
        1. Labor laws and legislation—United States—Popular works.
    2. Employee rights—United States—Popular works. I. Title.
    KF3319.6.M39 1989
    344.73'01—dc19
    [347.3041]   88-25232
                                                                    CIP

Printed in the United States of America

10 9 8 7 6 5 4 3

To
Professor Page Keeton

Preface

This book is about rights, specifically the rights people have at work. A century ago working people had no rights. Today they have many rights. Worker's compensation and unemployment compensation provide funds for injured or out-of-work people. State and federal civil rights acts protect against race, sex, and other types of discrimination. State and federal constitutions protect the free-speech and due-process rights of many employees.

At the same time there are new threats to the rights of working people. More and more employers want to invade the bodies and minds of their workers with drug and polygraph tests. Some employers intentionally injure their employees, something worker's compensation was not designed to deal with. Some employers think it is all right to ask employees to violate the law and to fire them when they refuse, or to fire employees simply because they have to serve on juries. The legal system is only now coming to grips with these problems.

Also, the work force has changed a great deal during the twentieth century. A work force that was once mainly blue collar producing products is now mainly white collar providing services. A work force that was once protected by union contracts is no longer protected as unions represent a smaller percentage of the work force each year. More and more women have joined the work force. The legal system has not kept up with these changes.

At the same time employers and supervisors hear about all the lawsuits by employees and feel no one cares that they have to meet a budget and provide products and services at competitive prices.

This book is an attempt to provide a general overview of employment law. Although most people do not know it, everyone who works has an employment contract. In Part One we will discuss this contract and how it is enforced.

Every year many people are fired, often through no fault of their own. In Part

Two we will discuss when people have the right to collect unemployment compensation and when they have the right to sue their employer because they have been fired for the "wrong reason."

During the last four decades state and federal civil rights laws have provided protection against discrimination based on race, sex, religion, color, national origin, age, handicapped condition, and other traits depending on the state. We will discuss civil rights in Part Three.

Three of our most fundamental rights are the right to speak freely, the right to due process, and the right to privacy. The way in which state and federal laws protect these rights is discussed in Part Four.

Part Five is concerned with laws that provide for a minimum wage and protect the rights of union members.

Part Six deals with rights all workers have after being injured at work, including the right to file for worker's compensation and the right, in some cases, to sue the boss.

Although this book gives an overview of all these subjects, there is no substitute for the advice of an attorney when the time comes. I hope that after reading this book, employers, supervisors, and employees will have a better idea of when "the time has come" to consult an attorney.

I have worked very hard to be as accurate as possible in describing statutes and court decisions. Nevertheless, there is always the possibility of error. There is also the possibility that a judge will not agree with my interpretation of a statute or court decision. No one should rely on a specific statement about the law contained in this book without talking to an attorney.

A book like this cannot be written without consulting many other books and articles. I would like to thank all those authors for their guidance. I would especially like to thank Henry Perritt for his thoughtful writing.

I would also like to thank all the judges who labored long to write the decisions that form the basis of this book. Although I may not always agree with their conclusions about what the law is, or should be, I have the greatest respect for their integrity and sincerity.

Bernice Borak, Doreen Cohen, Carol F. Justus, and Ed Shaw read earlier versions of this book and made invaluable comments. Nils and Kathleen Pearson gave me many ideas about the way this kind of book should be written. For all their suggestions I thank them. I also want to thank my mother, Marty McWhirter, for providing me with invaluable insights into how the Social Security system really works.

Rick Balkin became my agent at a time when I needed his help and guidance. I thank him for all his efforts. I also thank my editor, John Mahaney, for helping me cut the manuscript down to a readable length.

I also thank the Austin Writer's League. Every writer in Austin is better off because of the League and its many workshops.

I also thank all the school board members, school administrators, and teachers in Texas, and my former colleagues at the Texas Association of School Boards who taught me so much about the real world of employment law.

I want to thank especially George Chandler, who supervised my "legal internship" and taught me so much about the real world of the law.

Finally I must thank all the teachers I have had throughout my life, and all the students I have taught over the years. Many areas are discussed in this book because students posed thoughtful questions during class discussions.

I have dedicated this book to Professor Page Keeton in gratitude for his dedication to the teaching of the law.

DARIEN A. McWHIRTER

Austin, Texas
November 1988

Contents

employer, and the employee does not learn of its existence until after his hiring."

The company offered her a total of $3,000 for her invention, but the jury felt a reasonable royalty would be $520,313.

Unique employees like Olivia Newton-John and the San Diego Chicken have to worry about being ordered not to work for anyone else. The rest of us do not.

She threw a writing tablet at the boss and told him to "shove it up his ass." The judge said this was not misconduct.

Part Four   Constitutional Rights   123

10   The Right of Free Speech   125

The teacher said, "We'll either have to discipline the superintendent or put him back in one of those long midnight trains to Georgia."

11   The Right to Due Process   138

The justices said he was "entitled to oral or written notice of the charges against him, an explanation of the employer's evidence, and an opportunity to present his side of the story" before being dismissed.

12   The Right to Privacy   144

The judge said there must be some degree of individual suspicion "before the dignity and privacy of a teacher may be compromised by forcing him or her to undergo a urine test."

Part Five   Rights under Wage, Hour, and Labor Laws   157

13   Wages and Hours   159

She was a dancer at the Lonely Lady Club. During her eight-hour shift she was required to dance three times for about fifteen minutes each time. She was also expected to solicit private dances for which she received tips, her major source of income. The judge said she was an employee, not an independent contractor, and was protected by the wage-and-hour laws.

14 Labor Unions   170

The judge said, "There cannot be peaceful picketing, any more than there can be chaste vulgarity, peaceful mobbing, or lawful lynching."

Part Six   Rights after Injury   183

15 Accidental Injury and Worker's Compensation   185

The judge ruled that "the very work which the deceased was doing for his employer exposed him to a greater hazard from heat stroke than the general public was exposed to for the simple reason that the general public were not pushing wheelbarrow loads of sand in the hot sun on that day."

Your Rights at Work

Introduction

There are three players in the employment game. First, there are employers. By employer we mean the owner, the corporation, the entity that ultimately hires, fires, and gets sued. Second are the employees. In between are supervisors who are both bosses and employees depending on the circumstances. Suggestions will be made here to all three groups. By reading this book, not only will you learn about employment law and receive suggestions on what to do in particular situations, but you will also see what advice the other two groups are receiving.

This is not a do-it-yourself book. Although advice will be given, there is simply no substitute for the advice of an attorney who can apply the particular facts of your case to the law as it exists when your problem comes up.

This book is concerned with the legal rights of employees. Lawsuits come about because employees' legal rights are violated. These rights come from many different sources. The most fundamental source is the decision a judge makes when resolving disputes between workers and employers. When two people have a dispute and the statutes do not tell a judge how to resolve it, the judge must use his or her belief in what is fair to resolve the dispute. We call these decisions the **common law.** During the last two decades many judges have changed their minds about what is fair, so the law of employer and employee has changed. In most cases, employees have more legal rights as a result.

Employees also have rights because Congress or a state legislature has passed a statute giving them rights. The major statutes we will discuss are concerned with unemployment compensation, civil rights, wages and hours, labor unions, worker's compensation, and Social Security.

The most important source of rights for everyone is the U.S. Constitution and the constitutions of the various states. The main constitutional rights that will

1

concern us are the right to speak freely, the right to a hearing, and the right to privacy.

PRO-BOSS VERSUS FAIR STATES

Throughout this book we will talk about pro-boss states and fair states. A century ago the law in every state was biased in favor of the boss (by boss we mean employers and supervisors). The judges did not think anything employers did was unfair. There were no statutes protecting civil rights or providing unemployment or worker's compensation; constitutional provisions were not interpreted in a way that protected workers. Today there are only a dozen pro-boss states left. The pro-boss northern states are Indiana, Ohio, Pennsylvania, New York, Delaware, and Rhode Island. The pro-boss southern states are Louisiana, Mississippi, Alabama, Georgia, Florida, and North Carolina. By pro-boss we do not mean that employers and supervisors always win, but that the law is biased in their favor. The other states are fair states. Indiana, Ohio, Pennsylvania, Rhode Island, North Carolina, and Florida are all in the process of becoming fair states.

GOVERNMENT AGENCIES

Often we will tell you that a government agency deals with a particular area of the law. If it is a state agency, you may have to call your state senator's office for aid in figuring out which state agency will help you. If it is a federal agency, we will tell you the name of the agency and you can take it from there.

THE AMERICAN LEGAL SYSTEM

America has a federal system. That means each of the fifty states has its own constitution, its own statutes, and its own judicial system. The federal government also has its own constitution, statutes, and judicial system.

Most states have a judicial system with three levels. The first level is the district court. The district court holds the trial, determines the facts of the case, and applies the law to the facts in order to reach a decision.

The next level is the appeals court. There is no trial at the appeals court. The attorneys for both sides present arguments to a panel of judges, usually three, who then decide the case. In most of the cases discussed in this book, one side has appealed the district judge's interpretation of the law. The appeals court will decide what it thinks the law is and rule accordingly. At the federal level the appeals courts are called circuit courts.

Next comes the supreme court. The supreme court of each state has the final say concerning what the common law of the state is. It also has the final word on what the state constitution and statutes mean. The U.S. Supreme Court has the final word on what the U.S. Constitution and federal statutes mean.

HISTORICAL PERSPECTIVE

At various points in this book we will try to put the law in historical perspective. The law is constantly changing. It is usually easier to understand where it is now if we look at where it has been in the past and where it might be going in the future.

REFERENCES

Throughout this book we will provide you with references so that you can go to a library and read the statute or court decision for yourself. If we are referring to a statute, you will find the number of the statute in parentheses. For example (Ga. 7-14-32) means Title 7, Chapter 14, Section 32 of the Georgia statutes. If we are talking about a court decision, you will find a short form of the name of the case in italics and in parentheses. For example, (*Smith*) refers to the Smith case. If you turn to Smith in the References at the back of the book, you might find 428 S.W.2d 98 (Tex. App. 1983). The first number is a volume number in a set of court decisions, in this case the Southwestern Reporter Second Series. The second number, 98, is the page number. In the parentheses you will find the state the decision is from and the date the decision was made. If the decision was made by the state supreme court, only the state abbreviation appears (Tex. 1983). If the decision was made by an appeals court, App. will appear in the parentheses. Federal district court decisions are reported in the Federal Supplement, F. Supp., and the parentheses tells you the state the district court is in and the date of the decision (D.C. Okla. 1985). Federal appeals court decisions are reported in the Federal Reporter Second Series, and the parentheses tells you the number of the circuit court that handed down the decision and the date (5th Cir. 1981). If the decision is by the U.S. Supreme Court, only a date appears in the parentheses (1984).

TABLES

Throughout this book you will find tables that allow you to see how your state compares with other states. No one should make a final decision based on the information contained in the tables. The law is always changing. Consult an attorney familiar with the laws of your state about your particular situation.

Part One
Contract Rights

1

We All Have a Contract

Every employee has an employment contract. Most do not have a written or even an oral contract. The contract is "implied" from words and actions. For example, if an employer in the business of digging ditches says to a worker, "Hey, want a job?" and the worker responds, "Yeah," they have an employment contract. Implied in that brief conversation is that the employer will pay a reasonable wage, the location of the work is the town they are standing in, and the service to be performed is manual labor.

The difficult question is: How long is this contract supposed to last? Centuries ago the English judges assumed that the parties to an employment contract intended the contract to last one year. American judges do not make that assumption. They assume the parties intended the contract to be **at-will**, meaning the employee works "at the will" of the employer. The employer can fire the employee at any time for no reason. The employee can quit at any time for no reason.

The law works like your home computer. In many situations if you do not tell the computer something specific, the computer program "defaults" to the command most people want. The law does the same thing; it defaults to what the judges think most people intend when they enter into an employment contract. There are four basic terms that every employment contract has: wages, place of performance, work to be performed, and amount of time the contract is to last. The "defaults" for employment contracts are: the wages are reasonable wages; the location of the job is the place where the employee is; the work to be performed is anything the employee is capable of doing; and the length of time is at-will (*Mallory*).

In some states if the salary is stated as "so much per year," the judges assume that means the employer intended to hire the employee for a whole year. In a recent Tennessee case the employer quoted a salary as so much per year and the court enforced a one-year contract (*Ball*). In a recent Illinois case the letter confirming the job said "guaranteed salary for twelve months of $750 per week ($39K per annum)." The judges ruled this implied that the employer intended to hire the employee for one year (*Berutti*). Some states have statutes dealing with this. For example, a Georgia statute says that stating wages as so much per a period of time creates the presumption that the employee has been hired for that period of time (Ga. 34-7-1).

The judges have no trouble assuming the two parties intended that reasonable wages would be paid or that the employee would do whatever he or she was capable of doing. They have a lot of trouble assuming the parties intended the contract to last for any specific length of time. The time element can be one of three: at-will, for a definite term, or for an indefinite term.

What does it mean to have a contract for an indefinite term? In 1896 the Minnesota Supreme Court enforced a contract that said the employee had a job as long as he did his work efficiently and owned 50 shares of company stock. The court said the employee could not be fired as long as he met those conditions (*McMullan*).

In 1986 the Rhode Island Supreme Court refused to enforce a similar contract. The employee was hired to manage a new ski shop. The contract said he had a job as long as the ski shop was profitable. The ski shop was very profitable but the Rhode Island Supreme Court let the employer fire this employee because the judges felt this was just an at-will employment contract (*Bader*).

In fair states, written contracts for an indefinite term will be enforced. The judges in some pro-boss states think there is no such thing as a contract for an indefinite term; if contracts do not run for a specific period of time, then they are interpreted to be at-will. This may be changing. It appears the highest court in New York, a pro-boss state, is prepared to enforce written contracts for an indefinite term (*Weiner*). Whether this will cause judges in the other pro-boss states to reevaluate their position on this remains to be seen.

Even in fair states at-will is what the legal system defaults to. If the judge cannot figure out how long the employment contract is supposed to last, it is at-will. The vast majority of employees in America are at-will employees.

WRITTEN TERM CONTRACTS

Judges in all states will enforce an employment contract that runs for a definite length of time if it is in writing. An employee with a written term contract has a big advantage over an at-will employee. The employer cannot fire the employee during the term of the contract except as spelled out in the contract. Most contracts say that the employee can be fired only for "good cause." Even if the contract does not specifically say this, most judges assume that this is implied in any written employment contract. Union contracts are really nothing more than written term contracts that cover a large number of employees for a specific period of time.

There is a special problem that comes up with written contracts. Often the two parties have negotiated for a long period of time before the final contract is signed. It is hard to tell if the final written contract is intended to supersede all the prior discussions or if those discussions are intended to be part of the final agreement. That is why many people put a clause in the final written contract that specifically says it supersedes everything else.

What if the contract does not specifically say this? Then it is up to the judge to decide if the parties intended the final written contract to supersede the letters and conversations that came before it. Judges in pro-boss states tend to decide that the parties intended the final contract to be the entire agreement (*Pranzo*). In fair states the judges are more likely to find that the two parties did not intend the last written contract to be the whole agreement.

The case of Professor Martin Lewis, M.D., illustrates this problem (*Lewis*). Dean Clarence Peiss tried over several months to recruit Lewis to teach at Loyola University in Chicago. On September 20, 1979, the dean sent a long letter to Lewis with numbered paragraphs dealing with things like salary and tenure. In this letter the dean promised to submit Lewis for tenure at the first opportunity. Negotiations continued and on February 18, 1980, the dean sent another long letter to Lewis promising to submit Lewis for tenure in September 1981. Lewis accepted and on May 14, 1980, he received an appointment letter that stated his salary and appointed him professor of pathology from July 1980 through June 1981.

The dean did not submit Lewis for tenure in September 1981 as he had promised. Lewis did not receive tenure and was fired after three years. The university and the dean argued that the letters the dean sent in September 1979 and February 1980 should not be considered part of the contract. They argued that the contract consisted only of the one-page appointment letter. The court found that the appointment letter was not "expressive of the complete agreement and understanding of the parties" and ruled that the letters from the dean were part of the contract.

Employees should avoid signing contracts that say the written document contains the entire agreement when in fact it does not. An employee in the position Lewis was in should insist that the president of the university sign a contract that really contains the entire agreement, including all the promises the dean has made. Employers should make sure supervisors are not making promises the employer does not want to keep. Also, if the employer intends the final written contract to supersede all prior negotiations and promises, then the contract should say so.

How long can a written employment contract last? In California employment contracts cannot run for more than seven years (Calif. Labor Code sec. 2855), in Louisiana they are limited to five years (Art. 167, 2746 La. Civ. Code), and in North and South Dakota they are limited to two years (N.D. 34-01-02; S.D. 60-2-6). In other states there is no limit set by statute but the judges might not enforce an employment contract if it ran for too long a time. Seven years is probably safe because under old English law employment contracts were limited to seven years.

Every state has special statutes and legal doctrines that apply to written term employment contracts. For example, in Arkansas if a written employment contract is notarized and filed in the county records, it acts as a lien on the employer's property until the wages called for in the contract are paid (Ark. 51-501 to 510). Because every state is different both employers and employees should consult an attorney before signing a written employment contract.

ORAL TERM CONTRACTS

Oral contracts for a specified term are just as enforceable as written contracts if they do not violate the **Statute of Frauds.** The first Statute of Frauds was enacted in England in 1677. Today every state has its own version. This statute requires certain agreements to be in writing before the judges will enforce them. Technically, these statutes usually require that there be *something written and signed* by the party being sued. The provision that causes the most trouble in an employment setting is the requirement that an oral contract must be capable of being performed completely within one year from the day the agreement is made or it is not enforceable. An oral agreement to employ someone for more than one year would not be enforced in most courts because of the Statute of Frauds.

This provision has caused a lot of hardship to employees. Generally, judges in pro-boss states strictly enforce the Statute of Frauds (*Gatins*). Judges in fair states will find a way around the Statute of Frauds if enforcement of the statute would cause too great a hardship to the employee. For example, in one case an employee was hired in Los Angeles for a one-year job in Hawaii. He quit his California job and moved his family to Hawaii only to be fired two and half months later. Technically, the one-year contract violated the Statute of Frauds because it ran more than one year from the time the agreement was made. (An agreement made on December 30, 1989, to employ someone through December 31, 1990, technically violates the Statute of Frauds because it cannot be completed within one year of its making.) In this case, the Supreme Court of Hawaii enforced the oral contract, saying "injustice can only be avoided by the enforcement of the contract" (*McIntosh*).

Employers who do not intend to give employees oral contracts should instruct their supervisors accordingly. Employees should think twice before relying on an oral contract, particularly if it will run for more than a year from the time of the agreement.

Some people think an oral promise will not be enforced by a court unless there is some independent witness to the conversation. That is not true. It is up to the jury to listen to the testimony and decide who is telling the truth. If it is a case of the employer's word against the employee's word, then it is up to the jury to decide who is telling the truth (*Bernoudy*).

ORAL CONTRACTS FOR AN INDEFINITE TERM

Oral employment contracts that run for an indefinite term run into two problems. The first is the Statute of Frauds. The second is the reluctance of some judges to enforce employment contracts for an indefinite term.

In fair states the judges will not allow the Statute of Frauds to interfere with the enforcement of an oral employment contract for an indefinite period of time if there is any way the contract could end within one year of its making. In one Idaho case the court enforced a promise to employ the worker as long as the factory was in operation. The judge reasoned that the factory could close within one year so there was no Statute of Frauds problem (*Whitlock*). In an Oregon case the employer promised the employee a job for as long as there was "production to run." The court said the production could run out within one year and enforced the promise (*Seibel*).

What if the employer makes an oral promise that the employee will not be fired except for good cause or that the employee has a lifetime job? In many fair states the courts will enforce this promise despite the Statute of Frauds because the employee might die or give the employer good cause to fire him or her within one year. The question is not, did the contract end within one year? The question is, is there any way the contract could have ended within one year? This can lead to some strange results. In one case the court would not enforce an oral promise to employ the worker until retirement because "until retirement" is a definite period of time, is more than one year, and violates the Statute of Frauds. The court said it would have enforced an oral promise to employ the worker for life because he could have died within one year (*Hodge #1*).

That brings up the second problem, the reluctance of some courts to enforce employment contracts for an indefinite term. Many fair states will enforce oral employment contracts that run for an indefinite term. The only question is, did the employer really agree to employ this employee for an indefinite period of time (*Pugh, Shebar*)?

Judges in the pro-boss states (and some fair states) will enforce an oral promise to employ someone for an indefinite term only if the employee can prove not only that the promise was made but also that the employee gave up something special ("special consideration") in exchange for the promise. Promises of permanent employment, promises of lifetime employment, and promises to fire only for good cause are all promises to employ someone for an indefinite term.

Mr. Romack was an Indiana State Police Captain with 25 years' experience. When Public Service Company of Indiana offered him a job, he told them he had a permanent job with the state police and he would not consider working for them without a similar promise of permanent employment. When the company gave him an oral promise of permanent employment, Romack quit his job and moved his family.

He was fired three years later. The district judge ruled against Romack and the Indiana Appeals Court agreed with the district judge. Two appeals court judges did not feel that giving up a permanent government job with the state police was enough "special consideration" to justify enforcing this oral promise of permanent employment.

There were three appeals court judges, and one, Judge Conover, dissented. He argued that leaving a permanent job with the state police was enough "special consideration." He cited an Iowa case (Iowa is a fair state) where a tenured college professor gave up tenure at one university because he was orally promised tenure at another university. The Iowa Supreme Court held that giving up a permanent job with one employer is enough "special consideration" to allow enforcement of an oral promise of permanent employment with another employer (Collins #1). Judge Conover felt the same rule should apply in Indiana. The Indiana Supreme Court agreed with Judge Conover and ruled that Romack had provided enough "special consideration" (Romack).

The Alabama Supreme Court (another pro-boss court) has recently ruled that moving from one place to another or quitting a job is enough "special consideration" to allow enforcement of these oral promises (Murphree, Scott).

Why do some states require "special consideration" before they will enforce an oral contract for an indefinite term? Judge Cirillo of Pennsylvania recently answered that question (Green #1). He said there are two reasons why Pennsylvania judges will continue to require "special consideration" before they will enforce oral promises to employ people indefinitely. First, they are afraid that the employer did not mean permanent or lifetime even though that is what the employer said. They are afraid it might have been just a "casual aside." The other reason is that Pennsylvania judges do not trust juries, who are usually made up of employees, to make fair decisions in these cases. Because of these two problems Pennsylvania judges will continue to require some kind of "special consideration."

The Kentucky Supreme Court has come up with a compromise position. That court recognizes that the word "permanent" can have two meanings. On the one hand it often means that the work is not temporary. The employer is saying that there is work for the foreseeable future, but not promising this particular employee a job for the foreseeable future. Because this is what most employers mean when they use the word "permanent," Kentucky courts will not rule that more was intended without "special consideration" or other evidence that the parties meant that this particular employee would have a permanent job. On the other hand, promises to fire an employee only for good cause or to hire an employee for life are not capable of two interpretations. If the employer really made that promise, then Kentucky courts will enforce it without requiring "special consideration" (Synthetic Rubber).

Because of the possible confusion over the meaning of the word "permanent," everyone would be better off if employers and supervisors eliminated it from their vocabularies. If they mean "a regular job," they should say so.

IMPLIED EMPLOYMENT CONTRACTS

We have seen that most employees have an implied employment contract. The employee has simply accepted the job. Generally, if no specific term has been agreed to, the judges assume the parties intended to have an at-will employment contract. This is not always true, however. In fair states the judge will look at the negotiations of the two parties, the nature of the employment, and all the circumstances of the job before deciding whether or not the implied employment contract is at-will (*Allegri*).

Two California Appeals Court cases frightened a lot of employers. These judges ruled that if an employee has worked for the same employer for many years, that alone implies that the employee has something more than an at-will employment contract (*Cleary, Walker*). No other state has gone along with these California decisions. While most fair states are willing to look at all the circumstances to see if something more than at-will has been implied, it takes more than just a great many years on the job to find something other than at-will employment.

Judges in both fair and pro-boss states will not find that lifetime or fire-only-for-good-cause employment has been implied unless enough of the right kind of "very special consideration" exists. However, if the employee has given up something special, the judges figure something more than at-will employment must have been intended, even though the parties did not discuss it.

This is illustrated by a recent Indiana case (*Speckman*). David Speckman was the director of the Brookside Community Center for the city of Indianapolis. He was fired in December 1979. When he threatened to sue over this firing, the city rehired him in March 1981. Speckman was fired again in February 1982. This time he did sue. The court held that implied in his March rehiring was the promise that the city would fire him in the future only for good cause. Giving up his right to sue over the December firing was enough "very special consideration" to support a finding that he had an implied promise from the city to fire him only for good cause in the future.

Remember this is a problem only because there is no written contract. Even pro-boss judges will enforce an employment contract if it is in writing and for a definite term. For example, an Ohio Appeals Court enforced a written employment contract that promised to employ the worker until he was 65, was unable to work, or failed to perform his duties. The court said this was a written contract for a specified term which ended on the employee's 65th birthday (*Boundy*).

To summarize: Both fair and pro-boss states will enforce written employment contracts for definite terms. Judges in most fair states will enforce written contracts for indefinite terms. Most pro-boss states will not (finding them to be at-will contracts).

Both fair and pro-boss states will enforce oral employment contracts for less than one year. Both will generally not enforce oral employment contracts for more than one year because of the Statute of Frauds. Judges in fair states may ignore the Statute of Frauds if they feel justice and equity require them to.

Some fair states and all pro-boss states require "special consideration" before they will enforce oral promises to hire people for an indefinite period of time. More and more fair states are no longer requiring "special consideration" in these cases.

Finally, given the right circumstances, both fair and pro-boss states may find an implied promise to fire someone only for good cause. Judges will not find these kinds of implied contracts without some "very special consideration" (see Table 1–1).

In the past employers did not worry too much about the oral or implied promises their supervisors made. Employers should start worrying. More and more employees are winning these lawsuits and more and more states are changing long-standing legal doctrines that used to protect lazy employers with careless supervisors. Most employers would find it to their advantage to give their employees some kind of written contract. The contract could be for a specific term, or it could specify that the employee is hired at-will. Without a written contract an employer may well find that employees have been given oral or implied contracts that run indefinitely.

A PROMISE TO GIVE A CONTRACT

What if the employee does not actually have a contract because the employer promised to give him one and did not? There is a general rule in American law that promises to enter into a contract in the future will not be enforced. However, judges in the fair states will enforce a promise to enter into an employment contract if it would cause too great a hardship to the employee not to do so.

In a recent New Mexico case Marie Eavenson was offered a job. She quit her existing job, but when she showed up for work the new employer refused to hire her as promised. The New Mexico Supreme Court enforced the promise to hire her (*Eavenson*).

In an Arizona case, Mr. Lindsey was hired as the basketball coach at the University of Arizona. He was given a one-year written contract but he was

TABLE 1–1. Enforcement of Employment Contracts

	Fair States	Pro-Boss States
Written contract, definite term	Contract enforced	Contract enforced
Written contract, indefinite term	Contract enforced	Some enforce, some consider to be at-will
Oral contract, definite term, less than one year	Contract enforced	Contract enforced
Oral contract, definite term, over a year	Not enforced unless fairness requires it	Not enforced
Oral contract, indefinite term	Some enforce; some require "special consideration"	Require "special consideration"
Implied contract, indefinite term	Require "very special consideration"	Require "very special consideration"

orally promised that the contract would be renewed for at least three more years. The Arizona Appeals Court enforced this promise and affirmed the jury's award of $215,000 in damages (*Lindsey*).

What if the employee came to work because the employer promised to sign a written employment contract but the employer never got around to it and eventually fired the employee instead? Judges in the fair states will enforce an oral promise to give a written employment contract if they are reasonably certain what that written contract would have contained (*Alaska Airlines, Lovely*).

It is much harder for an employee to win a case involving a promise to give an employment contract in a pro-boss state. In every state it is always a good idea for an employee to get a written employment contract for a definite period of time *before* quitting their old job.

THE PROBLEM OF AUTHORITY

When employees want to enforce a contract against a corporation they come up against a fundamental question: Did the person making the contract for the corporation have the authority to do that? Courts will enforce a contract against a corporation if the person making the contract had actual or apparent authority to make the contract. The chairman of the board, acting pursuant to a vote of the board of directors, has the most actual authority. Generally, the president of the corporation also has actual authority to sign a contract and bind the corporation.

The idea of "apparent" authority was developed to keep corporations from having someone who seemed to have authority sign contracts that the corporation could get out of later. Judges will generally hold a corporation to promises made by people with apparent authority. Someone has apparent authority if a reasonable person under the circumstances would think that person had authority to bind the corporation.

Sheila Rancourt worked at a hospital in Waterville, Maine, for 16 years. She says that in March 1984 her supervisor, Dr. Littman, told her that she would "never have to worry about losing her job." She was fired three months later. The Supreme Court of Maine held that Dr. Littman did not have actual or apparent authority to bind the hospital to a lifetime employment contract (*Rancourt*). Other courts would not have agreed. If employers do not intend for supervisors to have this kind of authority, they should make that clear to the employees.

2
Employee Handbooks Are Contracts in Most States

During the 1980s a great battle was waged in the state courts of America over whether the promises made in employee handbooks are enforceable in court.

In the 1920s and 1930s employee handbooks appeared which spelled out the retirement, sick-leave, and fringe-benefit plan of the company. Judges found these to be promises of compensation and enforced them. There was no change in the at-will status of the employees. They could still be fired at any time for no reason. All these handbooks did was to spell out what the benefits would be as long as the employee remained with the company. Today, these retirement and benefit plans are enforced by a federal statute, ERISA, which will be discussed in Chapter 17.

In the 1960s and 1970s employee handbooks began to appear that either promised employees they would be fired only for "good cause" or set out a particular discipline procedure that the employer promised to follow.

The judges in several pro-boss states had no trouble dismissing these handbooks as unenforceable. Because the two sides had not signed the handbook before beginning the employment relationship, pro-boss judges in Indiana and Delaware ruled that employee handbooks were not contracts and therefore were not enforceable in court.

In Indiana, the S.S. Kresge Co. promised in their handbook that employees would receive three warnings before being discharged. When Ms. Shaw was fired without the three warnings, she sued. An Indiana Appeals Court, in 1975, held that Kresge did not have to live up to the promises made in the handbook (*Shaw #1*).

In Delaware the Kent General Hospital passed out a handbook that said employees would be fired only if they committed a Category One offense and listed the Category One offenses. When Mr. Heideck was fired for an offense not listed in Category One, he sued. The Delaware Supreme Court, in 1982, ruled in favor of the hospital (*Heideck*).

One New York case has caused some confusion because everyone knows the Highest Court in New York is the most pro-boss court in the country (New York calls its District Court the Supreme Court so we all have to talk about the Highest Court instead of the Supreme Court). In 1982, in the *Weiner* case, the New York High Court enforced an employee handbook. In doing so New York seemed to be breaking ranks with other pro-boss states like Indiana and Delaware. In a 1987 case the New York High Court cleared up the confusion (*Sabetay*). The court explained in *Sabetay* that it enforced the employee handbook in *Weiner* because the employer gave the handbook to Weiner before Weiner accepted the job in order to induce him to leave his old job. In other words, as far as the High Court of New York was concerned, the handbook was just a long, written employment contract between the employer and the employee. What the New York High Court is not willing to do is enforce a handbook if the handbook is given out after the employee comes to work.

Judges in most fair states are willing to enforce employee handbooks even though they are given to the employees after they start work.

In 1980 the Supreme Court of Michigan held that when an employer distributes an employee handbook that spells out the reasons employees can be discharged, the employer has given up the right to fire employees for other reasons (or no reason). The court said this was so, even though the handbook is "signed by neither party," "can be unilaterally amended by the employer," and "the employee does not learn of its existence until after his hiring." In other words, the Michigan Supreme Court did not care that the usual contract procedures had not been followed. It found this to be a contract. When the handbook was distributed, because the employees were at-will, they could have quit. Instead, they continued to work. The employer had made an offer that the employees accepted by not quitting (*Toussaint*).

In 1983 the Supreme Court of Minnesota agreed. The court made the employer follow the disciplinary procedure contained in the handbook (*Pine River*).

Some courts appear reluctant to enforce these handbook provisions because they do not understand why employers would write such things in a handbook. There is a concept in the law that judges should not hold insane or retarded people to their promises. Some judges seem to think that any employer who would give out handbooks promising to follow certain discipline procedures, or to fire employees only for good cause, must be either insane or retarded. Several recent cases illustrate the reasons employers give out employee handbooks.

In one case Canadian Pacific Airlines was trying to keep unions out at the time it issued the handbook. The Supreme Court of Hawaii found this to be a "sane" reason for giving out a handbook and enforced its provisions against the company (*Kinoshita*).

In another case the Supreme Court of Illinois was faced with a handbook that appeared to set up a system similar to a civil service system (*Duldulao*). Employees were given a 90-day probationary period, at the end of which they became permanent employees who could be terminated only after certain procedures had been followed. The court found that Saint Mary's Hospital had to compete for competent employees with government hospitals that provided their employees with civil service protection. Presumably Saint Mary's would have had to pay higher wages or offer some other inducement if it could not have provided a system similar to that of the government hospitals. The Illinois Supreme Court enforced the promises made in the handbook.

Given these precedents, the Supreme Court of South Carolina had no trouble enforcing the promises made in employee handbooks (Small). The South Carolina Supreme Court dealt with the argument that if courts enforce handbooks companies will stop putting them out by saying: "If company policies are not worth the paper on which they are printed, then it would be better not to mislead employees by distributing them."

By the summer of 1988 thirty state supreme courts (all but two in fair states) had ruled that employee handbooks are enforceable in court (see Table 2–1). Only four state supreme courts have specifically ruled otherwise: Delaware, Massachusetts, Missouri, and New York. Missouri and Massachusetts are the only fair states to have ruled against enforcing employee handbooks. Given this overwhelming acceptance of employee handbooks by the supreme courts of the fair states, it is reasonable to assume supreme courts in the other fair states will come to the same conclusion over the next few years. It is difficult to know what the other pro-boss states will do. Ohio and Alabama have broken ranks and enforced employee handbooks. Pro-boss states in the south may well find these handbooks enforceable because these courts do not like unions, and if employers can write enforceable employee handbooks, this can be used as a weapon in the war against unions. However, they may still refuse to enforce them because these handbooks could be viewed as contracts for an indefinite term and many pro-boss judges believe that anyone hired for an indefinite term is really an at-will employee.

Once a state supreme court decides employee handbooks are binding contracts, several interesting questions arise. Once the handbook is distributed, can it ever be changed, at least as regards employees who have worked under that particular handbook? Does the employee have to read the handbook before he or she can sue to enforce its provisions? Are provisions in the handbook that set out how the handbook will be interpreted enforceable? What if the handbook seems to promise the employees the moon, but has a disclaimer that says the handbook is not a contract?

If a handbook is a binding contract for an indefinite term, and says that employees can be fired only for good cause or for specific reasons listed in the handbook, then how can the employer alter that provision without violating that promise? Of course if the original handbook specifically said that the employer reserved the right to make changes in the future, that would be different. We usually suggest that employers put a date on the handbook. They should make it the 1989 handbook and state therein that the employer will revise it at the end of that period. However, this could cause problems in some pro-boss states. If a pro-boss state supreme court is refusing to enforce employee

TABLE 2–1.   Employee Handbooks

Employee Handbooks	Are/Are Not	Enforceable Contracts
*Alabama	Are	(Hoffman)
Alaska	Supreme Court has not ruled	
Arizona	Are	(Leikvold, Loffa)
Arkansas	Are	(Gladden)
California	Are	(Hepp)
Colorado	Are	(Keenan)
Connecticut	Are	(Finley)
*Delaware	Are not	(Heideck)
District of Columbia	Are	(Wheeler, Howard U.)
*Florida	Supreme Court has not ruled	
*Georgia	Supreme Court has not ruled	
Hawaii	Are	(Kinoshita)
Idaho	Are	(Watson # 1)
Illinois	Are	(Duldulao)
*Indiana	Are not	(Shaw # 1)
Iowa	Supreme Court has not ruled	
Kansas	Are	(Morriss)
Kentucky	Are	(Synthetic Rubber)
*Louisiana	Supreme Court has not ruled	
Maine	Supreme Court has not ruled	
Maryland	Are	(Staggs, Castiglione)
Massachusetts	Are not	(Action for Boston)
Michigan	Are	(Toussaint)
Minnesota	Are	(Pine River)
*Mississippi	Supreme Court has not ruled	
Missouri	Are not	(Johnson #6)
Montana	Are	(Gates, Kerr)
Nebraska	Are	(Lutheran, Johnson #3)
Nevada	Are	(Southwest Gas)
New Hampshire	Supreme Court has not ruled	
New Jersey	Are	(Woolley)
New Mexico	Are	(Vigil, Boudar, Lukoski)
*New York	Are not	(Weiner, Sabetay)
*North Carolina	Supreme Court has not ruled	
North Dakota	Are	(Aasmundstad, Sadler)
*Ohio	Are	(Mers, Hedrick)
Oklahoma	Supreme Court is not sure	(Hinson)
Oregon	Are	(Simpson #1)
*Pennsylvania	Supreme Court has not ruled	
*Rhode Island	Supreme Court has not ruled	
South Carolina	Are	(Small)
South Dakota	Are	(Osterkamp)
Tennessee	Supreme Court has not ruled	
Texas	Supreme Court has not ruled	
Utah	Supreme Court has not ruled	
Vermont	Are	(Sherman, Larose, Benoir)
Virginia	Are	(Hercules Powder)
Washington	Are	(Thompson #1)
West Virginia	Are	(Heck's)
Wisconsin	Are	(Ferraro)
Wyoming	Are	(Mobile Coal, Leithead)

*Pro-boss state. The law is constantly changing. Consult an attorney about your situation.

handbooks because they appear to be employment contracts for an indefinite time period, then putting a date on the handbook may make it enforceable. As always, employers should consult their attorneys before making any changes in the employee handbook.

What if the employer has not reserved the right to make changes in the future and now wants to change the handbook? That raises a very interesting legal question for which there is no answer because the courts have not yet ruled on this question. What should employees do in this situation? If they continue to work quietly without saying anything, the employer will argue that they accepted a new contract (handbook) the same way they accepted the old contract, by continuing to work. We suggest employees who like the old handbook send a letter to the employer by certified mail, return receipt requested, stating that they do not accept the new handbook and consider the old handbook to be their employment contract. How the courts will ultimately rule on this question remains to be seen.

Does the employee have to read the handbook in order to have it enforced? A number of state supreme courts have specifically said that it does not matter; they will enforce the handbook against the employer whether the particular employee read it or not (*Toussaint, Kinoshita*). The New Jersey Supreme Court said these handbooks should be interpreted "in accordance with the reasonable expectations of the employees" and that it should be presumed that employees have read the handbook (*Woolley*). Your state supreme court may not agree. Judges in your state may say an individual employee cannot have relied on the handbook until that individual employee actually read the handbook. Employees who work for companies with employee handbooks should get a copy as quickly as possible (before accepting employment if possible), make a note of when they read it, and keep a copy.

What if the handbook has special provisions concerning how it will be interpreted, such as calling for an employee committee to hear grievances concerning the handbook? We do not yet know how the judges in most states will view these kinds of provisions. The Michigan Supreme Court has refused to enforce provisions in a handbook that tried to take away the employee's right to sue in order to enforce the handbook (*Renny*). Other judges may say that if an employer unilaterally gives employees rights in a handbook, the employer should also be allowed unilaterally to say how those rights can be enforced.

What if the handbook has a disclaimer? In a Maryland case the Johns Hopkins Hospital handbook made a number of promises but it also had a disclaimer that said: "This handbook does not constitute an express or implied contract. The employee may separate from his employment at any time; the Hospital reserves the right to do the same" (*Castiglione*). The Maryland Appeals Court held that because of this disclaimer the hospital did not have to live up to its promises made in the handbook. The North Dakota Supreme Court has ruled the same way in a similar case (*Eldridge*).

This idea of disclaimers creates an interesting problem. Usually, if one person hands another person a contract that makes all kinds of promises but then takes them all back, we call that an ambiguous contract. Generally, judges interpret ambiguous contracts against the person who created the ambiguity.

The Fifth Circuit Court of Appeals held that an employer cannot "taketh" with a disclaimer what he or she appears to "giveth" in a handbook (*Aiello*). The case involved Linda Aiello, an 18-year employee with United Air Lines. When she was transferred from Ft. Lauderdale to Dallas, she was allowed to receive a reimbursement from the company for the cost of moving her two cars. She drove one car from Florida to Texas at a cost of $201.70. She submitted a bill for twice that amount, figuring it would cost about the same amount to move the other car. She was fired for asking to be reimbursed for expenses she had not yet incurred.

United Air Lines had an extensive collection of employee handbooks. The Transfer and Relocation Handbook did not specifically forbid putting in a request for an anticipated expense. The General Handbook said that employees would be fired only for good cause. The jury in this case specifically found that Linda Aiello had an express written employment contract (the handbooks) that required good cause for dismissal, and that she had not been fired for good cause.

The Fifth Circuit judges said that United Air Lines could not act as if these handbooks were binding contracts most of the time and then fall back on a general disclaimer when things did not go its way. Essentially, these judges said that employers cannot use a handbook with a disclaimer as an instrument of fraud on the employees.

The Kansas Supreme Court was also faced with a handbook that said employees could be fired only for good cause but had a disclaimer that said "nothing in this policy manual should be construed as an employment contract" (*Morriss*). The Kansas Supreme Court said this kind of general disclaimer was not enough to negate the specific promises made in the handbook.

Handbooks given to public employees have been enforced even in states that are not sure whether they will enforce handbooks for private employees (*Myrtle Springs*). These courts enforce government handbooks because they have the same legal force as any other government regulations.

Employers should not rely on general disclaimers and they should not make promises in the employee handbook that they do not intend to keep. If an employer wants to reserve the right not to follow the discipline procedure, then he or she should say so in the discipline procedure itself.

Employers should not make changes in employee handbooks without consulting an attorney and without considering both the legal and management ramifications of the changes. If you do not mean it, do not say it.

3

Special Contract Issues

IF EMPLOYEES INVENT THINGS

A number of special problems come up if employees invent things. What happens if employees bring their inventions with them when they start a new job? The question of who owns these inventions should be dealt with in the employment contract. If not, then the employee owns them.

Take the case of Mr. Michels. When he came to work for Dyna-Kote Industries, he brought with him several chemical formulas he had developed. There was a written employment contract but the question of who would own these formulas was not mentioned. When he left Dyna-Kote the company sued, trying to get the formulas back. The Indiana Appeals Court held that the formulas belonged to Michels when he came to work, and since there was nothing in the contract to the contrary, they still belonged to him when he left. The fact that he let the company use them while he worked for the company was irrelevant (*Michels*).

What if the employee agreed to sell her idea to the company but no price was ever agreed on? In one case Ms. Tate, a surgical nurse at the University of Minnesota, came up with the idea of covering the tips of metal surgical clamps with a plastic cover so that the suture material would not break when held by the clamps. She told her idea to a company called Scanlan International, which developed the product. Tate and Scanlan never agreed on what her royalty would be. At one point the company offered her a total payment of $3,000 in lieu of royalties. She sued and the jury felt a reasonable total royalty for her, given the circumstances, would be $520,313 (*Tate*).

If an employee develops an invention on company time, who owns the invention? If the employee was hired to design a specific invention, the employee must assign the patent to the employer. Otherwise, the company has what is called a **shop right** to use the product without paying the employee a royalty, but the invention belongs to the employee unless there is an agreement to the contrary (*Aetna-Standard*). That is why an employer who has employees inventing things should require them to sign a written employment contract that deals with this issue.

What if employers try to claim some right to inventions created by the employee after the employee has left? They usually cannot unless they can prove the employee did most of the inventing before leaving. What if the employer has a contract with the employee that says the employer owns whatever the employee invents, even after the employee stops working for the employer?

While working for Ingersoll-Rand, Armand Ciavatta signed an agreement promising to assign to the company any inventions he conceived within one year of ending his employment with the company. The New Jersey Supreme Court refused to enforce the agreement. Since the invention was not conceived until two months after Ciavatta left Ingersoll-Rand, this was not a case of someone working on an invention at the company and then quitting in order to patent it for himself. Because of this fact, and the fact that no company trade secrets were used, the New Jersey Supreme Court did not feel the legitimate interests of the company were harmed. Ciavatta owned the invention, not Ingersoll-Rand (*Ingersoll-Rand*).

Any employee who invents something at work should talk to an attorney. If there is no written contract dealing with this question, the employee may own the invention, not the employer.

A number of states have specific statutes that deal with these kinds of questions and limit the way these agreements can be written (Kan. 44-130; N.C. 66-57.1; Wash. 49.44.140; Cal. Labor Code 2870; Minn. 181.78). Only an attorney familiar with the laws in your state can make sure your rights (employee or employer) are protected.

IF EMPLOYEES WRITE OR CREATE THINGS

A copyright is just that, the right to copy something. If you buy a book, you have the right to read it, lend it to someone else, and burn it up. You do not have the right to copy it. Only the author has that right. The key question is: Who is the author?

Under the U.S. Copyright Act the author is the person who creates something in a tangible form (writes, paints, sculpts). The moment the thing is put in a tangible form, it is protected by the U.S. Copyright Act. Authors should routinely put a copyright notice on everything they create (the word *copyright*, the year, and your name). Anyone who is going to sell copies to the public should register with the copyright office. You can get the form at many post offices. (In some situations notice and registration are not required, but why not be safe?)

Under the copyright law, if an employee writes or draws something that is "within the scope" of his or her employment, the employer is considered to be the author and owns the copyright (17 U.S.C. sec. 101). If the person doing the work is an independent contractor, instead of a regular employee, then the independent contractor owns the copyright. Throughout this book we will be talking about employees and independent contractors. Basically, people who go to work every day and do whatever the employer tells them to do are considered to be employees. If they are hired to do a particular job unrelated to the employer's main business, like fixing the plumbing, they are considered to be independent contractors.

Of course, an independent contractor can sell the copyright to someone else, but the Copyright Act provides that anyone who sells a copyright can sue and get the copyright back 35 years later. If you write, paint, sculpt, and so on, you should keep track of the copyrights you sell. You may want to get them back and sell them again in your old age.

If there is any question about whether someone is an employee or an independent contractor, the issue of who owns the copyright should be dealt with in a written contract. A recent case illustrates how important this is (*Easter Seal Society*). The Easter Seal Society hired a company to film some Easter Seal Society events. The film was edited and used on a national Easter Seal telethon. There was no agreement about who owned the copyright on the film. The company later sold the film to a movie producer who used it in an adult movie called *Candy, the Stripper*. The Easter Seal Society sued and lost. The Fifth Circuit Court said the Easter Seal Society should have had a contract with the company that spelled out who would own the copyright to the film. They did not, so the copyright belonged to the company that made the film, not to the Easter Seal Society. The company was an independent contractor, not an employee, and therefore owned the copyright.

AGREEMENTS NOT TO COMPETE

Many employees are asked to sign agreements not to compete with their employer for a certain period of time after the employment relationship ends. Whether the court will enforce these agreements depends on a number of factors. We are concerned only with agreements that try to prevent employees from competing with their former employers. We are not talking about agreements that are part of the sale of a business. Courts will usually enforce these agreements, even for what seems to be a very long time (*Western Media, Bowan* #1—10- and 15-year agreements not to compete upheld as part of the sale of a business).

In a free-enterprise society, could there ever be any justification for allowing employers to keep their former employees from competing with them? There may be one. If an employee works directly with customers, the customers may come to associate the employee with the company. Think of the employee as glowing with the good will of the company. If this employee calls on these former customers right after quitting, the customers may get confused and transfer some of the loyalty they feel for the company to the employee in his or her new capacity as a competitor. In order to prevent this, courts will enforce agreements not to compete if the agreements are reasonable on three counts: time, area, and scope.

Time

How much time does it take for the good-will glow to wear off? A Minnesota Appeals Court felt it could not take more than a year. In a recent case the judges reduced the three years of no-competition called for in the contract to one. The court felt the customers would surely lose the identification between the employee and his former employer in one year (*Dean Van Horn*).

The court rewrote this agreement in order to save it. There is a general principle that if a private contract is important to the public interest, judges will rewrite it rather than just declaring it void. There was a time when many courts would do that with no-competition agreements. Recently more and more judges have decided that no-competition agreements are not important to the public interest and may even be contrary to the public interest in a society built on the idea of free enterprise. For these courts, if the agreement is not reasonable, they will not enforce it and they will not rewrite it.

Most courts seem willing to enforce no-competition agreements that last for one year after termination (*Wainwright's Travel, Unitel Corp.*).

Two-year agreements are less certain of enforcement. An Ohio Appeals Court found two years to be too long, given the public's need for a mobile work force and the need for free competition (*Snarr*).

Indiana and New Jersey Appeals Courts recently upheld two-year agreements not to compete, but both courts seemed to say that agreements not to compete are not enforceable against professionals such as attorneys and doctors because of the public's right to freely choose the professional they want to work with (*Field #1, A.T. Hudson*).

Geographic Area

The agreement must be reasonable as to geographic area. In two recent cases the courts found the area restriction to be too broad. The Illinois Appeals Court rewrote the agreement and reduced the area (*Total Health*). The Georgia Appeals Court refused to do that and declared the agreement void. In the Georgia case the employer tried to keep the employee from working in states he had never worked in while employed by this employer (*Kem*). In an Indiana case there was no geographic area restriction at all so the court declared the no-competition agreement invalid (*Com. Bankers*). If an employer wants an enforceable no-competition agreement, the geographic restriction must be reasonable. Generally, employees can be kept from competing only in areas where they worked for the employer.

Scope

The agreement must be reasonable as to scope. If the idea behind enforcing these agreements is that customers are blinded by the good-will glow, then these agreements should only restrict the employee's access to former customers. In one case the agreement was not limited to people the employee had actually had contact with while working for the former employer. The Nebraska Supreme Court refused to rewrite it or enforce it (*Polly*).

The Georgia Supreme Court felt the same way about an agreement that tried to keep the employee out of the insurance business "in any capacity." The court found that to be too broad (*National Settlement*).

Some employers argue they need these agreements to keep former employees from using trade secrets they learned with the company. However, an employer can always go to court to stop any former employee from using trade secrets whether or not there is an agreement about competition. Of course, the employer can keep the employee from using only bona fide trade secrets. The employer cannot use this in an attempt to keep the employee from working.

In a Texas case the company tried to keep a former vice president from competing against it by arguing he was using trade secrets. The judge found the things the company was concerned about—customer names and product prices—to be public information, not trade secrets. The judge said that the employer could not keep this former employee from using the general knowledge he obtained while he worked for the employer (*Numed*).

Recent Developments

Agreements not to compete are an American invention. These kinds of agreements were never enforceable in English law. During the 1980s more and more state supreme courts have questioned whether these kinds of agreements should be enforceable at all in a free-enterprise society. Judges in most states are becoming more and more restrictive. Where a three-year restriction would have been acceptable in the 1970s, it will probably not be enforceable in most states in the 1990s. In 1987 the supreme courts of West Virginia and Texas handed down decisions that make it even less likely these agreements will be enforced in the future.

The West Virginia case involved a chemist who had worked for a water-testing company (*Bostic*). The West Virginia Supreme Court refused to enforce the no-competition agreement. The court said these kinds of agreements are no longer enforceable in West Virginia unless the employer has some special "protectable interest" that can be protected only by such an agreement. The court said the need to protect trade secrets might qualify as a "protectable interest" but since no real trade secrets were involved in this case, the agreement was not enforceable.

The Supreme Court of Texas handed down two landmark decisions in 1987 (*Bergman*, *Mobile Auto Trim*). These decisions laid down four factors that must be present before an employee no-competition agreement will be enforced in

Texas. First, the agreement must be needed to protect the employer's good-will or trade secrets. Second, the time, area, and scope restrictions must be reasonable. Third, the agreement must not injure the public (it is not clear exactly what that means). Fourth, the employee must have received "something special," like special training, from the employer. Without that "something special" these agreements are no longer enforceable in Texas.

It is not clear what will qualify as "protectable interest" in West Virginia or as "something special" in Texas. What is clear is that in the 1990s no-competition agreements will no longer be favored by the courts.

Several states have special statutes that deal with these kinds of agreements. In Colorado, only "executives, managers, and professional employees" can be bound by no-competition agreements, and doctors cannot be bound (Colo. 8-2-113). In one case a Colorado employer tried to keep a dentist-employee from competing. The Colorado Appeals Court refused to enforce the no-competition agreement. The court pointed out that the statute says only professional "employees" can be kept from competing. In this case the employer had made this dentist sign an employment contract that specifically said he was an "independent contractor" (you will see later why some employers say this in employment contracts). The Colorado Appeals Court said "independent contractors" cannot be made to sign no-competition agreements and refused to enforce the agreement. Under the Alabama statute professionals cannot be bound by no-competition agreements (Ala. 8-1-1).

Employees should avoid signing no-competition agreements if at all possible. If everyone refused to sign them, they would disappear and that would be the end of it. Employers who want to have enforceable no-competition agreements should consult an attorney.

FRINGE BENEFITS AND EQUITY PARTICIPATION

Agreements concerning fringe benefits are difficult to write. An attorney should be consulted if at all possible. Recently the Rhode Island Supreme Court enforced an agreement that called for certain specific fringe benefits and provided that if the company ever provided "additional fringe benefits," the employee would have the option of having these additional benefits apply to him. The court held that a stock-option plan made available to other executives was "additional fringe benefits" to which the employee was entitled under the contract (*Miller*). Other courts might not have agreed, finding stock-option plans to be compensation, not fringe benefits. Of course this lawsuit could have been avoided if the term "fringe benefits" had been defined in the contract.

Agreements concerning equity participation by the employee are also difficult to write. In one case the contract said the employee would be given "vested participation in those future ventures of the Company where [he would] have operating responsibility." The judge found this too vague to be enforceable (*Weisman*).

If fringe benefits or equity participation are involved, both parties should consult attorneys. An attorney can make sure the contract calls for a real partnership or gives the employee an option to buy stock after the business gets started if that is what is intended. There are a great many possibilities. This is one of those situations where both sides can pay a little for an attorney now, or a lot for an attorney later.

STOCK OPTIONS

Some employees are given stock options. How does a stock option work? Suppose the stock of the company is presently selling for $10 a share. The company recognizes that if the price of the shares goes up over the next five years, it will be due in part to the hard work of the employees. Suppose the employer gives the employees the option of buying a certain number of shares during the five years at $12 a share. If in five years the stock is selling for $20 a share, the employees can exercise their option, buy at $12, sell at $20, and make money.

These plans are filled with potential problems. In some states a contract for a stock option has to be in writing because it involves the sale of securities.

Also the employee may be fired before the time comes to exercise the option. In one case the employee was fired five days before he had the right to buy stock under the stock-option plan. The Georgia Appeals Court ruled against the employee because the option plan said the option rights were granted "without restriction on the right of the company to terminate optionee's employment" (Lowe).

This employee might have won in a fair state. In a 1987 Texas case the employer's "reserve incentive plan" said that employees must be employed on December 31 to get their bonuses. Seven employees who were fired before December 31 sued for a prorated share of their bonuses. The Texas Appeals Court ruled that implied in a promise to give a bonus after many months or years of work is the promise to give the employees a reasonable chance to get to the point where they become eligible for the bonus. Since these employees were not fired for good cause, they had not been given that reasonable chance and were entitled to a prorated share of the bonus they would have received had they made it to December 31 (Enstar). Presumably employees work harder because of the promised bonus or stock option. This judge felt it would be unfair for the employer to receive that extra effort from the employees and then deprive them of the bonus.

PROFIT SHARING

In profit-sharing cases the problem is often determining what is **profit.** In one case the president of the company died and the company received $100,000 from a life insurance policy. The judge ruled that this money was not profit for the purposes of the profit-sharing plan (Henry). In another case the company made $700,000 on the sale of some property. The court found this was profit under the profit-sharing plan (*Siteman*).

Some commentators think that the first case is right and the second one wrong. They do not think employees should participate in windfalls like the proceeds from executive insurance policies or money made on the sale of property. It could be argued, however, that the money that was used to pay the premiums and buy the property would have been profit subject to sharing with the employees if the company had not bought the policy or the property in the first place. The company decided to gamble with the money instead. Since it was partly the employee's money the company was gambling with, why shouldn't the employees share in the proceeds when the gamble pays off?

COMMISSIONS

The biggest problem with commissions comes when the sale has been made but the salesman is fired before the goods are delivered. Should the salesman still get the commissions? To most people the answer would seem obvious. A commission is payment for making the sale and should be paid even if the salesman is fired before delivery. It was not so obvious to many American judges until a decade ago.

In a landmark case Mr. Fortune's contract with the National Cash Register Company called for a payment of 75 percent of the commission when he made the sale and the rest after delivery. Fortune made a $5,000,000 sale but he was fired before the machines were delivered. He sued for the rest of his commission. The Massachusetts Supreme Court ruled that implied in every employment contract is the implied promise from the employer to act in **good faith.** The court held that NCR could not fire Mr. Fortune just to deprive him of his commissions (*Fortune*).

This principle has come to be called the **procuring cause doctrine,** which says that employees who make the sale get the commission, even if they are fired before delivery (*Scheduling Corp., Kreinz*).

Delayed commission payments are a special problem in the insurance industry. Many insurance agents not only get a commission when they sell an insurance policy, but they also get another commission every year that policy is renewed. These agents usually do not "do" anything to earn that renewal commission. It simply comes to them as long as their customers remain with the company. What happens if the insurance agent is fired after having sold many policies? The Oklahoma Supreme Court answered that question in 1985 (*Farmers Ins.*). Mr. Hall had a contract with Farmers Insurance Exchange that allowed either party to terminate the contract with three months' notice. After a dispute between the parties, Farmers terminated the employment contract and offered Hall a check for $38,000 as compensation for future renewal commissions. The jury held that the actual value of the renewal commissions was $231,000 and that is what Hall was awarded by the Oklahoma Supreme Court. The Oklahoma Supreme Court agreed with the Massachusetts Supreme Court that implied in that kind of delayed commission arrangement was the promise to pay the future commissions unless the employee gave the employer good cause to end the employment relationship (see *Hinson*).

BONUSES

Bonus plans can often be difficult to enforce because they are so vague. However, a fair court will not let that deter it from enforcing these plans. After all, the plan is usually vague because the employer made it that way. For example, Mr. Lessley was recruited out of college. At the 1980 job interview the employer described his "golden handcuffs" bonus plan. He promised to set 10 percent of the income from each project aside to be distributed among the key employees. The exact distribution plan was left up to the employer. Did this make the promise too indefinite to be enforced? The Supreme Court of Kansas did not think so. The 10 percent was certain. The only question was which key employees got what part of the bonus fund. The employer had promised to distribute the bonus based on the quality and quantity of work put into each particular project. The Kansas Supreme Court said that implied here was the promise to exercise this discretion "honestly" and "faithfully." The court felt a judge and jury would be capable of figuring out what a faithful employer would do under the circumstances (*Lessley*).

Judges in fair states will enforce stock-option plans, profit-sharing plans, or bonus plans if there is any reasonable way to figure out what the employee deserves to get under the plan. Judges in pro-boss states do not work quite as hard to enforce these plans. In all states, the employees might find it worthwhile to hire an attorney to look over the plan before they work extra hard only to end up with nothing.

4

Writing and Breaking Employment Contracts

IF THE EMPLOYEE BREAKS A WRITTEN EMPLOYMENT CONTRACT

What happens if an employee breaks a written employment contract by quitting before the term is up?

The Employee Cannot Be Sent to Jail

Half a century ago many states had laws, called Labor Contract Acts, which provided that employees working under a written term contract could be put in jail if they tried to quit before the term was up. The U.S. Supreme Court declared those statutes unconstitutional in 1944 (*Pollock*). From time to time you hear on the news that a union leader has been put in jail. That relates to special laws that apply only to union leaders. No one else is going to jail for breaking a written term employment contract.

The Employee Cannot Be Ordered Back to Work

When the U.S. Supreme Court overturned the Labor Contract Acts, the court said an employee cannot be made to choose between working and going to jail. That violates the 13th Amendment's ban on involuntary servitude. When a judge orders employees back to work, they are being forced to choose between going to work or going to jail for contempt of court. A judge cannot do that. Again, special rules apply to unions. (Whether these special rules violate the 13th Amendment has not been decided by the U.S. Supreme Court.)

The Employee Cannot Be Stopped from Working for Others

Most employees cannot be prevented from going to work for another employer, even though there is still time left on a written contract, unless the employee is a movie star or a famous singer. From time to time you hear about some actor or singer who has broken a written term contract. The judge cannot order them to sing or act for the company they had originally agreed to sing or act for (that would be involuntary servitude), but the judge can order them to not sing or act for anyone else. Even the High Court of New York has agreed that a judge can do this only if the employee is "unique or extraordinary" (*ABC*). The idea is that when the employer hired this unique employee they were not just buying an employee, they were also trying to deprive the competition of this unique commodity. Employees such as Olivia Newton-John or the San Diego Chicken have to worry about this. The rest of us do not (*MCA Records, KGB*).

The Employee Can Be Sued for Money

The employee can be sued for money, but normally not a lot of money. The employer can sue only for the money he or she has really lost because the employee quit before the end of the contract term. Also, the employer has a duty to mitigate damages. That means the employer has to go out and hire someone else. The employer must bargain with that new employee and pay a reasonable salary. The employer can sue for the difference between what he or she was paying the former employee and what he or she has to pay the replacement until the contract term runs out.

The employer can also sue the employee for the cost of finding a replacement. This might involve an employment-agency fee and the cost of flying in a couple of candidates for interviews. Given the high cost of lawsuits, it is almost never going to be worth it to an employer to sue an employee who has broken a written employment contract.

Once in a very great while, an employer will try to sue the employee for a lot of money, arguing that because the employee quit, the employer had to go out of business or suffered some other terrible loss (this is called consequential damages). The Tenth Circuit Court has ruled that an employer can sue an employee for these kinds of damages only if the employee is "unique or irreplaceable" (*Eckles*). Again, movie stars have to worry about this; the rest of us do not.

The vast majority of employees will not be sued if they break an employment contract. At the same time, there is a belief in this country that people should live up to their promises. If an employee gets a reputation as someone who does not keep agreements, he or she may find it difficult to find anyone willing to sign a contract with them in the future. (Employers can get the same reputation.)

IF THE EMPLOYER BREAKS A WRITTEN EMPLOYMENT CONTRACT

What happens if the employer breaks a written employment contract? While employees usually break contracts by giving the employer good cause to fire them or by quitting, there are many things an employer can do that might constitute a breach of the contract.

Demotion or Reassignment

If the employer demotes or reassigns the employee, that may be enough. In a New York case Mr. Rudman was a textbook author who ran a small publishing company. He sold his company to Cowles Communications and signed a written employment contract that put him in charge of the division that published his textbooks. When Cowles tried to put other people in charge of that division, Rudman quit and sued. The High Court of New York said that a significant reduction in rank or duties constitutes a breach of contract. Rudman had every right at that point to quit and sue for his damages (*Rudman*).

Some companies handle this problem by "promoting" people out of the way. It is not a breach of contract to give someone more money and a better title. That is why some organizations have so many vice presidents.

Employees who have been demoted or reassigned in violation of a contract should talk to an attorney right away. If they wait for months, the judge may say that they accepted the demotion and waived their right to sue.

Do Nothing

Most people cannot sue if the employer decides to make them sit and do nothing. In a few cases the courts have said that part of what the employee bargained for was the chance to build up a reputation and the employer damaged that chance by not letting the employee work. These cases usually involve people in show business. In 1930 an actor in England was hired for the lead in a play. When the producer wanted to cast him in a smaller part, the actor sued and won (*Herbert*). A California court recognized that a radio disc jockey got more than just money from being on the air; he also increased his reputation (*Colvig*).

Employers in show business deal with this problem by putting what is called a "pay or play" clause in employment contracts. This clause says that the employer has the right to ask the employee to sit and do nothing and the employee agrees that this is acceptable. This kind of clause is now turning up in employment contracts for professionals and executives outside of show business.

Fired

In most cases the employee has been fired. An employer has a right to fire a term contract employee if good cause exists. What constitutes good cause is not always easy to determine. If someone is incompetent or insubordinate or habitually comes to work late, most judges would consider that good cause. Beyond that it can get complicated. Mr. Schuermann was accused of (and fired for) having an affair with the wife of another employee (*Schuermann*). The district judge ruled in favor of Schuermann, finding that this was not good cause to fire someone. The South Carolina Supreme Court sent the case back for trial. There was some evidence that Schuermann's employer had specifically told him not to have "affairs inside the company." The South Carolina Supreme Court felt that the jury should decide whether the employer really told him this and, if he did, whether breaking this rule was enough to constitute good cause for dismissal.

Money Damages

Generally an employee with a broken employment contract sues for money. There is a special rule that some courts use when an employment contract has been broken. The judge will not let the employee sue for "future lost wages," only wages that would have been earned by the time of the trial (*Lewis*).

Not all courts follow this special rule. In a case involving the breach of an employee handbook, the Michigan Supreme Court upheld an award of $100,000. Most of the money was for lost future wages (*Renny*). In another case involving the breach of an employee handbook, the Supreme Court of Nevada upheld an award of $382,000 (*K Mart*). Most of this was to compensate for lost future wages.

While the employee has a duty to look for another job (mitigate damages), he or she does not have to take any job that comes along. For example, Shirley Maclaine had a contract with 20th Century-Fox to star in a movie musical. Fox admitted breaking the contract, but argued that Shirley Maclaine had to mitigate damages by accepting their offer to star in a western instead. The court said Shirley Maclaine did not have to accept significantly different employment and a western is significantly different from a musical. Shirley Maclaine got the money and did not have to make the western (*Parker*). While employees have to look for another job, they do not have to take a significantly different job or a job in a different city.

Mental Anguish

Money for lost wages is usually about all an employee who sues for breach of contract is going to get. In rare cases the employees may receive damages for mental anguish if they can prove they really suffered anguish and that the employer was "willfull or wanton" in breaking the contract (*Hoffsetz*). Courts are generally willing to find the behavior willful or wanton if the employer acted not out of business necessity but simply to harm the employee.

Reinstatement

A contract employee is almost never going to get a court to order the employer to give him or her the job back.

Stipulated Damage Clauses

As you can see, it is often hard to figure out what the employee has lost by being fired, and what the employer has lost if the employee quits. Because of this people often put a clause in the contract that spells out how much each side has to pay if they break the contract. This is called a stipulated damage clause. The amount specified has to be a realistic estimate of what the real damages will be. It cannot be a penalty used to punish the person breaking the contract.

Employees would like a clause that says the employer has to pay the rest of the salary called for in the contract. Courts, at least those in fair states, will enforce a clause like this. In one case the Wisconsin Supreme Court enforced a clause that required the employer to pay the rest of the salary to the employee. The court said that because of this clause, the employee did not have to mitigate damages by getting another job. Because the real damages to the employee, including damage to reputation and mental anguish, are hard to calculate, the court felt this was a reasonable estimate of damages (*Wassenaar*).

A Colorado Appeals Court recently agreed. In this case the contract had a clause entitled *Termination*, which said that "in the event the Employment Agreement is terminated without cause by the Employer, the Employee shall be entitled to receive compensation to the end of the period of this Agreement." The Colorado Appeals Court said that this meant the employee did not have to get another job or mitigate damages. Once there is a stipulated damage clause of this type the employer has to pay the rest of the salary (*Drews*). In this case the employer tried to get the employee to come back to work. The Colorado Appeals Court said the employee did not have to go back once the employer had fired him. He could sue for damages instead.

Quantum Meruit

In a few cases it turns out there is no enforceable contract. The court will still make the employer pay the employee the reasonable value of his or her services for any work the employee has actually performed. This is called *quantum meruit*, which is Latin meaning "the value of the work." Once the employee has done work, the employer has to pay, even if the contract turns out to be unenforceable.

In one case a young dentist worked for an older dentist. The employment contract ran out in 1980 but the young dentist continued to work until 1982. The court awarded the young dentist money for the reasonable value of his services using *quantum meruit* (*Johnston*).

In another case Nanci Burns moved in with William Koellmer and began helping him manage his tennis club (*Koellmer*). After six years their relationship ended and she sued him for the value of the work she had done at the club. The jury awarded her money on the basis of *quantum meruit* even though there had never been any specific employment contract between Nanci and William.

Even if the employer never actually hired the employee, the employer may still have to pay the reasonable value of the labor done. An employer cannot watch a person do work and then not pay. The courts have ruled that the employer has to pay for the work if a reasonable person standing in the employer's place would have known that the person doing the work expected to be paid (*McCray*).

WRITING AN EMPLOYMENT CONTRACT

Having read this chapter, both employers and employees are in a position to write an employment contract. Both should consult an attorney before signing any employment contract. Anyone writing an employment contract should follow the rules given here.

1. **Never copy an employment contract out of a book.** On several occasions employees have come to me with written employment contracts that were very favorable to the employer. It turned out they had copied the contract out of a book and the employer had signed it without reading it. A sample contract will be provided at the end of this chapter that was written to favor the employee, but even that contract should not be blindly copied. This is one time where you can pay a little for an attorney now or a lot for an attorney later.

   The same advice goes double for employers. For example, in one case the employer copied a no-competition agreement out of a book and had the employee sign it (*Riffert*). There was nothing in this agreement about a geographical limit. Apparently, it kept the employee from competing anywhere in the world. Even the pro-boss judges in Pennsylvania would not enforce a no-competition agreement like that.

2. **Write the contract in plain English.** Both employers and employees are generally going to be better off with plain English. Most legal mumbo jumbo has been twisted over the last century to favor employers, and is now being twisted again to compensate for this bias. The result is that both parties will generally be better off avoiding legal mumbo jumbo altogether. If either side does not understand what an employment contract means, it should be rewritten. Otherwise, there are a lot of judges out there who simply will not enforce it. On the other hand, if the contract is written in plain English, California judges will enforce it even if it means the employee loses, and Delaware judges will enforce it even if it means the employee wins.

3. **Make sure the four basic terms are covered.** The four basic terms of an employment contract are time, service, compensation, and location. Make sure your contract says how long it is going to run. Generally, both parties will be better off if the contract runs for a definite number of years. You have seen that in some states if the contract is not for a definite term, the court will not enforce it. The contract should spell out what the employee is going to do and what the employer is going to pay. The place where the work will be done should also be specified in the contract.

4. **Consider integration clauses carefully.** An integration clause says that the written agreement is the entire agreement and supersedes all prior agreements, either written or oral. In some situations the employee may want to put in an anti-integration clause that says: THIS IS NOT THE ENTIRE AGREEMENT OF THE PARTIES. ALL PRIOR WRITTEN AND ORAL

STATEMENTS MADE BY THE EMPLOYER OR HIS REPRESENTATIVES ARE ALSO A PART OF THIS CONTRACT.

5. **Consider arbitration clauses carefully.** Many employment contracts have an arbitration clause that says the parties will submit any disagreement about the contract to an arbitrator. Generally, employers like arbitration clauses, and employees do not.

6. **If profits are supposed to be shared, get an attorney.** If the contract is simple you may be able to write it yourself. If the employee is supposed to get part of the profit, a stock option, complicated commissions, special bonuses, or anything else that will be difficult to calculate, both sides should get an attorney. This is another situation where both employers and employees can pay a little for an attorney now or a lot for an attorney later.

7. **Be exact whenever possible.** Avoid using vague phrases. If you know the exact day the employment is to begin and the exact amount of the salary, put it in the contract.

8. **Consider a stipulated damage clause.** You have seen that a stipulated damage clause can help when the contract is broken and it is difficult to figure out what the real damages are. Consider putting a stipulated damage clause in the contract.

9. **Consider a choice of law clause.** A choice of law clause says the contract will be interpreted under the legal doctrines of a particular state. If an employee is going to put a stipulated damage clause in, he or she may want to say that the law of Wisconsin will be used to interpret the contract, because the Wisconsin Supreme Court has approved the use of these kinds of clauses in employment contracts. What state employers should pick will depend on the kinds of clauses they put in the contract.

Now we shall see a sample contract that favors the employee. It is a contract for a fictitious client who is supposed to be a computer genius and has a number of special concerns.

The contract is written using the pronouns "I" and "you" and those pronouns are defined at the beginning. A contract written this way is easy to read. You will notice that the contract uses the word "shall" a lot. The word "shall" in a legal document means something must be done.

You will also see a special sentence in the contract that says the employee is not "unique." You have learned that bad things can happen to "unique" employees.

There is a sentence that requires the employer to pay if the employee gets sued because of his work. That is called **indemnification**.

Also included is a requirement that if one side has to complete a trial and wins, the other side has to pay the attorney fees. There are a number of ways this can be dealt with. This client wanted to deal with it this way.

It is usually best, if one party to a contract has a right, to give it to the other party as well. Remember, we may have to convince a judge that this is a fair contract. Giving a right to both sides helps us do that.

Remember the problem of authority. It is best to get the signature of the chairman of the board, with a statement from the secretary of the corporation that the board of directors voted to authorize that signature. In most employment situations that is not going to happen. The signature of the president of the corporation will usually be sufficient in most situations.

The law does not require notarization or witnesses. However, in some states if the contract is notarized it can be filed in the county records and acts as a lien on the employer's property to guarantee the payment of wages under the contract. Your attorney will advise you on this. Also, it never hurts to have a contract signed by witnesses.

A SAMPLE EMPLOYMENT CONTRACT

In this employment contract the pronoun "you" refers to XXX corporation, a Delaware corporation with its principal office in New York. The pronouns "I" and "me" refer to Fred Smoot, an individual residing at XXX St., Austin, Texas. The pronouns "we" and "us" refer to both the XXX Corporation and Fred Smoot.

I. EMPLOYMENT

You agree to employ me as a computer researcher. I agree to work for you as a computer researcher.

II. TERM

You shall employ me for five (5) years beginning on May 1, 1989, and ending on April 30, 1994.

III. DUTIES

I shall be a computer researcher. I shall do research into advanced computer architectures.

You shall furnish me with a private office above the first floor that has at least two hundred (200) square feet. This office will also have a window to the outside of at least nine (9) square feet.

You shall allow me access to the office twenty-four (24) hours a day.

You shall not impose any dress code on me or restrict me to certain working hours. I shall do a reasonable amount of work at the office if that is possible. You shall allow me to work at home when that is necessary because you have allowed too many distractions to interfere with my work at the office.

I shall not divulge any trade secrets to anyone without your permission. You will tell me when something I am working with is a trade secret.

IV. COMPENSATION

You shall pay me one hundred thousand dollars ($100,000) a year. You shall pay me in bimonthly installments on the first day and the fifteenth day of each month.

V. FRINGE BENEFITS

You shall provide me with fringe benefits equal to what you provide to other employees doing similar work. At a minimum you will provide me with medical insurance that pays for all medical expenses over five hundred dollars ($500) in any one year. If I am injured or disabled, you will pay me my full salary until I recover or Social Security begins paying me benefits. If I am sick you will pay me my full salary until I recover. The injury, disability, or illness does not have to be job-related.

You will provide me with a defined-contribution retirement fund. You shall take ten percent (10%) of my salary every paycheck, match that amount with company funds, and deposit the entire amount into my retirement fund. The fund shall be administered by a financial institution that is mutually agreeable to both of us. This fund will meet the requirements of the Internal Revenue Service so the amount taken out of my paycheck is not taxable as income to me. This retirement fund will vest, completely, immediately upon deposit.

VI. EXPENSE REIMBURSEMENT

You shall allow me to incur reasonable business expenses. You shall provide me with a company American Express card so that I do not have to do more than a reasonable amount of paperwork in accounting for these expenses. You shall allow me to attend at least three (3) computer conferences during each year of this contract. You shall reimburse me for the expenses involved in going to these conferences.

You shall reimburse me for all reasonable moving expenses I incur because I must move to your Dallas office. You shall not transfer me from the Dallas office without my express written permission. If I do agree to a transfer, you shall reimburse me for those moving expenses as well.

You shall indemnify me. You shall pay for all damages and attorney's fees that result from any lawsuits that arise out of my employment with you.

You shall allow me to present papers at computer conferences and universities. I shall keep any income I derive from these presentations. The time I spend attending conferences and presenting papers shall not be deducted from my vacation or personal leave.

You shall reimburse me for all business travel expenses. You shall send me on business trips only with my permission. I shall decide how much I travel, where I travel, what form of transportation I take, and where I stay when I travel.

VII. VACATION AND PERSONAL LEAVE

You shall allow me four (4) weeks' vacation for each year of this contract. I shall decide when to take my vacation. I do not have to give you advance notice of when I plan to take a vacation.

You shall allow me ten (10) normal working days as personal leave for each year of this contract. Personal days are days that I may take off to take care of personal business.

I shall be eligible for my vacation and personal leave from the first day I work for you.

You shall allow me to take off any days that are official holidays of the corporation. These days will not count as vacation or personal-leave days. At a minimum, official holidays will include: Christmas Day, New Year's Day, the Fourth of July, Labor Day, Memorial Day, Thanksgiving Day, and the day after Thanksgiving Day.

All unused vacation and personal-leave days shall carry over to the following years. You shall pay me my full salary for any vacation days I have not used when this contract ends.

VIII. TERMINATION

You may terminate my employment for good cause only. Only a judge and jury shall determine if I actually did what you accuse me of. Only a judge shall determine if my actions are good cause for termination. What you think I did and what you think constitutes good cause are irrelevant.

I may terminate this contract if you give me good cause to do so. I shall have good cause to terminate this contract if you merge or consolidate with another company.

You shall not require me to take any physical or mental examination. You shall not require me to take a drug test, a lie detector test, or any other test.

IX. STIPULATED DAMAGES

We both agree that the actual damages in a breach of contract case will be difficult to ascertain. Both of us may suffer damage to our reputations. It will be difficult to ascertain whether I get a comparable job or you have recruited a comparable employee. The expenses I incur in searching for another job, and you incur in recruiting a replacement, will be difficult to ascertain. Because of this we agree that the following stipulated damages are fair and reasonable. If I break this contact I shall pay you five thousand dollars ($5,000) to compensate you in full for your damages. If you break this contract you shall pay me the salary that remains to be paid under the terms of this contract. You shall not have to continue to provide me with fringe benefits or put money into the retirement fund.

X. BREACH OF CONTRACT

If for some reason a court will not enforce the stipulated-damages clause, then we both agree that our remedy will be limited to money damages. Neither you nor I shall ask for an injunction or court order of any kind. If either of us has to complete a trial because the other party has breached this contract, then the losing party shall pay the attorney's fees for the winning party.

You and I agree that I am not unique or irreplaceable. Other people are capable of doing my job.

XI. ASSIGNMENT

Neither you nor I can assign this contract without first obtaining the other's written permission. You agree that the president of the corporation has authority to act for the corporation in all things that relate to this contract.

XII. GOVERNING LAW

Both of us agree that Wisconsin law shall be used to interpret this contract.

XIII. CONCLUSION

This contract supersedes all other agreements between you and me. This contract contains our entire agreement.

Neither you nor I shall amend or alter this contract without the written permission of the other party.

If a court decides any of the provisions in this contract are void or not enforceable, the other provisions shall remain valid.

It shall not be a waiver if you or I fail to sue because of a breach of this contract. We may sue later for that breach or any other breach.

The titles in this contract serve only as a guide to the reader. They are not part of the substance of this agreement.

DATE—YOUR SIGNATURE—MY SIGNATURE

Employer Alterations

An employer would probably remove some of the items concerned with office size and fringe benefits. An employer would probably ask that stipulated damages be the same amount for both parties and might require disputes over the contract to be handled by arbitration. An employer who wants to add special clauses concerned with trade secrets, patents, copyrights, and competition should consult an attorney.

Part Two
Rights after Being Fired

5

Unemployment Compensation

THE PAST

After the Great Depression many economists felt that America needed a program to provide temporarily unemployed workers with money so that consumer spending would not drop drastically and recessions would not turn into depressions.

The Social Security Act of 1935 set up a federal unemployment compensation system. "Oh no," people cried, "not another giant federal bureaucracy!" In response to this outcry the federal government agreed to waive most of the federal unemployment tax in any state that set up its own unemployment system. Every state did just that. The focus at the time was on a national depression that had hit every state. No one was looking to a time in the 1980s when some states would go through severe recessions while other states would have booming economies.

STATE UNEMPLOYMENT COMPENSATION PROGRAMS

While every state has to meet minimum federal standards there are differences, and you will want to contact your state unemployment agency with any specific questions you may have. Throughout this chapter we are talking about the "average" state unemployment system.

CALCULATING BENEFITS

The amount an unemployed worker is entitled to receive every week is determined in a bizarre way. Suppose the worker is laid off in April 1989. Most states do not look at what he or she earned during the last full quarter of work (January to March), but look instead to the four quarters before the last full quarter. In this case that would be the four quarters of 1988. This four-quarter period is called the Base Period. Of these four quarters in the Base Period, the quarter with the highest wages is chosen. Let's suppose our fictional worker earned $4,000 during the best quarter in the Base Period. Divide this amount by 25 to get $160. That is our fictional worker's basic weekly compensation payment. The worker receives his or her best quarter of wages spread out over 25 weeks. There is a maximum weekly amount that differs from state to state. Some states require the worker to have earned a certain total amount over the entire Base Period to be eligible to receive compensation at all. Other states require the worker to have earned a minimum amount of money a week for a minimum number of weeks to be entitled to compensation. Weeks spent on sick leave count toward this total (*Lopata, Wiersma*).

Most agencies take a percentage of the total amount of wages earned during the entire Base Period, usually 27 percent. That is the maximum the agency will pay out to a worker in unemployment compensation.

A worker who is able to work part time is still entitled to some unemployment compensation. In at least 13 states the worker is also entitled to extra compensation if he or she has dependents, such as underage children or a nonworking spouse (Alaska, Connecticut, District of Columbia, Illinois, Indiana, Iowa, Maine, Maryland, Massachusetts, Michigan, Ohio, Pennsylvania, Rhode Island).

The amount of unemployment compensation depends on the amount of wages the worker earned while working. Even meals and lodging provided by the employer count as wages for calculating benefits (*Vermont Camping*).

The purpose of the unemployment compensation system is to keep consumer spending up, and provide financial help to people who are temporarily unemployed. If a worker has been fired but has income from other sources such as a pension, there are complex rules on whether he or she can collect unemployment compensation.

Who Can Get Benefits

People who quit usually cannot get unemployment compensation. There is an exception we will discuss in a moment, but don't count on it. An employee about to quit should consider consulting an attorney first. In some states, a worker who quits is disqualified from receiving unemployment compensation until he or she has worked for another employer for a certain period of time, usually six weeks. But there are exceptions to this. For example, the Ohio statute said if the worker quits to take another job and starts the new job within one week of quitting, the worker has to work only three weeks at the new job to be eligible for compensation. In one case the employee worked two weeks and received one week's severance pay. The Ohio Supreme Court, following the rule that these statutes are to be liberally interpreted, held that the severance pay counted and the employee had worked the required three weeks (*Radcliffe*).

While almost every worker in the United States is covered by unemployment compensation insurance, a few are not. In some states people who work for religious organizations are not covered. In many states agricultural workers are not covered.

Usually only employees can get unemployment compensation. Independent contractors and self-employed people do not qualify. If there is any doubt, judges will usually find someone to be an employee, not an independent contractor, and therefore entitled to unemployment compensation (*Rent-A-Mom, Rivera*).

Some years ago an enterprising teacher filed for unemployment compensation during summer vacation. That caused most states to amend their statutes. Today, in most states, if teachers have "reasonable assurance of employment" for the coming school year, they cannot get unemployment compensation during the summer. They do not have to have a signed employment contract.

What if the teacher has been fired but is getting paychecks during the summer because he or she had the pay spread out over the summer? The Ohio Supreme Court held that a teacher who was receiving delayed paychecks during the summer, and who had no reasonable assurance of employment for the fall, was entitled to receive unemployment compensation during the summer (*Cook #2*).

Generally, substitute teachers who work from day to day are entitled to unemployment compensation during school vacation periods (*Soliman, Hopewell*).

Extended Benefits

There are several provisions for extending benefits beyond the usual 25 weeks. If unemployment in the state reaches a certain level, people on unemployment may be entitled to extended benefits. Also, the Federal Trade Act of 1974 (19 U.S.C. sec. 2101) allows employees who have been laid off because of foreign competition to receive extended benefits. These employees may also be entitled to money to help them retrain for another occupation (*Poll, Jones #2*).

DENIAL OF BENEFITS

There are three main reasons why people are denied unemployment compensation benefits: they were discharged for misconduct, they quit without cause, or they are unemployed because of a labor dispute.

Discharged for Misconduct

Most unemployment compensation statutes deny benefits to anyone who is discharged for misconduct. Whether an employee engaged in a kind of misconduct that disqualifies him or her from getting unemployment compensation is the subject of most unemployment compensation hearings.

Incompetence is not misconduct. Making mistakes or not having the necessary job skills is not misconduct. However, if the employee has demonstrated an ability to perform in the past and stops performing competently, that would be misconduct. Also, if the employee lied on a job application, causing the employer to think the employee had the necessary job skills, that would also constitute misconduct (*Zadworny, Northwest Foods, Attisano*).

Negligence is not misconduct. In one case the employee was fired after having three accidents in five months. The Pennsylvania Appeals Court ruled that this was not misconduct because there was no evidence of a "conscious disregard of the employer's interests" (*Colonial Taxi*). A Washington Appeals Court explained that intentional or deliberate actions are required for misconduct to be present. An employee who had an accident because he was preoccupied with personal problems was not guilty of misconduct (*Darneille*).

Many cases involve employees who are fired for using obscene language. Whether or not using obscene language constitutes misconduct will depend on a number of factors including whether the employer has a rule against using obscene language at the workplace (*Browning-Ferris*).

Most courts say that one incident of vulgarity is not enough to justify discharging someone. For example, Mr. Armstrong was singing to himself in the break room when another employee came in and told him to shut his "Goddamn mouth." Armstrong responded by saying that he would "whip the ass" of that employee if he ever said anything like that to him again. That remark got Armstrong fired. The court did not feel this justified withholding Armstrong's unemployment compensation (*Armstrong*). On the other hand a Kentucky court felt that one incident involving an obscene gesture was enough to justify denial of unemployment compensation. The gesture was toward the manager (*Dye*).

The rule in Iowa is that an employee can use vulgar language if it is part of an isolated incident. In one case the Iowa Appeals Court judges disagreed on whether or not two "kiss my ass" remarks to two different supervisors thirty minutes apart constituted one incident or two. One judge thought it was all part of one incident, but the other two did not and ruled that the two separate incidents constituted misconduct (*Carpenter*). Oregon and Minnesota follow a similar rule. Isolated instances of vulgarity ("I've had enough of this shit") or hothead behavior (throwing the hammer on the ground) do not constitute misconduct (*Bunnell, McCoy*).

Courts usually look at the surrounding circumstances to see if the vulgarity was justified or provoked. In one case, Sara Kowal was put in a room with two other employees. The supervisor then proceeded to yell at them about their attitude (he felt they did not smile enough at work). Apparently this supervisor had a management style that involved a lot of yelling. Finally he asked Kowal if she liked her job. She threw a writing tablet at him and told him to "shove it up his ass." The Pennsylvania Appeals Court did not think that, given these circumstances, this was misconduct. The judges felt that "forty-five minutes of harassment" by the supervisor constituted "justifiable provocation" for Kowal's behavior (*Kowal*).

Many cases involve drugs and alcohol. In one case the court held that coming to work intoxicated was not misconduct because the employee was an alcoholic and could not control her drinking (*Denver*). In another case the employee was caught drinking at work. While this would usually be misconduct, the Minnesota Appeals Court felt that it was not in this case. This employee was an alcoholic who was undergoing treatment. The court ruled that misconduct caused by a chemical dependency which the employee was trying to control did not justify withholding unemployment compensation (*Dist. 709*).

As more and more employers attempt to control smoking at work, we expect this issue to arise for smokers as well as dope addicts and alcoholics. Of course there is an important difference. Cigarette smokers are not only lowering their own mental abilities, they are also interfering with the ability of their co-workers to function effectively. On the other hand, many smokers are just as addicted to cigarettes as alcoholics are to alcohol. It will be interesting to see how the courts deal with smokers who get fired because they refuse (or are unable) to obey the nonsmoking rules at work.

As the Massachusetts Supreme Court recently pointed out, the burden is on the employer to prove the employee was fired for misconduct. In a case involving excessive absenteeism caused by an alcohol problem, the court said the employer must prove that the employee is capable of controlling his or her alcohol problem. If the employee is really an alcoholic who cannot control his or her actions and who missed work because of the disease, that is not misconduct (*Shepherd*). The general principle is that if persons are unemployed because of circumstances beyond their control, they should receive unemployment compensation.

The issue with absences is usually whether the employee had a reasonable excuse. Being late to work because of heavy traffic or missing work because of illness is not misconduct (*Mendez #1, Manatawny Manor*).

Failure to obey reasonable employer rules is usually considered misconduct. These cases run the gambit from falsifying time cards to spitting on the floor and from sleeping on the job to threatening to shoot a co-worker (*Burlington, Bowers, Grant, Thompson #2*).

On the other hand, refusing to settle a worker's compensation claim, disputing the ownership of an invention with the employer, having wages repeatedly garnished, or defending against attack by a co-worker is not misconduct (*Dunkle, BMY, Great Plains, Peeples*).

Some of the cases would seem silly were it not for the fact that someone's unemployment compensation hung in the balance. In one case Kristen Hurst was fired because she ate some cookies that were about to be thrown away. The court said Hurst had not engaged in misconduct. Taking something of no value is not theft (*Hurst*).

One female employee was subjected to so much verbal and physical abuse by a co-worker that she grabbed a 25-pound roast beef and threw it at him (they worked in a meat market). The New Jersey Appeals Court found this to be a spontaneous reaction to "persistent, unremitting, and sexually offensive" behavior, not a deliberate attack, and therefore not misconduct (*Demech*).

Just breaking the employer's rules is not enough. As one court said, if it were, "then the employer would need only to establish rules so complex or so strict that any employee would ultimately fail to live up to every provision" (*Safety Med.*). The rules must be reasonable and generally enforced.

An employer has a right to ask employees to work on the weekend, and if they refuse, it is misconduct (*Frazee*). However, an employee's refusal to work on his or her Sabbath is not misconduct. Paula Hobbie was fired for refusing to work on her Sabbath. The U.S. Supreme Court ruled that the state of Florida could not withhold benefits. That would violate the freedom-of-religion clause of the First Amendment of the U.S. Constitution. Paula Hobbie got her unemployment compensation (*Hobbie*).

The misconduct must be "work-related." Employees fired for off-duty conduct usually get compensation. Before the off-duty conduct qualifies as "misconduct," it must have a nexus to work, it must harm the employer, and it must either violate an employer rule or clearly be harmful to the employer's interest (*Nelson*).

In most cases the courts are not enforcing some esoteric legal doctrine. Misconduct means what most people would think it means in the circumstances. Employers and employees who use a little common sense should not have any problem. See Table 5–1 for a summary of what is and is not misconduct in most states.

Quitting without Cause

The general rule is that people who quit their jobs do not get unemployment compensation. However, there is an exception in most states. If the employee

TABLE 5–1. What Is Misconduct?

Is Misconduct	*Is Not Misconduct*
Failure to perform work after having demonstrated ability to do the work	Incompetence; genuine inability to do the work
Deliberate damage to equipment; willful failure to follow safety rules	Accidents; negligence; errors that are not the result of reckless conduct
Unreasonable or excessive use of obscene language in violation of employer's rules	Isolated incident using obscene language
Excessive and unjustified absences and tardiness; failure to inform supervisor	Justified absences and tardiness
Lying; stealing; using equipment without permission of supervisor	Age; physical condition; illness; pregnancy
Failure to obey reasonable rules and follow reasonable orders	Failure to obey unreasonable rules and follow unreasonable orders
Unjustified assault on co-worker or supervisor	Justified assault on co-worker; self-defense
Spending too much time socializing at work after being told not to	Associating with co-workers or marrying co-worker in violation of employer's rules
Refusal to work on the weekend	Refusal to work on the employee's Sabbath day

has a good enough reason to quit, he or she can still get unemployment compensation. The states do not always agree on what is a good enough reason, but there are some general principles.

If the employer changes the duties of the employee, that may be a good enough reason to quit. Mr. Shingles was hired to be the pharmacist in a store near his home. Eventually the employer made him a floater, which required him to work at 12 different stores. On some days he had to commute 90 miles. Shingles quit, and the court allowed him to receive unemployment compensation. The court felt this was enough of a "substantial unilateral change in employment" by the employer to justify giving unemployment compensation to the employee (*Shingles*). In other cases, the courts ruled that a nurse who was demoted with a substantial reduction in pay had good reason to quit, as did a museum curator who quit rather than take the two half-time clerical jobs offered by the employer (*Ponderosa Villa, Holbrook*). Having to work 80 hours a week to meet deadlines and having to move to another town have also been found to be "unilateral changes" in the job description that were more than a reasonable employee has to accept (*Inside Radio, Donaldson*).

Not all "unilateral changes" in working conditions justify quitting. A temporary reduction in pay while the workplace is being renovated, not getting a big enough raise, and not being willing to commute to the new plant location are all not good enough (*Rodeen, LaBlanc, Lee*).

Some courts seem particularly willing to find good cause for quitting when the employer has gone back on a promise to the employee. An Indiana Appeals Court felt that not living up to the promise to train, promote, and give a raise to the employee justified quitting (*Gathering*). In another case, the employee took the job only because of the promise of eight hours a week of overtime work. When the employer failed to live up to that promise, the employee quit and the Minnesota Appeals Court allowed him to receive unemployment compensation (*Danielson Mobil*).

Some courts will rule against an employee if the employer makes the unilateral change in working conditions and the employee does not quit right away. This is a terrible rule because it encourages people to quit without giving the new conditions a chance. The Minnesota Rule is more reasonable. Minnesota courts will allow the employee to work under the new conditions for a while to see if an accommodation can be made. For example, John Baker was hired and told he would never have to work on the night shift. After six years the employer put him on the night shift. Baker complained to the employer and gave the employer time to correct the problem before quitting. The Minnesota Appeals Court refused to penalize Baker for continuing to work under the new conditions. Of course, if the worker continues to work under the new conditions for more than a few months, even a Minnesota court would probably rule that the employee had waived the right to complain and accepted the new working conditions (*Baker*).

Most courts will allow employees to quit to protect their health and safety. The High Court in Maryland allowed a teacher to quit because he was being harassed mercilessly by a gang of students (*Paynter*). Quitting because the draft from the air conditioner caused sinus headaches was good enough in another case. The employer refused to let the employee move her desk to avoid the draft (Goettler).

The battle between smokers and nonsmokers causes problems. In one case the court allowed an employee with allergic bronchitis to quit rather than work around people who smoked cigarettes (Lapham).

Generally, the employee must have a real health or safety problem, must inform the employer about the problem, and must be available to work if the employer corrects the problem (Allen #2).

Employees can quit rather than endure sexual or racial harassment. They should report the problem to the employer and give him or her a chance to correct it (St. Barnabas). If the supervisor is doing the harassing, this may not be necessary. A New Jersey Appeals Court did not think the worker had to complain to higher-ups when her own supervisor sexually and racially harassed her. She was the only "white chick" at work and was made to suffer because of it (Doering).

Some states require someone who has quit in order to take another job to work at that new job for a minimum number of weeks before being entitled to unemployment compensation. Not all states feel that way. Alice Brennan quit to take a new job only to have the new employer change his mind and not hire her. The Pennsylvania Appeals Court found that was good cause to quit and allowed her to receive unemployment compensation. The Idaho Supreme Court ruled the same way in a similar case (Brennan #2, Schafer).

Most states say the reason for quitting must be related to the job. Personal reasons do not qualify. This is illustrated by a 1987 U.S. Supreme Court decision concerning pregnant women. The court ruled that a state does not have to give preferential treatment to pregnant women. If a woman has to quit her job because of pregnancy, a state is free to deny her unemployment compensation because the reason for quitting was personal and not job-related (Wimberly).

The Pennsylvania statute used to say that the reason for quitting had to be job-related, but the Pennsylvania Appeals Court declared the law unconstitutional because it violated the equal-protection and due-process clauses of the state and federal constitutions. That landmark case involved a hospital employee who had to quit to stay at home in the evenings to care for her two children. She had been able to work evenings in the past because her oldest daughter was home and cared for the younger children. When her oldest daughter left home, she had no choice but to quit her night job. The court felt that it was unconstitutional to deny her unemployment compensation benefits when she had to quit for compelling personal reasons (Wallace).

The Pennsylvania legislature changed the statute in 1980 to allow employees to quit for compelling personal reasons and still receive unemployment compensation. Most cases involve people who have to move because their spouses have been transferred. In Pennsylvania, if the spouse has been transferred and there is no way the worker can continue to live with the spouse and work at the job, then quitting is justified. However, the worker may be penalized if he or she tries to live with the new conditions for a while. For example, one couple got married but they continued to work and live in different towns. When the wife finally quit her job to move in with her husband, the Pennsylvania court did not allow her to collect unemployment compensation. Apparently, if she had quit when she first got married, it would have been all right, but since she waited she could no longer say that her resignation was caused by compelling personal reasons (*Schechter*).

While most states will not allow an employee to quit for personal reasons, every state is different. Employees should consider consulting an attorney before giving up. They may find that there is a special provision in their state that applies to their situation. For example, the Washington statute allows people to quit because of domestic responsibilities. In one case the Washington Supreme Court allowed a person to collect unemployment compensation because she moved in with her new spouse (*Yamavchi*).

Sometimes it is hard to tell whether the employee quit or was fired. In one case the employee gave his two-week notice and the employer decided to go ahead and fire him before the two weeks were up. The court said the employee had been fired and was thus entitled to unemployment compensation (*Westport*). In another case the employer said, "How would you like to leave here?" and the employee replied, "Sounds like a wonderful idea." The court said that employee had quit and was not entitled to unemployment compensation (*Keast*). This can be particularly difficult when the employee resigns and then tries to take back the resignation. In one case Richard Nichols wrote a memorandum that said he would resign effective January 2, 1985, unless there was a change in management. There was a change in management but the employer would not let him take back his resignation. The court said the resignation was conditional, and since the condition happened, he had not resigned, he had been fired (*Nichols*). In another case the employee tried to revoke the letter of resignation before the deadline and the employer would not let him. The court said that an employee can revoke a resignation anytime before the actual date of separation unless the employer has taken real steps to replace the worker (*Pa. Labor*).

Unemployed because of a Labor Dispute

Most unemployment compensation statutes have some provision concerning people who are unemployed because of a "work stoppage" or "labor dispute." Often whether or not the employee gets unemployment compensation depends on how the court interprets these phrases. The Indiana Appeals Court said that once the strikers make an unconditional offer to return to work, the "labor dispute" is over and if the employer does not take them back they can collect unemployment compensation (*Allen #3*). The Vermont and Maryland Supreme Courts have ruled that during a strike or lockout the key question is whether or not there has been a "stoppage of work," which means that if the factory is still producing, the strikers get their unemployment compensation; if it is shut down, they do not (*Sinai Hosp., Pfenning*).

In Pennsylvania the rule is that employees who are on strike do not get unemployment compensation, but employees who are locked out do. It is not

always easy to know which is which. When 22,000 employees of the Philadel-
phia School District walked off the job, the Unemployment Compensation
Board said it was a strike and refused to pay them unemployment compensation. The Pennsylvania Supreme Court said it was a lockout because the city
had refused to live up to the union contract (Odgers).

Sometimes the decisions in this area seem unfair. In one case the union
employees went on strike. The nonunion employees showed up for work and
were turned away. The nonunion employees were denied unemployment compensation benefits because the Pennsylvania Appeals Court said their unemployment was caused by a strike, not a lockout. The court said this, even though
these employees were not on strike and would have gone to work if the employer had let them (Kearney). The labor department in South Dakota tried to
give unemployment compensation to nonstriking employees who had been
locked out but deny it to union employees who were on strike. The Eighth
Circuit Court would not allow this. The court said it would be a violation of
federal labor laws for the state to give unemployment benefits to nonunion
members and deny it to union members (United Steelworkers).

THE DUTY TO BE AVAILABLE FOR AND SEEK SUITABLE WORK

One of the purposes of unemployment compensation is to give an unemployed
worker time to find a job that matches his or her skill level. Society is not really
well served if skilled workers are forced by necessity to take the first menial job
that comes along. At the same time the unemployed workers have to look for
work. They cannot just sit around and do nothing, or spend their time on
personal projects. One worker spent 40 hours a week remodeling his parent's
home. The court ruled that spending full time on a project like that did not
constitute "being available for work." He did not get compensation (Bergstedt).

Some courts say the employee has to be "attached to the labor force." That
means ready, willing, and able to work. Workers who are not mentally, emotionally, or physically able to work are not entitled to unemployment compensation. Unemployment insurance is not temporary disability insurance (Kuna,
Borselli, Taylor).

What kind of job is suitable is often the key question. It depends on the
worker's training and experience, the location of possible jobs, and the probability that the employee will actually find work in his or her usual occupation.
Three cases involving teachers illustrate the point. One teacher refused to accept a substitute-teacher position that paid 40 percent less than her previous
job. Another teacher refused to take a ten-hour-a-week position as a part-time
tutor. Yet another refused to look for any kind of work other than teaching, even
though it was during the summer. In each case the courts said the teacher was
within her rights to refuse work of lesser skill and pay (Eddings, Simpson #2,
DaSilva).

Persons can go to college and get unemployment compensation. The key is
whether they are reasonably available for work. Often, if the workers had man-

aged to go to college and work before being laid off, they will get unemployment compensation. Of course, they must be "available for work" and "actively seeking work." In one case the worker was enrolled in school from 8:00 A.M. to noon. He contacted three or four employers a week and was willing to quit school if he found a job. The New Hampshire Supreme Court ruled that he was entitled to receive unemployment compensation (*Blanchard*). In another case a full-time college student who had held a job while attending college was laid off. The worker was willing to work any shift and to set up a course schedule to suit any employer. The Georgia Appeals Court said people on unemployment compensation do not have to be available to work "at all times and for all jobs." The court was satisfied that this worker was reasonably available for work (*Curry*).

The general rule is that persons on unemployment compensation have to be looking for work, not setting up their own business (*Rocke*). There is an exception to this rule. If the worker was (1) involved in self-employed activity before being fired; (2) continued this activity without substantial change after being fired; (3) remained available for full-time employment; (4) and the self-employment was not the primary source of income, then the worker can continue the self-employed activity after being fired (*Hanley*). Mr. Carey had been employed at the Blaw Knox Foundry for ten years before being laid off. For six years before being laid off, he and his wife had operated a store called Phyllis' Fabrics. He worked at the store after being laid off, but he also contacted potential employers and was actively looking for work. Mr. Carey met the test and was allowed to receive compensation (*Carey*).

The requirement that unemployed workers be available for suitable work makes for some interesting behavior. For example, when actors go to Hollywood the first piece of advice they get from their fellow actors is to hold out as long as possible for an acting job. If they get an acting job from which they are laid off, they can collect unemployment compensation and have to look only for another acting job. Once they accept a regular job such as being a secretary, they will have to accept those kinds of jobs as well when they get laid off from an acting job.

UNEMPLOYMENT TAXES

Employers pay taxes into the unemployment system based on the wages they pay out and the amount of money the unemployment compensation agency has to pay to their former employees. That gives employers an incentive to keep former employees from getting unemployment compensation payments.

INCOME TAXES

The money a worker receives as unemployment compensation is subject to federal income tax. The unemployment compensation agency will not withhold any money for the I.R.S. so remember to save for April 15th.

CLAIMS PROCEDURE

To file a claim the first thing employees have to do is go to the unemployment agency and fill out a form. The employees should take their Social Security card and identification with them. They will usually have to appear in person to file the initial claim. Employees should take the name and address of every employer they have worked for during the last couple of years. To most unemployment agencies "fired" means "fired for misconduct," so when they ask, do not say you were fired, say you were laid off.

The agency will contact the last employer to hear the other side of the story. Then the agency will make an initial determination. Once the initial determination has been made the loser can ask for a hearing. It is your responsibility to find out what the deadlines are and follow them. If the notice says you have 12 days to appeal, that usually means 12 days from the time the agency mailed the notice, weekends included (calendar days, not work days).

Both sides should consider getting an attorney to represent them. If the question is whether the employee quit or was fired, the burden is on the employer to prove the employee quit. If the employee was fired, the burden is on the employer to prove the employee was guilty of misconduct. If the employee quit, the burden is on the employee to prove he or she had a good reason to quit. Waiting too long after the good reason came up may cost the employee the case. If the employer waited too long to fire the employee after the misconduct, it may cost the employer the case (*Green #2, Curtis, Vernon*).

One reason for getting an attorney is that some states, such as Pennsylvania, will not allow hearsay evidence to be admitted at the hearing if it is objected to. Hearsay means *hear* and *say*. If someone is testifying to something someone else said, it is hearsay. The purpose of a hearing is to allow the hearing officer to see the witnesses and listen to the cross-examination. He or she cannot see someone who is not there and there can be no cross-examination of an absent witness. Anytime the other side wants to admit a piece of paper as evidence, you should object. That is hearsay. A piece of paper cannot be cross-examined. We would like to have the person who wrote whatever is on the piece of paper at the hearing. There are all kinds of exceptions to the hearsay rule but you cannot be expected to learn them. Just object to anything that looks like hearsay.

The Pennsylvania courts are very strict about this rule. In one case the employer did not show up at the hearing; he sent a written statement instead. Since that was just hearsay, the employee won (*Vann*). In another case a teacher had been fired for alleged improper conduct. The school board had held a hearing and wanted to submit the transcript of that hearing as evidence at the unemployment compensation hearing. The court said that the transcript could not be considered because it was hearsay and had been properly objected to by the employee's attorney (*Blue Mountain*). In Pennsylvania, even if the hearsay is admitted because it is not objected to, it must be corroborated by some other evidence. A decision cannot be based on hearsay alone (*Auddino*). Of course, this rule can work against the employee as well. In one case Mrs. Woods testified that her husband had been transferred and that he had no control over the decision. She tried to introduce a written statement to that effect but this was hearsay and was not admitted. She should have had both her husband and the husband's supervisor at the hearing so that they could testify in person (*Woods #2*).

Regular business records are usually going to be admitted into evidence under an exception to the rule that anything written on a piece of paper is hearsay. That means letters of reprimand and employee evaluations will usually be allowed at the hearing. However, the person in charge of these records or the supervisor who created them will have to be there to testify that they are what they appear to be. Documentation is often the key to whether or not an employer wins an unemployment compensation case. The same applies to employees. Employees should keep a logbook of everything that happens at work. Sandra Bird kept a logbook and the Oregon Appeals Court allowed it into evidence (*Bird*). Every major incident at work and every outlandish thing the supervisor tells an employee to do should go into the logbook. It may or may not be admissible at the hearing, depending on the state, but even if it is not admitted into evidence, the employee can use it to refresh his or her memory. A witness who can recall details sounds much more convincing.

On Appeal

The losing side may appeal. First you will appeal to a review board or the employment commission itself, and then to the courts. Since you may have only ten days to appeal (calendar days, not work days), you need to act fast.

Generally you can appeal one of four things: (1) the proper procedure was not followed; (2) your constitutional rights were violated; (3) the statute or regulations were not interpreted correctly; or (4) the finding of the agency was not supported by substantial evidence (*Spencer*).

COLLATERAL ESTOPPEL

In 1986 the High Court of New York handed down a ruling that will cause problems for years to come. The New York court ruled that once the hearing officer makes findings of fact in an unemployment compensation case both sides are stuck with those facts (*Guimarales*). This is called **collateral estoppel**. Collateral estoppel is a legal doctrine that says once the legal system determines a fact the parties involved are stuck with that fact. They cannot keep suing trying to change the legal system's mind. This doctrine makes sense where a case has been tried before a judge and jury. It does not make sense to give the factual findings of an unemployment compensation hearing the same weight. These hearings often last 15 minutes. Usually neither side has an attorney. The issues are very specialized and focus on the special terms of the unemployment compensation statute. Decisions in these cases should affect nothing except whether or not the worker gets unemployment compensation. To make them count for anything else is unfair to both employers and employees. In New York employees may not apply for unemployment compensation fearing the determination of the agency will keep them from winning a lawsuit later on. Employers may not challenge employees who apply for unemployment compensation for the same reason. If the employer does challenge the granting of compensation, then each side will probably need an attorney. The unemployment compensation hearing will become the most important hearing for both parties. Whoever wins at that hearing may well have won everything later on.

No other state supreme court has gone along with New York. The Colorado Supreme Court has rejected it along with the supreme courts of Indiana and South Dakota (*Salida Sch., McClanahan, Kolman*).

Employees thinking of suing their employer should consult an attorney before even filing for unemployment compensation. If they live in a state that agrees with New York, the attorney may want them either not to apply for unemployment compensation or to fight that case to the limit. And of course an employer living in New York, or in a state that agrees with New York, will want to consult an attorney before deciding whether to challenge an application for unemployment compensation.

THE FUTURE

We have an unemployment compensation system that ends at state borders. That may have been fine half a century ago but it is not fine today. During the 1980s some states were in recession while others were booming. Under the present system employers in boom states pay low unemployment taxes while employers in recession states pay very high unemployment taxes that they can ill afford. These increased taxes are just another factor preventing those states from recovering.

In an age of computers and closed circuit television most state unemployment agencies are still using the horse and buggy. These agencies can never do the job one big federal employment agency could do. An employer in Boston should be able to interview potential employees in Houston by closed circuit television. Basic-skills tests should be performed once and the results beamed around the country. The answer seems simple. Turn the system back into what it was to begin with, a federal system. With economies of scale this should result in fewer bureaucrats and lower costs. It should also result in increased effectiveness.

6

Wrongful Discharge and Contract Interference

WRONGFUL DISCHARGE

Some employees think they can sue their employer just because they have been fired. This is true if the employee has a term employment contract, a union contract, or a wonderful employee handbook. Most employees do not. They are at-will employees and can be fired for no reason at all.

They cannot be fired for an illegal reason. Throughout the twentieth century Congress and state legislatures have passed laws making it illegal to fire employees for certain reasons. Employees who think they have been fired because of their union membership should turn to Chapter 14. Employees who think they have been fired to keep them from getting their retirement or other company benefits should turn to Chapter 17. Employees who think they have been fired for reporting safety violations to OSHA should turn to Chapter 18. Employees fired because of their race, religion, sex, age, or handicapped condition should turn to Chapters 7, 8, and 9. Employees who have been fired for exercising their right of free speech should turn to Chapter 10. Employees fired because of a drug or lie-detector test should turn to Chapter 12.

Many judges feel these statutes have not been complete enough. Over time, cases have arisen where the state supreme courts felt that the law should protect an employee from discharge for "that reason" but no statute existed that afforded that protection. These courts invented the concept of **common-law wrongful discharge**. Most of these state supreme courts said that firing an employee for a particular reason violated the "public policy" of the state and was thus illegal. The landmark case came three decades ago in California. For many years this idea of common-law wrongful discharge remained just another strange idea of the California judges. During the 1980s more and more state supreme courts came to believe that in some situations courts should declare a particular reason for firing someone to be illegal, even if the legislature had not gotten around to doing so.

Of course, not all state supreme courts feel this way. The Highest Court in New York has rejected this idea, and has said it is up to the New York Legislature to add to the list of reasons employers cannot fire employees. Most pro-boss state supreme courts have refused to recognize the concept of common-law wrongful discharge. So far, Indiana is the only exception. In this chapter we will discuss the major areas in which courts in most fair states will find a discharge to be illegal, even if the legislature has not gotten around to passing a statute to that effect.

Refusing to Commit an Illegal Act

The first common-law wrongful discharge case was the California case of *Petermann v. International Brotherhood of Teamsters*. In 1959 Petermann was told by his supervisors at the Teamsters Union to perjure himself before a legislative committee. When he refused, and told the committee the truth, the Teamsters Union fired him. The California Appeals Court found this to be contrary to the "public policy" of the state of California. The court said it would be "obnoxious to the interests of the state" to allow an employer to fire an employee for this reason. Over the years more and more states have come to accept the concept that employers cannot fire employees just because they refuse to commit an illegal act (*Tameny, Trombetta*).

The clearest case is when the employer tells an employee to do a clearly illegal thing. For example, the Texas Supreme Court had no trouble finding a case of wrongful discharge when a seaman was allegedly fired for refusing to pump the bilges of the boat into the water in violation of the federal environmental laws (*Sabine*).

The Massachusetts Supreme Court recognized the concept of wrongful discharge in a case involving a refusal to commit perjury, while the Indiana Supreme Court allowed a truck driver to sue because he was fired when he refused to drive an illegally overweight truck (*DeRose, McClanahan*). The Minnesota Supreme Court recognized this concept when it refused to allow a gas-station attendant to be fired because he refused to put leaded gas in an unleaded engine in violation of federal law (*Phipps*).

This area of wrongful discharge gets more difficult when the employee is ordered to violate a sense of morality rather than a specific statute or regulation. For example, Dr. Pierce was an at-will employee doing drug research for Ortho. She was assigned to help test an antidiarrhea drug called Loperamide. In order to make the drug easier to take saccharin was added. Pierce objected to the use of saccharin and refused to participate in the drug testing. She was asked to choose another project to work on, but she resigned instead and filed a wrongful discharge lawsuit. She lost. The New Jersey Supreme Court said that she did not have the right to refuse to "conduct research simply because it would contravene . . . her personal morals." The New Jersey Supreme Court said that the case would certainly have been different if she had been asked to violate a statute, a regulation, a constitutional provision, or a professional code of ethics. Since she was not asked to violate any of those things, she had no case (*Pierce*).

Given these decisions, it is reasonable to expect that the supreme courts in most fair states would consider it wrongful discharge for an employer to fire an employee because the employee refused to commit an illegal act.

Whistleblowing

A number of state supreme courts have extended this concept of wrongful discharge to protect employees who were fired because they exposed the illegal activities of their fellow employees or supervisors.

First, there are the cases where the employees reveal illegal activity to the proper governmental authorities. In one case a bank employee was fired for reporting violations of the banking laws to government officials. The West Virginia Supreme Court found this to be a wrongful discharge because it violated public policy (*Harless*).

Other courts have ruled the same way when faced with employees who were fired for reporting possible criminal activity to the local police or threatening to report patient abuse at a nursing home to state officials (*Palmateer, McQuary*).

Some courts have gone a step further and recognized wrongful discharge when the employee has been fired for reporting problems to someone in the company, not to the government. In one case a quality-control inspector complained to his superiors that substandard raw materials in food products violated food and drug laws. The Connecticut Supreme Court found this discharge to be a violation of public policy and therefore wrongful (*Sheets*). The Supreme Court of Hawaii found it to be wrongful to fire the company comptroller because he discussed possible antitrust violations with the company attorney (*Parnar*).

While courts in most fair states appear to be willing to protect people who blow the whistle to a government official, there is some question whether they should do the same when the employee has blown the whistle to higher management within the company. Is this something courts have any right to interfere with? Of course, if the courts protect only the employees who blow the whistle to governmental agencies, employees are not going to tell upper management first and those executives are not going to have a chance to correct the problem internally. In 1988 the Kansas Supreme Court said it did not matter; the employee would be protected if the report is made to either higher management or a government agency (*Palmer*).

If what the employee is complaining about is not a violation of law, the courts may not find it to be a violation of public policy to discharge him or her for exposing it. For example, in one case the employee complained to his superiors within the company about "questionable accounting practices" and was fired because of this complaint. The Michigan Supreme Court refused to find this to be a case of wrongful discharge. The employee was complaining about being forced to violate his professional code of ethics, which the Michigan Supreme Court did not feel was important enough to be protected by the concept of common-law wrongful discharge (*Suchodolski*).

If that employee could have cited a statutory provision, he might have had better luck. In an Illinois case the chief financial officer of a company was allegedly opposed to certain accounting practices because he felt they violated federal securities law (*Johnson #1*). The Illinois Appeals Court found this to be a case of wrongful discharge, even though this employee complained only to other company officials. This court said the behavior complained of did not have to be illegal. What mattered was whether the employee believed in good faith that it was illegal.

The High Court of New York has refused to recognize any kind of common-law wrongful discharge for whistleblowing, a fact that led the New York Legislature to pass a statute on the subject. A number of other states have passed similar statutes (see Table 6–1).

While a few of these statutes protect all employees, most protect only state or government employees from discharge. These statutes vary greatly. Some are very limited. For example, Rhode Island's statute protects only public employees who report violations of law. Delaware's statute protects only state employees and public-school employees who blow the whistle to the state Office of Auditor of Accounts. Whistleblowing to anyone else or whistleblowing by any other kind of employee is not protected by the Delaware statute.

Other statutes are much broader. For example, New Jersey's statute protects all employees who either report illegal activity or refuse to engage in illegal activity. Maine and Minnesota have statutes similar to New Jersey's. The Arizona, Kentucky, and Maryland statutes protect public employees who report mismanagement and waste as well as illegal activity.

Many of these statutes allow the employee to sue and collect damages including attorney fees, but often the employee has only a short time to sue (60 or 90 days).

The New York whistleblower statute protects all employees who disclose illegal activity either to their supervisor or to a public body, but the activity must present a "substantial and specific danger to the public health or safety." It also protects employees who refuse to engage in illegal activities that threaten the "public health or safety." An employee in New York has a year to sue and may receive reinstatement, back wages, and attorney fees. On the other hand the law states that "a court, in its discretion, may also order that reasonable attorneys' fees and court costs and disbursements be awarded to an employer if the court determines that an action brought by an employee under this section was without basis in law or in fact."

Any employee thinking of blowing the whistle should consult an attorney first. The statutes listed in Table 6–1 may change, and more may be added. Some of these statutes require the employee to blow the whistle in a very particular way (or to a particular agency) if he or she wants the protection of the statute. All things considered, it may not be worth it to blow the whistle in many states given the court decisions and statutes that apply.

TABLE 6–1. Whistleblower Statutes*

Alabama	None
Alaska	None
Arizona 38-531,532	Protects public employees who disclose information to public bodies about violations of law and regulations, mismanagement, gross waste, or abuse of authority.
Arkansas	None
California Labor Code 1102.5	Protects all employees who disclose information to public agencies about violations of law and regulations.
Colorado 24-50.5-101 to 107	Protects public employees who disclose information.
Connecticut 31-51m	Protects all employees who disclose information to public bodies about violations of law or regulations. 90 days to sue—can be awarded attorney fees.
Delaware 29-5115	Protects state and school employees who disclose to the Office of Auditor violations of law or regulations. 90 days to sue.
District of Columbia	None
Florida 112.3187	Protects public employees who disclose information to public agencies about violations of law or regulations or neglect of duty. The activity disclosed must present a danger. 90 days to sue.
Georgia	None
Hawaii	New statute 378-61.
Idaho	None
Illinois	None
Indiana 22-5-3-3	Complex—see an attorney.
Iowa	New statute 19A.19
Kansas	None
Kentucky 61.101 to 103	Protects public employees who disclose information to public agencies about violations of law or regulations, waste, fraud, or danger. 90 days to sue.
Louisiana	None
Maine 26-831 to 840	Protects all employees who disclose information about violations of law or refuse to commit violations of law.
Maryland Art. 64A sec. 12G	Protects public employees who disclose information about violations of law, gross mismanagement, or danger.
Massachusetts	None
Michigan 15.361 to .369	Protects all employees who disclose information about violations of law or regulations. 90 days to sue.

*Laws protecting employees may also protect employees of government contractors. Disclosure of false or confidential information may not be protected. Disclosure procedures can be complex.

The law is constantly changing. Consult an attorney about your situation before you disclose information.

TABLE 6–1. (Cont.)

Minnesota 181.931 to .935	Protects all employees who disclose information about violations of law or refuse to commit violations of law. Employees who sue can collect attorney fees.
Mississippi	none
Missouri	New statute.
Montana	none
Nebraska	none
Nevada	none
New Hampshire 275-E	Protects all employees who disclose information about violations of law or refuse to commit violations of law.
New Jersey 34:19-1 to 19-8	Protects all employees who disclose information about violations of law or refuse to commit violations of law. One year to sue—can be awarded attorney fees. Must give boss written notice and a chance to correct.
New Mexico	none
New York Labor sec. 740	Protects all employees who disclose information about violations of law or refuse to commit violations of law. The activity disclosed must present a danger. Both worker and boss can collect attorney fees.
North Carolina	none
North Dakota	none
Ohio	New statute 4113.51.
Oklahoma	none
Oregon	none
Pennsylvania	New statute 43-1421.
Rhode Island 36-15	Protects public employees who disclose information about violations of law or regulations.
South Carolina	New statute 8-27-10.
South Dakota	none
Tennessee	none
Texas Art. 6252-16(a)	Protects public employees who disclose information about violations of law. 90 days to sue.
Utah 67-21	Protects public employees who disclose information about violations of law or regulations or a waste of pubic funds. 90 days to sue.
Vermont	none
Virginia	none
Washington 42.40	Protects state employees who disclose information about improper activity.
West Virginia	none
Wisconsin 230.80 to 89	Protects public employees who disclose information. 60 days to file complaint.
Wyoming	none

Exercising a Legal Right or Performing a Legal Duty

In many states the supreme court has decided an employee cannot be discharged for exercising a right created by statute or for performing a duty required by statute. The classic cases are: (1) being fired for filing a worker's-compensation claim (exercising a legal right) or (2) being fired for having to serve on a jury (performing a legal duty). Some states have statutes that specifically protect people from discharge in these situations. Many state supreme courts have found these discharges to be wrongful even without a specific statutory provision.

In 1973 the Indiana Supreme Court was the first to hold, without a statute, that it was wrongful discharge to fire a worker simply because he or she filed a worker's compensation claim (*Frampton*). Since then almost every state supreme court to rule on this issue has agreed. While the employee cannot be fired simply because he or she filed a worker's compensation claim in most states they can still be fired if they are no longer able to do the work (*Clifford*). (The employee may have a handicap-discrimination claim; see Chapter 9).

What if the employer thinks the employee is about to file for worker's compensation and fires him or her before he or she can file? In 1988 the Illinois and Kansas Supreme Courts said that was still wrongful discharge (*Hinthorn, Chrisman*).

In 1975 the Supreme Court of Oregon found that is was against public policy for employers to fire employees because they had to serve on a jury (*Nees*). Most other state supreme courts have agreed.

The interesting question becomes, what other legal rights or duties will the courts also protect in this way?

A New Jersey court held that it was wrongful to discharge a pharmacist who refused to leave the drug counter unsupervised. He had a duty under state law to ensure that the counter was supervised at all times (*Kalman*). A California Appeals Court held that it was wrong to discharge an employee because he was trying to achieve a reasonably smoke-free workplace for himself (*Hentzel*).

A difficult question has been, while an employee may have a legal right to sue the employer, does the employer have a right to fire the employee in response or would that be wrongful discharge? The only state supreme court to face this issue so far is the Supreme Court of West Virginia in 1987. The case involved a dog catcher who sued his employer for overtime pay (*McClung*). The court ruled that he had a constitutional right to take his problem to court and could not be fired just because he did so. The court affirmed an award of $40,000 in compensatory damages, $35,000 in punitive damages, and attorney fees. An Illinois Appeals Court has ruled that it is wrongful discharge to fire an employee just because he filed a claim for wages (*Brazinski*).

While this may seem unfair to some employers, it is certainly within the logic of wrongful discharge. Many statutes that give employees legal rights, such as the civil rights statutes, specifically state that it will be considered wrongful discharge for an employer to fire an employee simply because the employee has filed a complaint under the statute with the appropriate agency.

Whether courts will extend this logic to cover employees who file other kinds of lawsuits remains to be seen.

Exercising Private Rights

What if the employee is discharged not for exercising rights created by law but for exercising rights spelled out in company policy? We have already seen that the Massachusetts Supreme Court would not let NCR fire a salesman simply to deprive him of his commissions (*Fortune*). A Connecticut Appeals Court held that an employer may not fire someone simply to avoid paying bonuses (*Cook #1*). An Illinois Appeals Court ruled that a company may not discharge workers just to keep them from receiving disability payments pursuant to the employee handbook (*DeFosse*). A Pennsylvania Appeals Court ruled in 1988 that an employee cannot be fired just to keep pension rights from vesting (*Mudd*).

Many of these cases involve employees who feel they have been discharged because they applied for benefits under the company benefit plan or filed a claim under group insurance plans. These cases are now controlled by the federal statute ERISA discussed in Chapter 17. In other cases it will depend on whether the state supreme court thinks employee handbooks are contracts. If they do then these rights will probably be enforced.

Many employees are also shareholders. The Virginia Supreme Court has held that company executives may not discharge or threaten to discharge at-will employees in an effort to control the way they vote their stock as corporate shareholders (*Bowman*). An employee who works for a company that sells stock to the public should buy at least one share. As shareholders employees have many rights, such as the right to examine the company records that they do not have as employees.

Other Public Policy Reasons

In the cases we have been discussing the courts are saying that they will not allow an employer to discharge an employee for "that" reason because it would violate public policy. For example, the New Hampshire Supreme Court said employers may not discharge employees for doing something that is encouraged by public policy or for refusing to do something that is condemned by public policy (*Howard*).

How do we know what is encouraged or condemned by public policy? The New Jersey Supreme Court said that we will find statements of public policy in statutes, government regulations, court decisions, and constitutions (*Pierce*). This can lead to a wide variety of decisions depending on the court.

The Eighth Circuit Court held that a woman who was fired for refusing to have sex with her foreman had been fired in violation of Arkansas public policy. The court said it violated the policy against prostitution (*Lucas*). The Vermont Supreme Court found it to be a violation of state public policy to fire employees just because they were over the age of fifty (*Payne*). The New Hampshire Supreme Court held that being fired for refusing to lie to the company's president violated the public policy in favor of truthfulness (*Cilley*).

Several courts have said that we can find public policy in the state and federal constitutions. Wrongful discharge related to the exercise of free speech is covered in Chapter 10, the demand for due process in Chapter 11, and the invasion of employee privacy in Chapter 12.

Some courts have held that to fire someone for no other reason that to hurt him or her is wrongful discharge (*Tourville*). Others have said that a discharge motivated by bad faith or malice may constitute wrongful discharge (*Monge*). Still others have said an employee can sue if the "way" in which he or she is discharged is particularly unkind (*Kostaras*).

What one person thinks is a violation of public policy may not coincide with what the judges think violates public policy. For example, Sandra McCartney thought it violated public policy for her employer to fire her simply because she was looking for a job with the competition. The Pennsylvania Appeals Court did not agree and refused to find her discharge to be wrongful (*McCartney*).

Montana's Wrongful Discharge Statute

One state supreme court tried to go beyond this idea that a discharge must violate a specific public policy in order to be wrongful. The Montana Supreme Court said that employers had a general duty to treat employees fairly, and if they violated that duty the employees could sue. What difference does it make whether we talk in terms of public-policy violations or this broader duty to be fair? While the Connecticut Supreme Court has recognized that an employer cannot fire an employee in violation of public policy, the court said it was not a violation of public policy for an employer to fire employees charged with wrongdoing without investigating the charges. The judges also said that the employer did not have a duty to give the employees a hearing before dismissal (*Morris*).

The Montana Supreme Court, recognizing a general duty to treat employees fairly, ruled that an employer did have a duty to investigate charges made against employees before firing them (*Crenshaw*). This was too much for the Montana Legislature, which passed a law overriding this decision in 1987 (Mont. 39–2–901).

The law is called the Montana Wrongful Discharge from Employment Act. The act begins by saying that except for the provisions of the act, an employee employed for "no specified term" may be terminated at the will of the employer. The act says that a discharge is wrongful if: "(1)it was in retaliation for the employee's refusal to violate public policy or for reporting a violation of public policy; (2) the discharge was not for good cause and the employee had completed the employer's probationary period of employment; or (3) the employer violated the express provisions of its own written personnel policy."

The law limits damages to four years' lost wages and requires the employee to exhaust the internal company appeal procedures if those procedures meet the requirements of the act. The act does not apply if specific wrongful discharge statutes like the civil rights statutes apply or if the employee has a written contract for a specified length of time (including union contracts). The act also allows either side to offer to arbitrate the dispute. If the other side refuses an offer to arbitrate and loses in court, it must pay the attorney fees for the side that offered to arbitrate.

The act appears to do three things (we will not know for sure until the Montana Supreme Court has a chance to interpret the act). First, it appears to get rid of this idea that employers have a duty to treat their employees fairly in any general sense. This would eliminate the duty to give employees charged with wrongdoing a hearing. Second, while the act specifically protects employees who refuse to violate public policy or report public-policy violations, it appears to take away any protection for employees who are discharged for exercising their legal rights unless another statute specifically protects employees from wrongful discharge in that case. Third, the act appears to eliminate the possibility of suing for violation of an oral employment contract. While the act allows people to sue for violation of the company handbook or a "written contract of employment for a specified term," oral employment contracts appear to be no longer enforceable in Montana. Also, because the act refers specifically to "written contracts of employment for a specified term" an individual with a personal written contract for an unspecified term (fire only for good cause, for example) would apparently be unable to sue in Montana to enforce the contract.

From the point of view of employers this is a very good statute. Employers in Montana no longer have to worry about outspoken supervisors who say things to employees that the employer does not mean. Employers are now free to discharge employees who exercise their legal rights unless there is a specific statute to the contrary. (ERISA and other statutes would protect employees in many situations.)

The statute is not all bad news for employees. The act makes it clear that the Montana Legislature believes employee handbooks should be enforceable in court. The legislature has also agreed with many legal commentators that implied in the notion of a "probationary period" is the idea that once the probationary period is over the employee can be fired only for "good cause." However, there is no requirement that employers have a probationary period and no limit on how long the probationary period may be.

Implied and oral employment contracts appear to be no longer legally enforceable in Montana. Montana employees will find their protection in written statutes, written constitutions, written regulations, written handbooks, written personnel policies, written union contracts, or individual written contracts for a specific term.

The Montana Wrongful Discharge from Employment Act is a compromise between employers and employees. Other state legislatures will be called upon to make similar compromises in the years to come.

Table 6–2 contains a summary of how the fifty state supreme courts feel about this question of common-law wrongful discharge. As you can see, all the pro-boss state supreme courts (except Indiana) who have dealt with this issue

TABLE 6–2. Common-Law Wrongful Discharge*

†Alabama	No	(Reich, Bender Ship, Opp Cotton)
Alaska	Yes Whistleblowing	(Knight)
Arizona	Yes Refuse to commit illegal act; whistleblowing	(Wagenseller) (Wagner)
Arkansas	Yes Whistleblowing	(Oxford)
California	Yes Refuse to commit illegal act	(Petermann, Tameny)
Colorado	Supreme Court has not ruled	
Connecticut	Yes Whistleblowing	(Sheets)
†Delaware	Supreme Court has not ruled	
District of Columbia	High courts have not ruled	
†Florida	Supreme Court has not ruled	
†Georgia	No	(Georgia Power, Gibson)
Hawaii	Yes Refuse to commit illegal act; whistleblowing	(Parnar)
Idaho	Yes	(Watson #1)
Illinois	Yes Whistleblowing; exercising a legal right	(Palmateer) (Kelsay, Hinthorn)
†Indiana	Yes Refuse to commit illegal act; exercising a legal right	(McClanahan) (Frampton)
Iowa	Supreme Court has not ruled	
Kansas	Yes Whistleblowing; exercising a legal right	(Palmer) (Anco, Chrisman)
Kentucky	Yes Exercising a legal right	(Firestone Textile)
Louisiana	No (not a common-law state—legislature must act)	
Maine	Supreme Court has not ruled	
Maryland	Yes	(Adler)
Massachusetts	Yes Refuse to commit illegal act	(DeRose)
Michigan	Supreme Court has not ruled	
Minnesota	Yes Refuse to commit illegal act; whistleblowing; exercising a legal right	(Phipps) (Freidrichs) (Brevik)

*The law is always changing. Consult an attorney about your situation.
†Pro-boss state.

TABLE 6–2. (Cont.)

†Mississippi	No	(Kelly)
Missouri	Supreme Court has not ruled	
Montana	Has wrongful discharge statute	
Nebraska	Yes Exercising a legal right	(Ambroz)
Nevada	Yes Exercising a legal right	(MGM)
New Hampshire	Yes Exercising a legal right	(Monge, Cilley, Cloutier)
New Jersey	Yes	(Pierce, Velantzas)
New Mexico	Yes	(Vigil)
†New York	No	(Murphy)
†North Carolina	Supreme Court is not sure	(Sides)
North Dakota	Yes Exercising a legal right	(Krein)
†Ohio	No	(Phung)
Oklahoma	Supreme Court is not sure	(Hinson)
Oregon	Yes Exercising a legal right	(Nees, Delaney)
†Pennsylvania	Supreme Court has not ruled	
†Rhode Island	Supreme Court has not ruled	
South Carolina	Yes Exercising a legal right	(Ludwick)
South Dakota	Supreme Court has not ruled	
Tennessee	Yes Exercising a legal right	(Clanton)
Texas	Yes Refuse to commit illegal act	(Sabine)
Utah	Supreme Court has not ruled	
Vermont	Yes	(Payne)
Virginia	Yes Exercising a private right	(Bowman)
Washington	Yes	(Cagle)

West Virginia	Yes
	  Whistleblowing; exercising a le-
	  gal right
		(Harless)
		(Wiggins)

Wisconsin	Yes	(Wandry)
Wyoming	Supreme Court has not ruled	

have ruled that there is no such thing as common-law wrongful discharge. Several pro-boss states have not yet specifically ruled on this question, but we would expect them to go along with the other pro-boss states and say that it is up to the legislature to deal with this question.

Every fair-state supreme court that has faced this issue has ruled that there is such a thing as common-law wrongful discharge. We would expect the supreme courts in the other fair states to agree when it is their turn to face the issue head on.

Damages for Wrongful Discharge

Most courts agree that common-law wrongful discharge is a tort. That means an employee can sue for all the damages that have resulted from the discharge. If the employee has suffered mental anguish, he or she can sue for it. If the employer's behavior meets the requirements for punitive damages, the employee can sue for that. The difficult question in these cases has been to what extent an at-will employee who has been wrongfully discharged can recover lost wages. There are three possible approaches.

A court could say that the employee would have worked for many more years if it had not been for the wrongful discharge, and should be paid the wages he or she would have earned over those years. That was the approach of the Wyoming Supreme Court, which took into account the fact that the employee had 26 years to go until retirement, that the average employee worked for this company for 12 years, and that this employee had worked for the company for 8 years. The court decided that this employee would probably have worked for this company for 8 more years, and based an award for lost wages on this figure (*Panhandle*).

Or a court could say that because the employee is at-will, he or she could have been fired the next day for no reason at all and therefore is not entitled to any award for lost wages as part of the damages (*Wagenseller*).

Most courts will probably reject both of these approaches. To make an award based on an estimate of how long a particular employee would have worked for a particular employer would be too speculative for most courts. On the other hand, not to allow any award for lost wages would make this whole area of wrongful discharge meaningless. Most courts will probably take a middle approach. Having been wrongfully discharged, the employee has to mitigate damages by getting another job. Most juries are capable of deciding how long a reasonable person with this employee's skills should take to get another job and the court should make an award for those lost wages. In a 1986 case the Washington Supreme Court upheld an award of $102,152 in a common-law wrongful discharge case. Fourteen thousand of that was for lost wages; the rest was for emotional distress (*Cagle*).

Then there is the question of reinstatement. Many of the statutes that create a type of wrongful discharge provide a remedy that includes reasonable damages and reinstatement. For example, the Oklahoma statute states it is wrong to discharge someone just because he or she filed a worker's compensation claim. Under the statute, if an employee is fired for that reason, the court is required to award reasonable damages and order the employee to be reinstated. The Oklahoma courts have done just that (*Williams #1*). While courts have no trouble ordering employers to reinstate employees when a statute authorizes it, they have been reluctant to order reinstatement for common-law wrongful discharge.

Punitive damages punish people who intentionally hurt others. If the employer acted maliciously, the court may award punitive damages. However, in some states, before the court will award punitive damages against a corporation a special test must be met. In a New York case, a corporation executive defamed an employee (*Loughry*). The jury awarded $55,000 to compensate for the damage done to the employee's reputation, and $133,000 as punitive damages. The executive involved was a bank vice president. The Highest Court in New York held that before anyone can get an award of punitive damages against the corporation, he or she has to show that someone in management either "authorized or participated in" the conduct in question, or that someone in management "consented to or ratified" the conduct. In this case the person who committed the act was only a vice president. The New York High Court said that was not good enough. Since he was not "management," the court eliminated the punitive-damages award against the corporation. Some states, such as Alabama and California, have statutes that prevent awarding punitive damages against an employer unless the employer knew the employee was unfit, or the employer authorized, ratified, or knowingly participated in the evil conduct (Ala. 6–11–1 to 30; Cal. Civil Code sec. 3294).

In many cases the employer will offer the employee a chance to resign. Every employee, even company executives, should think twice before they agree to resign. It is very difficult to sue for wrongful discharge if you have not been "discharged" (but it is not impossible).

Any employee asked to sign a release should consult an attorney before doing so. A release means you can forget any lawsuits against the employer. Before you give up your rights, make sure you know what your rights are.

Preemption

There may be times when employees will not be allowed to sue because of preemption. Preemption may mean that there is some administrative procedure the employee should have followed instead of suing in court or that because the state legislature or Congress has dealt with a problem in a specific statute, everyone is stuck with the provisions of that statute, and the courts will not allow recovery under the general principles of the common law. The point is that employees need to discuss their case with an attorney as soon as possible because their situation may be covered by an existing administrative procedure or statute.

Administrative Preemption   If employees sue under a statute that gives them a right to sue but requires them to bring the case to some administrative agency first, they are probably stuck with that procedure. For example, in two recent cases from Illinois and Massachusetts, employees were suing for age discrimination but failed to take their complaints to the relevant administrative agencies before going to court. Both courts held that the employees were required to follow the administrative procedure first, and because they had not, they lost (*Pistner, Mouradian*).

These courts are correct in stating the general rule. If a specific statute requires employees to go to an administrative agency, then they cannot recover under that statute without following the required procedure. If there is some other statute they can also sue under, or the court believes this behavior violates the common law, then the employees may not have to go through the administrative procedure if they do not want to (*Payne*).

The best example of this is the Civil Rights Act of 1866 and the Civil Rights Act of 1964. The Civil Rights Act of 1866 did not have an administrative agency to enforce its provisions. The 1964 Act requires employees to go to the EEOC (Equal Employment Opportunity Commission) before they can sue in federal court. The federal circuit courts have said that employees do not have to go to the EEOC if they are claiming a violation of the old act, but do if they are suing under the new act (*Hines*).

Usually, since an employee will want to sue under every available statute as well as the common law, it will be to their advantage to follow any administrative procedure available to them. If for some reason they cannot go to the administrative agency—for example, they waited too long—they may be able to sue under some other statute or the common law and still get a remedy.

Statutory Preemption The other aspect of this that both employers and employees must be aware of is the question of state statutory preemption. When a legislature passes a statute, the question often comes up: Is this statute in addition to the common law or is it intended to preempt the old common law and change the law on this subject? The Montana Wrongful Discharge from Employment Act clearly is intended to preempt the common law. That means all the wrongful-discharge decisions made by the Montana Supreme Court before the passage of that statute are out the window. The common law has been preempted by the legislature, and an employee will have to find a remedy in that, or some other statute, if he or she wants to sue an employer for wrongful discharge.

In some states it is an open question whether the whistleblower statutes that have been passed are in addition to the common law as declared in state supreme court decisions or have preempted the common law.

Then there is the question of federal preemption. This doctrine flows from the fact that federal law is the supreme law of the land. If Congress passes a statute, and it is constitutional, it is the supreme law of the land and every law that contradicts it is by implication made null and void. Also, if Congress wants to, it can preempt the field. That means all state statutes and state court doctrines dealing with that area of law are no longer of any force, whether they contradict the federal law or not.

It is not always easy to tell whether Congress intended to preempt an area of law. The U.S. Supreme Court has decided that when Congress passed ERISA, it intended to preempt that area. That means if an employee has a problem with the way an employer administers the employee benefit program (medical insurance, disability, and so on), the employee has to sue under the provisions of ERISA, not state law (see Chapter 17).

During the 1980s many state and federal judges decided that federal labor law preempted state common-law wrongful discharge for workers covered by union contracts. That meant that these workers were not allowed to sue for the kinds of wrongful discharge discussed in this chapter. Other judges said they could, and this disagreement caused a great deal of confusion. In June 1988 the U.S. Supreme Court cleared up the confusion with a unanimous decision. The justices ruled that workers covered by union contracts can sue for wrongful discharge under state common-law principles just like everyone else (Lingle).

INTERFERENCE WITH CONTRACT

Pennzoil had a contract to buy Getty Oil. Texaco talked the owners of Getty Oil into selling out to Texaco instead of Pennzoil. The jury awarded Pennzoil $7.5 billion in compensatory damages (the money Pennzoil was out because they did not get the benefit of the contract) plus $3 billion in punitive damages. The Texas Appeals Court reduced the punitive damages to $2 billion (Texaco). The Texas Supreme Court upheld that decision.

The same principle applies to employment contracts. If a third party comes along and interferes with an employment contract, usually by talking the employer into firing the employee, the employee can sue the third party just as Pennzoil sued Texaco. Remember, every employee has an employment contract. Even if the employees are at-will, they can still sue anyone who talks the employer into firing them (Eib, Deauville, Hooks).

Take the case of Karen Lewis. Soon after she went to work for the Oregon Beauty Supply Company, she started dating the owner's son. When she told the owner's son she wanted to see other men, he harassed her at work until she quit. The Oregon Appeals Court found this to be a case of interference with a contract (the court called it interference with an economic relationship). It did not matter that Lewis was an at-will employee; she still had a contract with her employer that was interfered with by the employer's son. The court upheld an award of punitive damages against the son (Oregon Beauty).

In another case the executive director of legal aid in Hawaii was charged with misappropriation of funds. Before the investigation could be completed the Legal Services Corporation in Washington D.C. said if the director were not fired, it would stop funding the Hawaii legal-aid office. The fired executive director sued the Legal Services Corportion for interference with his employment contract and defamation and received an award of $337,500 (Locricchio).

The law understands if one of the two parties to a contract has to break the contract. The law does not understand when some third party comes along and talks one of the parties into breaking the contract.

The law also does not like people who interfere with other important relationships, such as a person's relationship with government. In one case the employer told the Maryland Unemployment Compensation Agency that Julianna Ellett had quit, which would make her ineligible for unemployment compensation. This turned out to be a lie. The Maryland Appeals Court found this to be interference with a government relationship (the court called it interference with perspective advantage) and allowed Ellett to sue the employer (*Ellett*).

In another case the employer got a government agency to revoke the employee's license to work. That also qualified as interference with a government relationship and the employer was held liable (the court called this interference with an advantageous relationship) (*Willis*).

What if the employer is a corporation and the person who interferes (by firing the employee) is the employee's own supervisor? Can the employee sue the supervisor? Yes, but to win, the employee has to prove that the supervisor fired the employee for personal reasons. A supervisor has every right to fire an employee for business reasons.

In a Vermont case several Bennington College adminstrators talked Bennington College into firing Professor Lyon (*Lyon*). The Vermont Supreme Court held that Professor Lyon could sue Bennington College for breach of contract and the administrators for interference with contract. The Vermont Supreme Court said that if the administrators made their recommendation for business reasons, fine; if they did it for personal reasons, then they would be held liable. It would be up to the jury to decide.

A Pennsylvania Appeals Court has ruled that employees cannot sue their own supervisors for interference with the employee's contract, but in 1988 a Georgia Appeals Court ruled that they can (*Daniel Adams, Yaindl, Favors*).

People usually cannot sue a party to a contract, in this case the company, for interfering with its own contract (*Michelson, Mailhiot*). Dudley Post found a way around this when he sued Wang for both breach of contract and interference with contract (*Wang*). Post had a contract with Wang to help reduce Wang's income taxes by finding provisions in the tax laws that Wang could take advantage of. He did a very good job and saved Wang hundreds of thousands of dollars. Eventually Wang hired a full-time tax man, Mr. Joseph, who talked other executives at Wang into firing Post even though there were several years left on his contract. The trial judge said in his decision that Joseph did this "with the intent to advance his own interests within the corporation. His interference constituted a willful act calculated to obtain the benefits of Post's contract with Wang without cost and in disregard of known contractual arrangements."

While Post could sue Wang for breach of contract, and Joseph for interference with contract, the trial judge would not let Post sue Wang for interference with its own contract (that is generally going to be the case). The Massachusetts Supreme Court found a way around this problem in this case. It held that Joseph's behavior violated the Massachusetts Deceptive Trade Practices Act. Because Joseph was trying to advance Wang's interests, as well as his own, when he did deceptive things (lied to other executives at Wang about Post's performance under the contract), Wang could be made to pay the damages. A deceptive trade practices act is usually intended to protect consumers. Yet if you read the language of most acts literally, they say anyone who has been injured by a deceptive practice (in this case Joseph's lies were the deceptive practice) can sue for damages. Technically Post had a contract with Wang, and Wang not only broke the contract but did something deceptive in the process. The Massachusetts Supreme Court did not care that Post was not a consumer but an employee (in this case, technically, he was an independent contractor). The deceptive trade practices act requires the judge to at least double the amount of damages. The Massachusetts Supreme Court sent the case back so that the trial judge could decide how much the damages should be increased. Some attorneys find this case a little hard to swallow. After all, deceptive trade practices acts are designed to punish people who lie to consumers. In this case the only people lied to were Wang's own executives. In a sense, Wang had to pay extra damages to Post because it lied to itself.

Part Three
Civil Rights

7
Racial and Religious Discrimination

THE PAST

In 1857 Dred Scott, a Missouri slave, sued to have himself declared a free man because he had been taken by his master through free territory. The Supreme Court said any law that purported to make slaves free without compensating the slave owners violated the U.S. Constitution because this amounted to a taking of private property without compensation (*Dred Scott*).

Abraham Lincoln was elected President in 1860. On April 12, 1861, Fort Sumter was shelled and the Civil War began. On January 1, 1863, Lincoln signed the Emancipation Proclamation freeing the slaves in the Confederate States. Robert E. Lee surrendered on April 9, 1865, and President Lincoln was assassinated six days later. The period of Reconstruction left us three Constitutional Amendments and the Reconstruction Civil Rights Acts.

Thirteenth Amendment

The Thirteenth Amendment says "neither slavery nor involuntary servitude, except as a punishment for crime whereof the party shall have been duly convicted, shall exist within the United States, or any place subject to their jurisdiction." It was with this amendment that the former slaves really became free.

Some southern states dealt with the new freedmen by arresting them. A former master could then buy a convict for the length of his prison term by putting up the amount of his fine. The U.S. Supreme Court declared that activity unconstitutional in 1914 (*Reynolds #1*).

Fourteenth Amendment

The Fourteenth Amendment says "no State shall make or enforce any law which shall abridge the privileges or immunities of citizens of the United States; nor shall any State deprive any person of life, liberty or property without due process of law; nor deny to any person within its jurisdiction the equal protection of the laws."

To enforce this amendment and protect the rights of the new citizens, Congress passed a series of Civil Rights Acts in 1866 and 1867 called the Reconstruction Civil Rights Acts, but these statutes were soon forgotten.

As the twentieth century progressed, the U.S. Supreme Court decided that the Fourteenth Amendment made the Bill of Rights of the U.S. Constitution applicable to state and local governments. This means a government employer cannot fire employees for exercising their right of free speech, deny them the due process of law, or invade their privacy (*Slochower*) (see Chapters 10, 11, 12).

It also means that governments must treat people equally. For example, in 1978 the U.S. Supreme Court struck down an Alaska statute that required companies using state oil leases to hire residents of Alaska before hiring people from other states. This law denied the citizens of other states the "equal protection" of the law (*Hicklin*).

Fifteenth Amendment

The Fifteenth Amendment says "the rights of citizens of the United States to vote shall not be denied or abridged by the United States or by any State on account of race, color or previous condition of servitude."

Some states required voters to own property, pay poll taxes, and pass literacy tests. The U.S. Supreme Court declared the property ownership requirements and poll taxes to be unconstitutional in the 1960s (*Reynolds #2, Hill, Harper*). Congress passed the Voting Rights Act in 1970, which outlawed literacy tests as a requirement for voting, and the Supreme Court upheld the statute (*Oregon*).

The Reconstruction Civil Rights Acts

The Civil Rights Acts passed during Reconstruction were forgotten for almost a century. Then, in 1968, they were rediscovered and declared valid by the U.S. Supreme Court (*Jones #1*).

The section we are concerned with is section 1981, which says "all persons" shall have the same right to "make and enforce contracts" as "white citizens" (42 U.S.C. sec. 1981). Everyone agrees that this section prevents states and local governments from passing statutes or ordinances that would allow judges to be race conscious when interpreting or enforcing contracts. The difficult question is, did Congress intend also to prevent private people from being race conscious when they entered into private contracts? In 1975 the U.S. Supreme Court said Congress did intend this section to reach private people and that this statute could be used to force private employers to extend the same right to make employment contracts to blacks that they extend to whites. In other words, the court said section 1981 of the Reconstruction Civil Rights Act prohibits racial discrimination in employment (*Railway Express*).

The next year the court said this section also prevented discrimination against whites (*McDonald*). In 1987 the court made it clear that this section applies to all racial discrimination, even discrimination against Arabs and Hispanics (*St. Francis*).

TITLE VII OF THE 1964 CIVIL RIGHTS ACT

President Kennedy proposed a Civil Rights Act in 1963. It was passed in 1964 and went into effect in July 1965. The part concerned with employment discrimination is commonly called Title VII. The main section of Title VII reads as follows:

(a) It shall be an unlawful employment practice for an employer:

(1) to fail or refuse to hire or to discharge any individual, or otherwise to discriminate against any individual with respect to his compensation, terms, conditions, or privileges of employment, because of such individual's race, color, religion, sex or national origin, or

(2) to limit, segregate, or classify his employees or applicants for employment in any way which would deprive or tend to deprive any individual of employment opportunities or otherwise adversely affect his status as an employee, because of such individual's race, color, religion, sex or national origin. (42 U.S.C. sec. 2000e-2)

The EEOC

The Equal Employment Opportunity Commission (EEOC) was created to administer the 1964 Civil Rights Act. It performs four major functions: writing regulations interpreting the act; investigating possible discrimination; trying to negotiate a settlement when individuals file complaints; and filing lawsuits to stop discrimination.

Who Can Sue?

The 1964 Civil Rights Act outlaws discrimination based on "race, color, religion, sex or national origin." While the act says its main purpose is to "open employment opportunities for Negroes in occupations which have been traditionally closed to them," the Supreme Court has held that it protects everyone from racial discrimination, including whites and American Indians (*McDonald, Weahkee*).

The act also outlaws discrimination based on national origin. That means an employer cannot discriminate based on "the country where the person was born" or "the country from which his or her ancestors came" (*Espinoza*). The act also outlaws sex and religious discrimination.

Who Can Be Sued?

Businesses The 1964 Civil Rights Act applies to businesses if they have at least 15 employees during at least 20 weeks in the year. The act also requires that the employer be engaged in a business that "affects commerce," but almost any business "affects commerce" today.

Religious and Educational Organizations Religious and educational organizations are listed as employers and are covered by the act. However, Title VII specifically allows religious organizations (including schools affiliated with religious denominations) to discriminate on the basis of religion.

Governments The act applies to state and local governments. It also applies to federal civil servants, but they follow a different procedure from the one described in this chapter.

Employment Agencies and Labor Unions Employment agencies and labor unions are specifically covered by the act. Licensing agencies like state bar associations and medical boards are also covered (*Tyler*).

What Is Discrimination?

The 1964 Civil Rights Act outlaws discimination in hiring, firing, and working conditions. Some employers tried to get around this with sex-plus or race-plus rules. For example, one company had a rule against hiring women with preschool-aged children (*Phillips*). The U.S. Supreme Court said this was illegal. While employers can say "employees with children" need not apply (unless a state law forbids this), they cannot say "women with children" or "blacks with children" need not apply. While employers can say "employees cannot be married" (unless a state law forbids this), they cannot say female employees cannot be married (*TWA, Sprogis, Airline Stewards*).

Employers cannot segregate employees into jobs or work units on the basis of race, color, religion, sex, or national origin. It makes no difference if the jobs are equal; separate but equal is not allowed. Employers cannot have separate restroom or eating facilities for blacks and whites or sponsor separate social functions (*Jacksonville Terminal, Firefighters*). Having Hispanic employees serve Hispanic customers and Anglo employees serve Anglo customers is also illegal (*Rogers*).

Employers cannot harass employees because of their race, color, religion, sex, or national origin. If the harassment is inflicted by other employees, the employer is still liable if he or she knew about it and did not try to stop it (*Higgins*). In some cases the employee has quit rather than put up with harassment or discriminatory conditions. For example, in one case an employee quit rather than attend an employer-sponsored religious service. The Fifth Circuit Court said this was an illegal activity and allowed this employee to sue. To the courts, being forced to quit (constructive discharge) is just the same as being fired (*Young*).

The 1964 Civil Rights Act outlaws not only intentional discrimination but also unintentional discrimination. Even if a rule appears to be race or sex neutral, if the rule has an **adverse impact** on a minority group, it may still be illegal discrimination. In one case the employer would not allow employees to transfer from one job group to another. In the past only members of one race had been allowed to apply for certain jobs. This no-transfer rule continued the effect of past discrimination and was illegal (*Lee Way*). In another case the employer discriminated in favor of workers who had worked under past union contracts. Since black people had not been allowed to join the union in the past, this perpetuated past discrimination and was illegal (*Sheet Metal Workers*).

The landmark "adverse impact" case was *Griggs v. Duke Power Co.* The Duke Power Company required a high-school diploma and passing scores on two standard tests, the Wonderlic Intelligence Test and the Bennett Mechanical Comprehension Test, before it would consider an applicant for a job, any job. These requirements kept more blacks than whites from getting jobs at Duke Power. The district judge ruled that Duke Power had not discriminated because there was no intent to discriminate. The U.S. Supreme Court overruled this decision, saying "the act proscribes not only overt discrimination, but also practices that are fair in form but discriminatory in operation." While the 1964 Civil Rights Act specifically allows employers to use tests, the tests must not be "intended, designed or used" to discriminate. The Supreme Court held that a test that had an adverse impact on a protected group was "used" to discriminate and thus violated the act.

The court said an employer could use a test that had an adverse impact on a protected group if the employer could prove the test accurately predicted job performance. The test must "measure the person for the job, not the person in the abstract." There are only two ways an employer can meet this requirement. First, the test can measure a skill used on the job. A mailman has to be able to read and a secretary has to be able to type. Second, the test can be proved to predict job performance accurately. There is only one scientific way to prove that. The test must be given to a group of applicants who are then all hired. After a time, the job performance of the employees is objectively measured and compared with the test results. If there is a significant correlation between the quality of job performance and the test results, then the test can be used, even if it discriminates against a protected group. Very few employers have been willing to scientifically validate job tests in this way.

How does an employee prove adverse impact? In the *Griggs* case statistics showed that 12 percent of blacks in North Carolina had high-school diplomas compared with 34 percent of whites. That was enough to prove adverse impact. When height and weight requirements were imposed on prison-guard applicants, national census data showed that the requirements eliminated 97.76 percent of the women and 58.87 percent of the men who might have applied. The U.S. Supreme Court said that had an adverse impact on women (*Dothard*).

In some cases the judges have decided that a diploma or other requirement was "obviously" required for the job and allowed its use without special proof that it predicted job performance. For example, one court felt a high-school diploma was an obvious requirement for being a police officer (*Castro*). However, different courts do not always agree on what is an "obvious" requirement. The California Supreme Court felt that the ability to pass an agility test was obviously related to being a good police officer but the Ninth Circuit Court did not agree and demanded proof that agility correlated with job performance (*Hardy, Blake*).

A requirement that has an adverse impact on a minority group may be allowed if the employer can prove there is a good reason for the requirement. For example, Safeway Stores were allowed to have a no-beard rule even though in this particular case it had an adverse impact on blacks. The judges felt the desire to maintain a good public image was a good enough reason for the rule (*Woods #1*). The U.S. Supreme Court allowed the New York City Transit Authority to automatically reject job applicants who were on methadone maintenance in order to maintain the public's confidence in public transportation even though this requirement had an adverse impact on minorities (*Beazer*).

The EEOC has written guidelines on the kinds of questions employers can ask job applicants. The employer cannot ask different questions of different groups. The employer cannot ask about age ("How old are you?"), race, sex, religion ("What church do you go to?"), or national origin ("What kind of name is that?"). Employers can ask if the job would conflict with religious observance ("Can you work on Saturday or Sunday?"). Employers cannot ask women about their children or their plans for having a family, but they can ask if job applicants have any physical limitation that might prevent them from being able to do the job.

Proving Discrimination

Employees do not have to prove that the employer intended to discriminate under Title VII, only that they were discriminated against. What's the difference?

The U.S. Supreme Court explained the process in *McDonnell Douglas*. Employees must prove:

1. that they are within a protected class;
2. that they applied for the job;
3. that they were qualified for the job;
4. that they were not hired (or fired);
5. that the employer then hired someone of a different race, color, religion, sex, or national origin.

If the employee can prove these five things, he or she wins, unless the employer can prove a "legitimate reason" for not hiring or firing this person. If the employer can prove that, then he or she wins unless the employee can prove the reason is "merely a pretext" covering up the fact that the employer intended to discriminate (*Sweeney #1*). Employees do not have to prove they are the most qualified for the job, only that they have the basic qualifications. However, an employer can defend himself by proving someone more qualified was actually hired (*Flowers*).

If a group of employees engage in the same misconduct and the employer fires only those of a particular race or sex, that is obviously discrimination. In one case two white employees were dismissed while a black employee accused of the same theft was not. The U.S. Supreme Court ruled that this was a clear case of racial discrimination (*McDonald*). In another case a group of black police officers proved that white officers who were also accused of taking bribes were not investigated and were not fired. The judge found that the bribe-taking charge was just a pretext for firing black police officers and ordered them reinstated (*Corley*).

During the 1970s class-action lawsuits and complex statistics were used to prove discrimination. In the 1980s many federal judges were less willing to allow one worker to represent many members of a class that might include all blacks who applied for jobs or promotions with a particular company during a particular period of time. Also, many federal judges were less willing to allow statistics to be used to prove discrimination. Both class-action lawsuits and the use of statistics may have been given new life in June 1988 with a unanimous decision from the U.S. Supreme Court in *Watson*. The case involved statistics showing that over a four-year period 16.7 percent of whites and 4.2 percent of blacks who applied were offered jobs. An expert on statistics testified that the odds against this happening by chance were ten thousand to one. The Supreme Court ruled that these kinds of statistics could be used to prove discrimination even though the supervisors testified that they did not discriminate and several black employees testified that they were treated fairly (*Watson #2*).

This case is important for another reason. During the 1980s many employers stopped using objective tests in making hiring or promotion decisions because the tests kept out a higher percentage of minorities and the employer could not prove that the test validly predicted job performance. These employers began to rely solely on the subjective decisions of their supervisors. In the *Watson* case those subjective decisions resulted in the rejection of 95.8 percent of black job applicants. The U.S. Supreme Court ruled that these "subjective tests" are also in violation of Title VII if they result in discrimination unless they can be shown to validly predict the quality of job performance. That will be impossible to prove in most cases, and this fact leaves us all to wonder what selection method is legal under Title VII. Will flipping a coin be the only legally acceptable method? On the other hand, if all other methods are in reality just disguised race discrimination, with no scientific basis for their use in making personnel decisions, perhaps flipping a coin should be the only legal method of employee selection. Remember, if the test, objective or subjective, does not result in discrimination (the same percentage of minorities pass the test), it is not illegal and can be used, regardless of its validity. Stupid tests are not illegal; only nonvalid tests that result in discrimination are illegal.

When Discrimination Is Legal

Title VII specifically allows discrimination that is the result of a bona fide seniority or merit system (42 U.S.C. sec. 2000e-2(h)). This is allowed even if the bona fide seniority system perpetuates past discrimination (*Teamsters*). At the same time, federal judges have the power to grant artificial seniority to people who have been the victims of past discrimination (*Franks*). That means that if persons apply for a job and are turned down, and then win in federal court, the judge can give them the seniority they would have had if they had been hired in the first place.

Title VII also allows discrimination if sex, religion, or national origin is a "bona fide occupational qualification" (BFOQ) reasonably necessary to the normal operation of that particular business (42 U.S.C. sec. 2000e-2(e)). Please note: Race is not on that list, only sex, religion, and national origin.

To qualify as a BFOQ the favored sex or religion must possess a quality essential to the job. For example, only women can be wet nurses. Just because customers prefer one sex over the other is not good enough. The airlines argued that customers preferred women stewardesses over male stewards but the judge said that was not a BFOQ (*Diaz*).

Procedures under Title VII

Congress created a procedure that is far more complex than it needed to be. A complaint (called a "charge") must be filed with the EEOC within 180 calendar days after the discriminatory act. In a state that has its own human rights commission an employee may file a charge with either the EEOC or the state commission. The state may give employees more than 180 days to file the charge with the state commission.

The best approach for most employees is to file a complaint with the EEOC within the EEOC's 180-day time limit. The EEOC will send the case to the state commission, the state commission will do whatever it does, and then it will send it back to the EEOC.

The U.S. Supreme Court has ruled that if a state has a human rights commission the deadline for filing with the EEOC is automatically extended to 300 days instead of 180 (*Com. Office Prod.*). To see how this works take the case of Michael Mennor. He filed his charge with the EEOC within 300 days of the discriminatory act (he was fired for complaining about the way his employer treated Hispanic employees) but more than 180 days after the discriminatory act. The EEOC sent this complaint over to the Texas Human Rights Commission, which sent it back because Texas law requires the injured person to file with the Texas commission within 180 days. Mennor was too late under Texas law. The EEOC then processed this complaint. Mennor eventually was reinstated with back pay and the Fifth Circuit Court approved of this procedure (*Mennor*).

Once the case gets to the EEOC, that agency has 180 days to try to negotiate a settlement between the employer and the employee. If the EEOC decides not to sue for the employee (they almost never do), then they will give the employee a right-to-sue letter (*Stebbins*). Once an employee has a right-to-sue letter, he or she must file a lawsuit in federal court within 90 days (*Lynn*). If an employee misses this deadline, he or she may still be able to get another right-to-sue letter from the state human rights commission and sue in state court under the state civil rights act.

Title VII versus the Reconstruction Act

There are two civil rights acts at the federal level, Title VII and the Reconstruction Civil Rights Act. Many people can sue under both and usually will. Anyone suing for race discrimination can sue under both acts. People suing private employers for sex or religious discrimination can sue only under Title VII. What difference does it make? Under Title VII the injured person must go to the EEOC quickly, within 180 or 300 days. That is not true when suing under the Reconstruction Act. If victims of racial discrimination miss the deadlines under Title VII, they may still be able to sue under the Reconstruction Act.

Persons suing under Title VII get up to two years' back pay and are reinstated to their old job. People using the Reconstruction Act can sue for their entire damages. For example, in one case the court awarded $123,000 for emotional damages, $176,000 for lost wages, and $300,000 for punitive damages (*Rowlett*).

Someone suing under Title VII does not get a jury, while someone suing under the Reconstruction Act does. On the other hand, someone suing under the Reconstruction Act has to prove intentional discrimination, while someone suing under Title VII can prove adverse impact or meet the *McDonnell Douglas* test (*Catlett*).

The amount of back pay awarded under either statute will be reduced by the amount of money the employee earned, or could have earned, while not working for this employer. It will also be reduced by the amount of Social Security and unemployment compensation received (*Steamfitters*).

Under both statutes, if the employee wins, the employer has to pay the employee's attorney fees.

In a few cases employees have sued only under the Reconstruction Civil Rights Act and skipped all the EEOC procedure. This is perfectly all right (*Patsy, Trigg, Crawford*). However, most attorneys would prefer to sue for everything they can when they finally get their day in court. They prefer to go through the EEOC and state human rights commission procedures first.

In some states the state human rights commission will hold a hearing at which the facts will be decided. In 1986 the U.S. Supreme Court ruled that if a state hearing officer makes a decision on the facts (whether the discharge was motivated by race, for example), that decision has "collateral estoppel" effect on a case brought under the Reconstruction Civil Rights Act but does not have "collateral estoppel" effect on a case brought under Title VII (*Elliott*). Collateral estoppel means that once a fact is decided the parties involved are stuck with that decision. Because employees may be stuck with the facts as they are found to exist by the state human rights commission (as far as their Reconstruction Civil Rights Act case is concerned), they will want to discuss their case with an attorney as quickly as possible and before doing anything on their own. The attorney may decide to skip the state human rights commission and may even decide to skip the EEOC.

The rest of this chapter is about reverse discrimination, affirmative action, racial harassment, religious discrimination, the new immigration law, and state civil rights laws. Readers interested in age or handicap discrimination can skip to Chapter 9. Readers interested in sex discrimination should read the rest of this chapter before going on to Chapter 8.

REVERSE DISCRIMINATION

Can a white man sue because of race or sex discrimination? Section 1981 of the Reconstruction Civil Rights Act says "all persons" shall have the same right to contract as "white citizens." That would seem to suggest that white men cannot sue under Section 1981. Title VII says it is unlawful to "discriminate against any individual" or to deprive "any individual" of employment opportunities. That is certainly broad language. At the same time Congress said the purpose of the act was to help blacks. Could it be interpreted to help whites also?

In 1976 the U.S. Supreme Court said that both acts protect white men as well as everyone else. The case involved two white male employees who were fired for stealing while a black employee charged with the same offense was not fired. The court said the company could fire all three, or keep all three, but it could not fire the white men and keep the black man (*McDonald*). Men have also been able to prove discrimination in cases involving sex discrimination (*Martinez, Diaz*).

In the decade since that decision was handed down federal courts have wrestled with how to protect the rights of white men. As you have seen, the standard procedure in a Title VII case is to start by showing that the employee is a member of a protected group. White men are not members of a protected group. This places an extra burden on white men to show that there is some evidence of discriminatory intent on the part of the employer. This usually means that facts have to be a little more outrageous than would be the case if the employees were not white men.

In one case a white man was fired by a black-oriented radio station in Houston because he did not have the right "voice." The judge said this was a pretext for racial discrimination and awarded back pay and reinstatement (*Chaline*).

When the black principal of South Oak Cliff High School in Dallas, Texas, fired Norman Jett, the white-male head football coach, Jett sued for race discrimination under the Reconstruction Civil Rights Act (Oak Cliff is a predominantly black section of Dallas). Jett had coached at South Oak Cliff High School for 20 years. The District Court awarded $450,000 in actual damages and

$112,870 in attorney's fees. The jury found violations of Jett's due process and free-speech rights as well as racial discrimination (*Jett*).

How did Jett prove racial discrimination? He showed he was part of a racial minority at South Oak Cliff High School, that he was well qualified for the job, and that he was replaced by a less-qualified black football coach. The school district presented evidence that it had legitimate reasons for firing Jett, but the jury apparently believed Jett, not the school district.

It is probably easier for a white man to prove discrimination when he is fired than when he is not hired or not promoted. Two 1986 cases show that a white man can win cases involving failure to promote or failure to hire.

When the fire chief of the District of Columbia, a black man, promoted a black man to be assistant fire chief the deputy chiefs sued for race discrimination. There were five deputy chiefs below the level of assistant chief, all white. The black man who received the promotion was a battalion chief, a level below that of deputy chief. The district judge found the five white candidates at the deputy-chief level to be superior in terms of "seniority, education, and experience" to the black man who was promoted. The Circuit Court said that the white men had proved a case of reverse discrimination (*Bishopp*).

In another case, the judge found Dennis Walters had been the victim of racial discrimination because the city of Atlanta did not hire him to be the director of the Cyclorama (*Walters*). The Cyclorama is a giant painting 50 feet high and 350 feet in circumference that depicts the Civil War battle of Atlanta. When Walters first visited it at the age of six, he was so impressed he decided he would work at the Cyclorama when he grew up. In the 1970s the Cyclorama was closed for restoration. It was reopened in 1981 and the city established a list (called a register) of eligible applicants for the position of director. Seven applicants were on the register, all white. Walters was listed as "well qualified." The seven were interviewed by city officials and three were recommended to the Parks Commissioner, Geraldine Elder. Walters, who had worked for the Georgia Historical Commission and the North Carolina Museum of History, was one of the three. When Ms. Elder found out all the applicants were white, she asked for a new register. At that point Walters sued under Title VII and the Reconstruction Civil Rights Act. Meanwhile, Ms. Elder appointed as acting director a black woman who had campaigned for Mayor Young. This woman was fired in 1982 for poor performance.

A new register was established in 1982. Walters was again listed as "well qualified" and was again among the three candidates recommended. David Palmer, a black man, was first listed as "unqualified," but this was changed to "qualified" because he had two years of experience in food-product marketing. Elder hired Palmer instead of Walters.

In 1983 the new Parks Commissioner, Carolyn Hatcher, fired Palmer when she found him holding two full-time jobs in violation of city regulations. She then hired Carole Mumford to be the director. Ms. Mumford had been listed as "qualified" on the 1982 register.

The district judge and the jury found intentional racial discrimination. Walters was awarded the pay he would have received if the city had hired him in 1981, and he was given the job of director of the Cyclorama. Because he had sued under the Reconstruction Civil Rights Act the jury was allowed to award him full compensatory and punitive damages. They awarded him $150,000 for mental anguish and $7,000 for punitive damages (this punitive-damages award was reduced to $2,000 by the circuit court). The attorney's fees award was over $60,000. The circuit court ended its decision by saying:

> The relief awarded in this case places Walters in an unusual position. He has, with the aid of the federal courts, achieved his lifelong ambition. The irony of Walters' use of statutes enacted in the wake of the Civil War is lost on no one. Walters and the City must now live together. As did the Union and the Confederacy, the parties must bind their wounds and make peace.

AFFIRMATIVE ACTION

There is one defense to a civil rights lawsuit by a white man that is not available in other cases. Employers can defend themselves by proving the discrimination is part of a bona fide affirmative action plan. There are four rules that apply to affirmative action plans. These rules exist because it takes five votes to win a case at the U.S. Supreme Court. Justices Marshall, Blackmun, and Stevens always vote for affirmative action. Two more votes must be gotten before an affirmative action plan will be accepted by the court. Each of the rules is associated with one of the other justices.

The O'Connor Rule: The Plan Cannot Help the Majority

Mississippi Women's University was founded in 1884 as the Mississippi Industrial Institute and College for the Education of White Girls. A century later Joe Hogan wanted to attend Mississippi Women's University to work on his B.A. in nursing but the school refused to admit him because of his sex. Justice O'Connor, writing for a majority of the court, held this was a plain violation of the equal-protection clause of the Fourteenth Amendement. Mississippi argued that the single-sex admission policy was an affirmative action plan to compensate for past discrimination against women. Justice O'Connor did not buy this argument, given that 98 percent of all nurses are women. She ruled that people cannot have affirmative action plans that protect the group that occupies most of the positions in a profession (*Hogan*).

The White Rule: The Plan Cannot Cause White Men to Be Fired

The City of Memphis, Tennessee, had hired many new black firemen when a budget crisis forced it to cut back on personnel (*Stotts*). If the city laid off on the basis of seniority, most of those laid off would be black. The federal district judge ordered the city to forget seniority and lay off more whites than blacks.

Justice White, writing for the majority, held that this violated Title VII, which specifically allows the use of bona fide senority systems.

Justice White acknowledged that the Supreme Court had allowed federal judges to award back seniority to individuals who had been denied employment for discriminatory reasons (*Teamsters*). He said judges were not allowed to award seniority to people, such as these newly hired firemen, who had not been the specific victims of past discrimination. This would take seniority away from whites who had legitimately earned it, which is not allowed.

In 1986 Justice White again used his rule to strike down an affirmative action plan (*Wygant*). Four justices were in favor of the plan and four opposed it. Justice White held the deciding vote and wrote his own opinion. The Jackson School Board and the Jackson Teacher's Union had signed an agreement that would protect minority teachers from layoffs. This plan would have resulted in the laying off of tenured white teachers instead of minority teachers who had worked for only a short time. Justice White held that to fire whites because of their race was racial discrimination and could not be excused by an affirmative action plan.

The White Rule is that there is a fundamental difference between not being hired and being fired. An affirmative action plan can prevent some whites from being hired but it cannot cause whites to be fired.

The Brennan Rule: Voluntary Plans Are Favored

Justice Brennan, in his separate opinion in the *Bakke* case in 1978, argued that voluntary affirmative action plans would be necessary if the goals of the 1964 Civil Rights Act were ever to be attained. Over the years he seems to have convinced a number of his fellow justices that voluntary affirmative action plans are good things. As Justice Brennan said in a recent opinion: "We have on numerous occasions recognized that Congress intended for volunatry compliance to be the preferred means of achieving the objectives of Title VII" (*Local 93*).

The Powell Rule: Quotas Are Not Favored

The *Bakke* case was decided in 1978 but it still confuses people. Mr. Bakke applied to the University of California at Davis Medical School. The school had an affirmative action plan that set aside a fixed number of positions for minority applicants even though it had no history of racial discrimination. The school was simply trying to correct what it saw as a racial imbalance in the medical profession. Four justices liked the plan and four did not. Justice Powell wrote his own decision and struck down the plan. (Because he cast the deciding vote in *Bakke*, his rule is still important even though he is no longer on the court.)

Justice Powell rejected the use of strict quotas because the institution did not have a history of past racial discrimination. However, Justice Powell recognized that one acceptable goal was served by the plan, the goal of having a diverse student body. Powell, a former school-board president, found this to be an acceptable goal of an educational institution. He ruled that in an educational context, race or ethnic background could be a "plus" in the individual applicant's file. The general rule that seemed to emerge from his opinion was that racial quotas are bad but some race consciousness is acceptable, at least as regards student admission policies.

These four rules are important for two reasons. First, they do appear to represent general rules that the Supreme Court follows when dealing with affirmative action plans. Second, Justices Marshall, Blackmun, and Stevens like affirmative action plans. They must get two more votes. Brennan will usually vote with them, which makes the other rules very important. We can see how these rules apply to two types of affirmative action plans: court-ordered plans and voluntary plans.

Court-Ordered Affirmative Action Plans

Title VII specifically orders federal judges not to use affirmative action plans just to correct an imbalance between the percentage of minority members working for a particular employer and the percentage of qualified minority members in the work force (42 U.S.C. sec. 2000e-2j).

That means federal judges can order affirmative action only when they determine the employer has intentionally discriminated against a minority group. Once the judge determines this has happened, he or she can order a number of remedies, with mandatory racial quotas being the most extreme. In two recent cases the Supreme Court upheld mandatory racial quotas ordered by federal district judges.

In one case the district judge found the union guilty of past intentional race discrimination and ordered an affirmative action plan to bring the level of nonwhite members up to 29 percent (the percentage of nonwhites in the relevant labor pool, New York City). Justices Brennan, Marshall, Stevens, and Blackmun found this plan to be acceptable (*Local 28*).

Justice Powell wrote his own opinion supporting the quotas in this case. He felt the union's "egregious" past behavior made an extreme remedy appropriate. He went down his own personal list of questions:

1. Are there alternative remedies? No.
2. How long will the plan last? A short period of time.
3. Is the plan related to the percentage of minority members in the relevant labor pool? Yes.
4. Does the plan allow for a waiver of the quotas by the judge if in good faith the quota cannot be met? Yes.
5. Does the plan lay off whites? No.

Because of the answers to these questions Justice Powell approved this particular court-ordered affirmative action plan, even though it contained racial quotas.

In a 1987 case, the district judge found the Alabama Department of Public

Safety to be guilty of egregious intentional racial discrimination (*Paradise*). The department had promoted very few black officers. The judge ordered the department to promote one black officer for each white officer promoted until 25 percent of the corporals were black. Justice Powell, again in a separate opinion, found that his list of five requirements had been met.

When it came to court-ordered affirmative action plans, Justice Powell cast the deciding vote several times. The legal community is waiting to see how Justice Kennedy feels about these plans.

Voluntary Affirmative Action Plans

In 1979 the U.S. Supreme Court approved a voluntary affirmative action plan. The union and the employer had agreed that half of the people admitted into the employer's training program would be black until the percentage of black employees in the plant was the same as the percentage of black workers in the local labor pool (*Steelworkers #1*).

The justices liked this plan because it was temporary, did not lay off any white workers, and allowed some whites to continue to enter the training program.

In 1986 six justices approved a plan worked out between the city of Cleveland and the firefighter's union (*Local 93*). The plan called for more minority members to be promoted during the next round of promotions. Again, the plan was temporary, did not lay off whites, and allowed some whites to be promoted.

In 1987 the Supreme Court decided the case of *Johnson v. Santa Clara County, California* (*Johnson #2*). In 1978 Santa Clara County voluntarily adopted an affirmative action plan for women and minorities. The plan did not have quotas, but it allowed sex and race to be considered when making hiring and promotion decisions. The long-range goal of the plan was to have the percentage of women and minorities in various job categories reflect the percentages in the relevant labor pool.

When the job of road dispatcher opened up, none of the 238 people holding jobs in the skilled-craft category was a woman. Diane Joyce, a white woman, and Paul Johnson, a white man, applied for the job. It would have been a promotion for either person.

Nine applicants were deemed qualified and were interviewed. Seven scored above 70 on the interview. Johnson was tied for second place with 75 and Joyce was next on the list with 73. A second interview was conducted by three agency supervisors, who then recommended Johnson.

The affirmative action officer recommended Joyce. The director of the county transportation agency promoted Joyce, and Johnson sued. The director testified that he considered the experience, test scores, and expertise of both applicants along with the affirmative action plan.

The plan did not have quotas and it did not have a set ending date. Brennan, writing for the majority (Marshall, Blackmun, Stevens, and Powell), held that the plan was justified because of the gross underrepresentation of women in a "traditionally segregated job category." This plan met all the rules. It was designed to help a true minority (O'Connor Rule); it did not lay off white men

(White Rule); it was voluntary (Brennan Rule), and it did not use quotas (Powell Rule).

Justice O'Connor wrote a separate opinion agreeing with the majority. She said this was a clear case because 36 percent of the relevant labor pool were women and none of the people in this job category was a woman.

This case appears to have answered a number of questions about voluntary affirmative action plans.

1. Is there a different standard for government employers? No, governments can set up affirmative action plans.

2. Does the employer have to admit past intentional discrimination before setting up a voluntary affirmative action plan? No, if that were required, few employers would do so.

3. Does the plan have to have specific quotas? No.

4. Does the plan need to be written and formally adopted by the agency or company? Yes. Informal, unwritten affirmative action plans are just another name for reverse discrimination (*Lilly*, *Lehman*).

5. Can the employer make up a plan for any job category? No, only where there is a "manifest imbalance" in a "traditionally segregated job category."

6. Can the employer adopt rigid quotas without admitting past intentional discrimination first? No one knows (*Valentine*, *Setser*, *Warsocki*).

Only time will tell whether the appointment of Justice Kennedy to the Court will change these answers.

RACIAL HARASSMENT

When people think of harassment lawsuits under the civil rights acts, they tend to think of sex harassment. However, employees can also sue for racial harassment. If an employer is making an employee's life miserable because of the employee's race, the employee can sue under Title VII, which forbids discriminating against individuals with respect to the "conditions" of employment. However, an employee who sues under Title VII for racial harassment does not get much. He or she cannot get back pay or be reinstated because they were not fired. They get an injunction from a federal judge ordering the harassers to stop harassing people and the employer has to pay the employee's attorney's fees. Without an award for other damages such as mental anguish or punitive damages, there is very little incentive for someone to sue for racial harassment. In some cases the employee may be able to sue also for assault or battery and recover real monetary damages. We will discuss this further in the section on sex harassment in Chapter 8.

During the 1988–1989 session the U.S. Supreme Court will hear the case of *Patterson v. McLean Credit Union*. The case involves whether or not someone who is suing for racial harassment can also use the Reconstruction Civil Rights Act and receive a real damage award along with the injunction. The circuit court ruled that people cannot use the Reconstruction Civil Rights Act in a racial harassment case because that act does not say anything about the "conditions" of employment. The circuit court decision was very narrow and the Supreme Court was apparently about to affirm it in the spring of 1988 with a four-to-four vote. Instead five justices asked that the case be re-argued during the 1988–1989 session (Rehnquist, White, Scalia, O'Connor, and Kennedy) apparently so that Justice Kennedy can cast the deciding vote.

Justices Brennan, Marshall, and Stevens objected to this tactic. Nevertheless, in 1989, Justice Kennedy may write the most important decision of his judicial career. His options are to:

1. affirm the circuit court on the narrow grounds that the Reconstruction Civil Rights Act does not mention "conditions" of employment;
2. overrule a decade of Supreme Court decisions that have held that the Reconstruction Civil Rights Act applies to private employers;
3. or decide that the Reconstruction Civil Rights Act does reach cases of racial harassment because it outlaws racial discrimination in hiring and firing and if an employer harasses an employee in an attempt to force that employee to resign, that is a kind of indirect firing (constructive discharge) that should not be tolerated.

There is something that too many people forget when discussing affirmative action, racial harassment, and the correct interpretation of the Reconstruction Civil Rights Act. Both liberals and conservatives on the U.S. Supreme Court are willing to enforce the will of Congress. Both agree that Congress has the power under the Thirteenth, Fourteenth, and Fifteenth Amendments to do almost anything to end racial discrimination in the United States. When Congress passed the Civil Rights Act of 1964, no one remembered the Reconstruction Civil Rights Act of 1866. It has been up to the federal judges to decide how to deal with two statutes that take very different approaches to the same problem. The Reconstruction Act was passed at a time when allowing people to sue for money damages was the answer to every problem. The 1964 Act was passed at the height of the "let's create a federal agency to solve every problem" era and the EEOC was born. Congress could of course take a look at both acts and write a new civil rights statute that deals with these apparent conflicts. If Congress is unhappy with Justice Kennedy's opinion, it may have to do just that.

RELIGIOUS DISCRIMINATION

Title VII and most state civil rights laws protect people against religious discrimination. The religion does not have to be an established denomination but it must involve a "sincere and meaningful belief" (*Seeger*). Religions that are "patently devoid of religious sincerity" are not protected (*Theriault*). Atheists are protected (*Young*).

Title VII and most state civil rights acts do allow religious discrimination if the employer is unable to "reasonably accommodate" the religious observance without "undue hardship" to the business.

Reasonable accommodation does not amount to much. For example, courts have held that an employer is not required to force employees with seniority to work so that the religious employee can have his or her Sabbath day off (*Hardison, Albuquerque*). As a North Carolina Appeals Court said, if the cost of accommodation is more than de minimis (a little bit), the employer does not have to do it (*Pilot Freight*).

In 1986 the U.S. Supreme Court allowed a school district to deny a teacher six days off for religious observance. The school-district rules allowed teachers to take up to three days off for religious observance. While teachers also had "sick-leave days" and "personal-business-leave days," the district did not allow these leave days to be used for religious observance. The U.S. Supreme Court upheld the school district's rule (*Ansonia*).

However, the employer cannot treat different religions differently. In one case the employer allowed one employee to have Saturday off to observe his Sabbath, but would not allow another employee to have Sunday off to observe her Sabbath. The Ohio Appeals Court said the employer could not discriminate between religions (*South Wind*).

The U.S. Constitution and most state constitutions require governments not to interfere with people's religion, including discriminating against government employees because of their religion. At the same time, these constitutional provisions require the government not to encourage one religion over other religions. These two requirements often conflict.

When Janet Cooper, a public-school teacher in Oregon, became an adherent of the Sikh religion, she began wearing white clothes and a white turban to school. Since an Oregon statute says teachers shall not wear religious dress to school, Cooper's teaching certificate was revoked. The Oregon Supreme Court recognized her right freely to exercise her religion, but the court also recognized that as a teacher Cooper was an authority figure representing the government. The government is supposed to be neutral in religious matters and her wearing of religious dress compromised that neutrality. The Oregon Supreme Court upheld the revocation of her teaching certificate (*Cooper*). Some Christians have objected when teachers have been told not to wear Christian jewelry while teaching public school. They point to the small size of the jewelry, but there is no way to draw a line between jewelry and Cooper's white dress. Either they both go or they both stay, and the courts have uniformly decided they both go.

In 1985 the U.S. Supreme Court struck down a Connecticut statute as unconstitutional because it encouraged the "establishment of religion." The statute gave all employees an absolute right to take their Sabbath day off from work and required private employers to honor that right (*Caldor*).

Title VII allows religious organizations to discriminate on the basis of religion. This clearly applies to employees hired to work for the church or for a church school. In 1987 the U.S. Supreme Court said it also applied to other nonprofit activities carried out by a church. The case involved the Mormon Church in Salt Lake City. The church ran a gym that was open to the public but hired only Mormons. The justices said this was acceptable under Title VII. The justices left open the question whether a church engaging in for-profit activity could discriminate on the basis of religion (*Amos*).

THE NEW IMMIGRATION LAW

During 1987 and 1988 America tried to come to grips with the immigration problem by allowing millions of illegal aliens to apply for citizenship. The new federal law also makes it a crime for employers to hire illegal aliens and requires them to keep records on proof of citizenship for everyone they hire. That means we all must present either a passport or a Social Security card and a driver's license when we apply for a job (8 U.S.C. sec. 1324). The new statute also states:

> It is an unfair immigration-related employment practice for a person or other entity to discriminate against any individual (other than an unauthorized alien) with respect to the hiring, or recruitment or referral for a fee, of the individual for employment or the discharging of the individual from employment—
> (A) because of such individual's national origin, or
> (B) in the case of a citizen or intending citizen, because of such individual's citizenship status.

This statute makes it clear that employers must treat everyone the same. They cannot ask some people for proof of citizenship and not others. We suggest that everyone get a passport. They are the best proof of citizenship.

For many years a debate has raged in the federal courts over whether illegal aliens can be discriminated against, not just in employment but in other areas of life as well. In 1987 the Fifth Circuit Court overturned its past decisions in this area and ruled that discrimination against illegal aliens in all aspects of life is now authorized by this section of the immigration act (*Bhandari*). The case involved a bank that refused to give credit to an illegal alien. How the other circuit courts and the U.S. Supreme Court will rule on this remains to be seen.

STATE CIVIL RIGHTS STATUTES AND CONSTITUTIONAL PROVISIONS

Table 7–1 provides a summary of the state civil rights statutes and constitutional provisions. As you can see, in some cases, state law protects much more than just the "race, color, religion, sex, or national origin" protected by Title VII. A number of states prohibit discrimination based on marital status or parenthood. Others prohibit discrimination based on mental disorder or mental retardation. Still others prohibit discrimination based on sexual orientation, personal appearance, or political affiliation.

The Washington D.C. civil rights statute protects against discrimination based on "personal appearance." In one case Eliza Jenetis was hired to work in the Washington D.C. office of Atlantic Richfield by Rachel Morgret, the office manager (*ARCO*). Soon after Jenetis came to work, Morgret began to criticize the way she dressed. Apparently Morgret did not like the way Jenetis's blouses fit (too tight) and Jenetis was fired. While the statute prohibits discrimination on the basis of personal appearance, it allows employers to set dress standards if the standards are uniformly applied to a class of employees for a reasonable business purpose. The Washington D.C. Human Rights Commission found that ARCO did not have a uniform standard of dress and that Jenetis's style of dress was not very different from that of her co-workers. Eliza Jenetis got her job back.

Employees who cannot sue under Title VII because their employer does not employ the necessary 15 people may be able to sue under the state statute. Some state statutes reach employers with as few as three or four employees while a few reach all employers no matter how many employees they have.

In some cases the state statute allows for more damages than the federal law. For example, the Minnesota civil rights statute allows the state civil rights agency to award up to three times the actual damages as a penalty against the employer (*Anderson*). In Kentucky employees can get up to five years' back pay (*Owensboro*).

Whether to pursue the case under the state statute or the federal statutes is an important question that every employee will want to discuss with an attorney.

During the 1980s the states have taken the lead in dealing with civil rights problems. It is ironic that today many attorneys feel their clients are better off suing under state civil rights laws than under the federal statute, even in states that once belonged to the Confederacy.

TABLE 7–1. State Civil Rights Statutes*

Alabama	None
Alaska 18.80.220	Race, color, religion, sex, national origin, age, handicap, marital status, change in marital status, pregnancy, parenthood.
Const. Art. 1, sec. 1.3	Const. protects against race, color, creed, sex, or national-origin discrimination by government.
Arizona 41-1461, 1463	Race, color, religion, sex, national origin, age, handicap (boss must have 15 employees).
23-340, 341	Equal pay for women.
Const. Art. 2, sec. 13	Const. guarantees equal protection for all.
Arkansas 81-333, 624	Equal pay for women.
82-2901	No handicap discrimination in public employment or employment supported by public funds.
12-3501 to 3504	No age discrimination in public employment.
Const. Art. 2, sec. 3.18	Const. guarantees equality under the law.
California Gov't Code 12940 to 12945	Race, color, religion, sex, national origin, ancestry, age, handicap, marital status, pregnancy, medical condition (boss must have 5 employees).
Const. Art. 1, sec. 7	Const. guarantees equality under the law.
Art. 1, sec. 8	Const. protects against race, sex, creed, color, or ethnic-origin discrimination by government.
Colorado 24-34-402	Race, color, creed, sex, national origin, ancestry, age.
8-5-102	Equal pay for women.
Const. Art. 2, sec. 29	Const. protects against sex discrimination by government.
Connecticut 46a-60, 70	Race, color, religious creed, sex, national origin, age, ancestry, mental disorder, mental retardation, marital status, physical disability (boss must have 3 employees).
31-75	Equal pay for women.
Const. Art. 1, sec. 1 Art. 1, sec. 20	Const. guarantees equal rights. Const. protects against race, color, religion, ancestry, or national-origin discrimination by government.
Delaware 19-710 to 718	Race, color, religion, sex, national origin, marital status (boss must have 4 employees).
19-1107A	Equal pay for women.
District of Columbia 1-2512, 1-2505	Race, color, religion, sex, national origin, age, handicap, marital status, personal appearance, sexual orientation, family responsibilities, matriculation, political affiliation, pregnancy, childbirth.
Florida 760.10	Race, color, religion, sex, national origin, age, handicap, marital status (boss must have 15 employees).
448.07	Equal pay for women.
Georgia 34-1-2; 34-6A-1 to 6	Age, handicap.

*The law is always changing. Consult an attorney about your situation.

TABLE 7–1. (Cont.)

34-5-1 to 7	Equal pay for women.
Const. Art. 1, sec. 1	Const. guarantees equal protection of the law.
Hawaii 378-2	Race, color, religion, sex, ancestry, age, physical handicap, marital status, arrest record.
Const. Art. 1, sec. 2	Const. guarantees equal rights.
Art. 1, sec. 3.5	Const. protects against sex, race, religion, or ancestry discrimination by government.
Idaho 67-5909	Race, color, religion, sex, national origin, age (boss must have 10 employees).
44-1701 to 1704	Equal pay for women.
56-707	Government may not discriminate against handicapped.
Const. Art. 1, sec. 2	Const. guarantees equality under the law.
Illinois Ch. 68 sec. 1-101 to 9-102	Race, color, religion, sex, national origin, ancestry, age, marital status, unfavorable military discharge (boss must have 15 employees). Handicap (boss must have 1 employee).
Const. Art. 1, sec. 17, 18, 19	Const. protects against discrimination because of race, color, creed, national ancestry, sex, or handicap by private employers or government.
Indiana 22-9-1-1 to 22-9-2-11	Race, color, religion, sex, national origin, ancestry, handicap (boss must have 6 employees). Age (boss must have 1 employee).
22-2-2-4	Equal pay for women.
Const. Art. 1, sec. 23	Const. guarantees equal privileges for all.
Iowa 601A.6	Race, color, religion, creed, sex, national origin, handicap, age (18 or over), pregnancy, childbirth (boss must have 4 employees).
19A.18	The state will not discriminate because of political opinion, religion, race, national origin, sex, or age.
Const. Art. 1, sec. 6	Const. guarantees equal privileges for all.
Kansas 44-1009 44-1113	Race, color, religion, sex, national origin, ancestry, physical handicap (boss must have 4 employees).
Const. Bill of Rt., sec. 1	Const. guarantees equal rights.
Kentucky 344.040 207.150	Race, color, religion, sex, national origin, age, handicap (boss must have 8 employees).
337.420	Equal pay for women.
Const. Bill of Rt., sec. 3	Const. guarantees equality under the law.

TABLE 7–1. (Cont.)

Louisiana 23:1006	Race, color, religion, sex, national origin (boss must have 15 employees).
23:972	Age (boss must have 20 employees).
23:1002	Sickle-cell trait (boss must have 20 employees).
Maine 5-4572	Race, color, religion, sex, national origin, ancestry, age, handicap.
26-628	Equal pay for women.
Const. Art. 1, sec. 6-A	Const. guarantees equal protection of the law.
Maryland Art. 49B, sec. 16, 17	Race, color, religion, sex, national origin, age, physical or mental handicap, marital status, pregnancy, childbirth (boss must have 15 employees).
Art. 11, secs. 55A to 55H	Equal pay for women.
Const. Dec. of Rt., art. 46	Const. protects against sex discrimination by government.
Massachusetts Ch. 151B, sec. 4	Race, color, religion, sex, national origin, ancestry, age, handicap (boss must have 6 employees).
Ch. 149, sec. 24A	Age (boss must have 1 employee).
Ch. 149, sec. 105A	Equal pay for women.
Michigan 37.2202	Race, color, religion, sex, national origin, age, height, weight, marital status.
37.1202	Handicap (boss must have 4 employees).
408.397	Equal pay for women.
Const. Art. 1, sec. 2	Const. guarantees equal protection of the law. Const. protects against religion, race, color, or national-origin discrimination by government.
Minnesota 363.03 181.81	Race, color, religion, sex, national origin, age, disability, marital status, status with regard to public assistance.
181.67	Equal pay for women.
Const. Art. 1, sec. 2	Const. guarantees equal protection of the law.
Mississippi 25-9-149	The state as employer may not discriminate because of race, color, religion, sex, national origin, age, or handicap.
79-1-9	A corporation may not interfere with the social, civil, or political rights of its employees.
Missouri 213.010 to .126	Race, color, religion, sex, national origin, ancestry, age, handicap (boss must have 6 employees).
290.400 to .460	Equal pay for women.
Const. Art. 1 sec. 2	Const. guarantees equal rights under the law.
Montana 49-1-101 to 49-4-511	Race, color, religion, sex, national origin, age, handicap, marital status.
39-3-104	Equal pay for women.

TABLE 7–1. (Cont.)

Nebraska 48-1104	Race, color, religion, sex, national origin, marital status, disability (boss must have 15 employees).
48-1001	Age (boss must have 25 employees).
48-1219 to 1227.01	Equal pay for women.
Nevada 613.330	Race, color, religion, sex, national origin, age, handicap (boss must have 15 employees).
608.017	Equal pay for women.
New Hampshire 354-A:8	Race, color, religion, sex, national origin, age, handicap, marital status (boss must have 6 employees).
275:37	Equal pay for women.
Const. Pt. 1, art. 1	Const. guarantees equality under the law.
Pt. 1, art. 2	Const. protects against race, creed, color, sex, or national-origin discrimination by government.
New Jersey 10:5-12 to 29.1	Race, color, creed, sex, national origin, ancestry, age, handicap, marital status, dishonorable discharge, atypical hereditary cell, or blood type.
Const. Art. 1 sec. 5	Const. protects against religion, race, color, ancestry, or national-origin discrimination by government.
New Mexico 28-1-7	Race, religion, creed, sex, national origin, ancestry, age, handicap (boss must have 4 employees).
Const. Art. 1 sec. 18	Const. protects against sex discrimination by government.
New York Exec. sec. 296	Race, color, creed, sex, national origin, age, disability, marital status (boss must have 4 employees).
Labor sec. 194	Equal pay for women.
Const. Art. 1, sec. 11	Const. protects against race, color, creed, or religious discrimination by government.
North Carolina 143-422.2	Race, color, religion, sex, national origin, age, handicap (boss must have 15 employees).
95-28.1	Sickle-cell or hemoglobin C trait (boss must have 1 employee).
Const. Art. 1, sec. 1	All people are created equal.
North Dakota 14-02.4-01 to 21 34-01-17	Race, color, religion, sex, national origin, handicap, marital status, public assistance status (boss must have 10 employees). Age (boss must have 1 employee).
34-06.1	Equal pay for women.
Ohio 4112.02; 4101.17	Race, color, religion, sex, national origin, ancestry, age, handicap (boss must have 4 employees).
Oklahoma Tit. 25, sec. 1302	Race, color, religion, sex, national origin, age, handicap (boss must have 15 employees).
Oregon Ch. 659	Race, color, religion, sex, national origin, age (18 or over), handicap, marital status, expunged juvenile record.
Pennsylvania Tit. 43, sec. 955	Race, color, religion, sex, national origin, ancestry, age, handicap (boss must have 4 employees).
Tit. 43, sec. 336.1	Equal pay for women.
Const. Art. 1, sec. 26	Const. protects against discrimination by government.

TABLE 7–1. (Cont.)

Rhode Island 28-5-7	Race, color, religion, sex, ancestry, age, handicap (boss must have 4 employees).
28-6-1 to 21	Equal pay for women.
South Carolina 1-13-80	Race, color, religion, sex, national origin, age (boss must have 15 employees).
South Dakota 20-13-10	Race, color, religion, sex, national origin, ancestry, disability.
60-12-15, 16	Equal pay for women.
Const. Art. VI, sec. 18	Const. guarantees everyone equal privileges and immunities.
Tennessee 4-21-401	Race, color, religion, creed, sex, national origin, age (boss must have 8 employees).
8-50-103	Handicap (boss must have 1 employee).
50-2-202	Equal pay for women.
Texas 5221K	Race, color, religion, sex, national origin, age, handicap (boss must have 15 employees).
Const. Art. 1, sec. 3a	Const. protects against race, color, sex, creed, or national origin discrimination by government.
Utah 34-35-6	Race, color, religion, sex, national origin, age, handicap (boss must have 15 employees).
Const. Art. 1, sec. 2	Const. guarantees equal protection of the law.
Vermont Tit. 21, sec. 495	Race, color, religion, sex, national origin, ancestry, age, handicap, place of birth.
Virginia 51.01-41	Handicap.
40.1-28.6	Equal pay for women.
Const. Art. 1, sec. 11	Const. protects against race, religion, color, sex, or national origin discrimination by government.
Washington 49.60.180	Race, color, creed, sex, national origin, age, handicap, marital status (boss must have 8 employees).
Const. Art. 1 sec. 12	Const. guarantees equal privileges for all.
West Virginia 21-5C-7(b) 5-11-9	Race, color, religion, sex, national origin, ancestry, age, handicap (boss must have 6 employees).
21-5B	Equal pay for women.
Wisconsin 111.31 to 34	Race, color, creed, sex, national origin, ancestry, age, handicap, marital status, sexual orientation, arrest record, conviction record, National Guard membership.
Wyoming 27-9	Race, color, creed, sex, national origin, ancestry, age, handicap (boss must have 2 employees).
27-21-301	Equal pay for women.
Const. Art. 1, sec. 3	Const. protects against race, color, sex, or individual-circumstances discrimination by government.

8

Sex Discrimination

EQUAL PROTECTION

The Fourteenth Amendment guarantees to "any person" the "equal protection of the laws." A century passed before women were included in the definition of "person."

This changed in 1971, when a unanimous U.S. Supreme Court struck down an Oregon statute that said "males must be preferred to females" in choosing the administrator of an estate (Reed). The court said this violated the equal-protection clause of the Fourteenth Amendment because it discriminated against women. In 1973 the court struck down a rule that allowed male members of the armed forces to have their wives receive dependent benefits automatically while female military personnel had to prove their husbands were actually dependent on them for support (Frontiero).

In 1975 and 1977 the court struck down provisions in the Social Security Act that allowed widows to receive benefits denied to widowers (Weinberger, Califano).

Today it is clear that governments cannot discriminate against people because of their sex.

THE EQUAL PAY ACT

In 1963 Congress passed the Equal Pay Act as an amendment to the Fair Labor Standards Act originally passed in 1938 and discussed in Chapter 13 (29 U.S.C. sec. 206(d)). Because the law covers almost every employer, it will include some employers that are too small to be covered by Title VII. The Equal Pay Act prohibits the employer from discriminating

> between employees on the basis of sex by paying wages to employees in such establishment at a rate less than the rate at which he pays wages to employees of the opposite sex . . . for equal work on jobs the performance of which requires equal skill, effort, and responsibility, and which are performed under similar working conditions, except where such payment is made pursuant to (i) a seniority system; (ii) a merit system; (iii) a system which measures earnings by quantity or quality of production; or (iv) a differential based on any other factor other than sex. (29 U.S.C. sec. 206(d)(1))

The Equal Pay Act allows an employer to have different pay scales in different facilities (called "establishments"). However, a federal judge may treat these different facilities as one "establishment" if he or she feels that is necessary in order to achieve the purposes of the Equal Pay Act (*Goose Creek*).

While the act requires equal pay for equal work, that does not mean the work must be identical. When jobs are "substantially equal," equal pay must be provided (*Shultz*). Judges have decided the work of male tailors is equal to that of female seamstresses and the work of male barbers is equal to that of female beauticians (*City Stores, Usery*).

In theory, to prove a violation of the Equal Pay Act, an employee must prove four things are substantially equal: (1) skill, (2) effort, (3) responsibility, and (4) working conditions. Federal judges have refused to get bogged down in these factors. The real test is: do the jobs look basically alike?

If the males perform "extra" duties, federal judges will allow them to be paid more if the extra duties are (1) real; (2) regularly performed; (3) substantial; and (4) a type of work that justifies higher wages (*Shultz, American Can, Fairmont*).

The employer can justify unequal pay for equal work with any one of four reasons (the act calls them defenses): (1) a seniority system; (2) a merit system; (3) the quantity or quality of production; or (4) "any factor other than sex."

The justification must be legitimate. For example, two banks paid men more than women for clerical work. At one bank the men were part of a bona fide training program. The federal judge allowed the bank to pay the male trainees more (*First Victoria*). Another bank argued it also had a training program, a secret, informal training program open only to men. The judge did not allow that bank to pay men more for the same work (*Security*).

An employee who has been the victim of unequal pay can skip the EEOC and file a lawsuit directly in federal court. If she wins she gets the difference between what she was paid and what she should have been paid for the previous two years, attorney's fees, and a federal court order forcing the employer to pay women equally in the future.

Over half the states also have equal pay acts. In those states a victim has a choice of suing under either the federal or the state statute (see Table 7–1).

TITLE VII

In 1964, when it looked as if the Civil Rights Act was going to pass, a group of Congressmen decided they had a sure-fire way to stop it. They added "sex" to the list that already included "race, color, religion, and national origin." The act passed anyway.

These opponents then added the "Bennett Amendment." This amendment says: "It shall not be an unlawful employment practice . . . to differentiate on the basis of sex in determining . . . wages . . . if such differentiation is authorized by" the Equal Pay Act (42 U.S.C. sec. 2000e-2(h)).

Both acts allow discrimination based on seniority and merit. While the Equal Pay Act allows "factors other than sex" to justify discrimination, the U.S. Supreme Court has said these must be legitimate factors and cannot be just an excuse for discriminating against women (Gunther). With this interpretation the Bennett Amendment has not been much of an obstacle to women suing under Title VII.

Everything said in Chapter 7 about Title VII applies to women. The complaint must be filed with the EEOC within the time limit and the employee receives two years' back pay, reinstatement, and attorney fees if she wins. Generally, women who are being discriminated against on the basis of pay will want to proceed under both the Equal Pay Act and Title VII. This means going to the EEOC before suing in federal court. When the employee ultimately gets her right-to-sue letter and sues, the judge can figure out which law applies and proceed accordingly. Of course a woman can sue under Title VII for everything any other minority-group member can sue for: not being hired, being fired, being segregated, and being harassed.

THE RECONSTRUCTION CIVIL RIGHTS ACT

You saw in Chapter 7 that people can sue private employers for race discrimination under both Title VII and Section 1981 of the Reconstruction Civil Rights Act. This allows them to receive full damages including mental-anguish and punitive damages. The general belief is that women cannot sue private employers under Section 1981. A good argument can be made that this general belief is wrong. Section 1981 protects "persons" just as the equal-protection clause of the Fourteenth Amendment protects "persons." When the U.S. Supreme Court decided in 1971 that women are "persons" under the Fourteenth Amendment they, by implication, also decided that women are "persons" under Section 1981.

THE LEGEND OF COMPARABLE WORTH

Once upon a time a group of female government employees realized they were performing high-skill jobs for low wages while some male government employees were performing low-skill jobs for high wages. These female employees convinced a number of cities and states to hire consultants to study the "comparable worth" of these jobs. The consultants found that when they compared male-dominated jobs with female-dominated jobs for skill, effort, and responsibility, the women were doing high-skill work for low pay. As a result a number of cities and states raised the wage scales for female-dominated jobs. Many did not.

Some of the factors the consultants looked at were the same as those listed in the Equal Pay Act (skill, effort, responsibility). Some female government employees decided if the states would not implement the findings of these comparable-worth studies, they would ask federal judges to force them to do so under the provisions of the Equal Pay Act. They took this idea to several circuit courts in the 1970s and lost (Columbia, Angelo, Christensen, Lemons). The judges said they would not compare apples with oranges (secretaries with janitors). If the jobs did not look alike, the judges would not order equal pay.

In 1981 the U.S. Supreme Court breathed new life into the comparable-worth concept with the Gunther case. The case involved female jail guards who were paid 70 percent of what the male jail guards were paid. A consultant told the county that the women's jobs were "worth" 95 percent of what the men's jobs were "worth" but the county refused to raise the women's pay scale. These jobs looked very similar. The U.S. Supreme Court said this was not a "comparable worth" case but a case of intentional sex discrimination and sent it back to the lower court for further proceedings. No one was sure what the Gunther decision meant, but some women hoped it meant that comparable worth was a legitimate concept under the Equal Pay Act. The American Federation of State, County, and Municipal Employees (AFSCME) brought a comparable-worth lawsuit against the state of Washington in the Ninth Circuit Court in 1985 and lost (AFSCME). The judges said what they had said in the 1970s: they would not compare apples with oranges. The case did not reach the U.S. Supreme Court because the state settled out of court, agreeing to raise women's salaries by almost half a billion dollars between 1986 and 1992 (female secretaries will eventually make as much as male janitors).

Many critics have argued that the women shot themselves in the foot with these lawsuits. Many cities and states canceled comparable-worth studies because they did not want to be sued in federal court if they decided not to implement all of the recommendations.

What the federal judges said to women is exactly what they said to blacks and other minorities: Apply for jobs dominated by white males. For many racial minorities this meant leaving low-skill jobs for jobs requiring high skill and responsibility. Many women feel they have been forced to leave jobs requiring high skill and responsibility for lower-skill jobs that pay more.

The federal judges ruled that Congress intended the law of supply and demand, not the opinions of consultants, to determine wage levels for various jobs. That has happened over the years. Today America faces a shortage of teachers, nurses, and secretaries. Eventually, as the supply of applicants for these jobs declines, the pay and working conditions must improve to attract the necessary workers.

SEXUAL HARASSMENT

Federal judges arrived at the concept of sexual harassment two ways. First, the judges said that if an employer made an employee's life so miserable the employee could not take it any longer and quit, the judges would consider that the equivalent of being fired (constructive discharge). Second, Title VII says employers cannot discriminate with respect to the "conditions" of employment. The judges decided sexual harassment constituted a condition of employment that penalized women.

In 1977 three different federal circuit courts ruled that sexual harassment violated Title VII. Each case involved a woman who had been fired because she refused the sexual advances of her male supervisor. The courts asked if these women would have been fired if they had not been women. The answer was no, so the firings violated Title VII (*Tomkins, Barnes #1, Garber*).

In 1980 the EEOC defined sexual harassment:

> Unwelcome sexual advances, requests for sexual favors, and other verbal or physical conduct of a sexual nature constitute sexual harassment when (1) submission to such conduct is made either explicitly or implicitly a term or condition of an individual's employment, (2) submission to or rejection of such conduct by an individual is used as a basis for employment decisions affecting such individual, or (3) such conduct has the purpose or effect of unreasonably interfering with an individual's work performance or creating an intimidating, hostile, or offensive working environment. (29 C.F.R. sec. 1604.11(a))

Parts (1) and (2) of this definition outlaw what has come to be known as "quid pro quo" sexual harassment. Part (3) of the regulation outlaws conduct that interferes with a person's work performance or creates a hostile working environment. This has come to be called "hostile environment" sexual harassment. Through the 1980s circuit court after circuit court agreed that creating a hostile working environment for women constituted sexual harassment and violated Title VII.

When Sandra Bundy was subjected to repeated sexual advances by her supervisors, she complained to their supervisor, who said "any man in his right mind would want to rape you." The District of Columbia Circuit Court ruled that this was sexual harassment (*Bundy*).

Barbara Henson, a police dispatcher, finally resigned after two years of sexual harassment by the police chief. The court said this was constructive discharge and a violation of Title VII (*Henson*).

Deborah Katz, an air-traffic controller, had to undergo vulgar sexual epithets at work. She complained to a supervisor, who did nothing about it. The court found this to be "hostile environment" sexual harassment (*Katz*).

With sexual harassment firmly established as something women could sue for under Title VII, two questions have occupied the judges: What exactly constitues sexual harassment, and when can the company be held liable for the acts of its employees and supervisors?

It is easy to define "quid pro quo" sexual harassment. Defining "hostile environment" sexual harassment has not been easy. Federal judges have ruled that the following is not "hostile environment" sexual harrassment:

1. a supervisor who flirts (*Bouchet*);
2. a supervisor who asks for a kiss (*Jackson*);
3. a supervisor who calls the employee the Dolly Parton of the office (*Downes*);
4. a supervisor who calls female employees "honey, babe, and tiger" (*Volk*).

A number of cases have revolved around the supervisor's personality. In one case the supervisor told a lot of off-color jokes around the female employees. The judge said the supervisor just had a "bumptious personality" so this was not sexual harassment (*Buddle*). In another case the judge felt the embarrassing remarks by the supervisor were not "severe or persistent" enough to constitute sexual harassment (*Reichman*). In yet another case the judge decided the supervisor was just "crude and vulgar" and used words like "cunt" and "tits" all the time but did not mean anything by them (*Rabidue*).

Federal judges have ruled that the following is "hostile environment" sexual harassment:

1. being forced to wear revealing clothes (*Sage Realty*);
2. being rubbed up against by the supervisor and having to listen to him talk about sex all the time (*Bohen*);
3. having the male supervisor peer over the bathroom stall while the female employee is going to the bathroom (*Mays*);
4. having to listen to abusive language and having sexually oriented drawings posted at work (*Zabkowicz*);
5. having the supervisor keep track of the female employee's menstrual cycle on his office calendar and being asked by the supervisor when the employee was "going to do something nice" for him (*Coley*).

In December 1987, what may be the most famous sexual-harassment case was settled out of court. Louette Colombano, a San Francisco police officer, quit in 1984 after the harassment got to be too much. The harassment began when Colombano told police officials and the press that her fellow officers hired a prostitute to perform oral sex on a handcuffed rookie officer at a party for new recruits. This resulted in the firing of five officers, the introduction of an ethics course for police, and the reorganization of the police department. This incident even inspired an episode on "Hill Street Blues." Colombano settled for

$257,000 cash and the continuation of her disability pension (*San Francisco Chronicle*, Dec. 30, 1987, A3).

Collecting from the Company

The issue in many sexual-harassment cases has been whether the company can be held liable for harassment carried out by supervisors or employees without company approval. The Eleventh Circuit Court held that the company can be held liable for sexual harassment only if "higher managment knew or should have known of the sexual harassment and failed to take remedial action" (*Henson*). They require this even if a supervisor is the harasser. On the other hand, the Third Circuit Court has decided if a supervisor takes part in the harassment that is enough to hold the company liable (*Craig*).

In 1986 the U.S. Supreme Court handed down its first decision in a sexual-harassment case (*Meritor*). In a decision written by Chief Justice Rehnquist the high court acknowledged that "hostile environment" is a kind of sexual harassment forbidden by Title VII. In this case the D.C. Circuit Court (their opinion was under review) had agreed with the Third Circuit Court that a woman who is being harassed by her supervisor did not have to complain to higher management before the company could be held liable. Chief Justice Rehnquist's decision is confusing on this issue. The opinion says that the D.C. Circuit Court "erred in concluding that employers are always automatically liable for sexual harassment by their supervisors." However, he went on to point out that this company did not have a policy against sexual harassment and the company grievance procedure required the employee to file a grievance with the very supervisor who was sexually harassing her. This was too much for Chief Justice Rehnquist, who held the company liable for the harassment.

Chief Justice Rehnquist's opinion holds out the possibility that if a company has a policy against sexual harassment, and a grievance procedure that allows the harassed employee to go directly to higher management, the company might not be held liable for the damages. In a special concurring opinion Justice Marshall (joined by Brennan, Blackmun, and Stevens) said that a company is always liable for sexual harassment by supervisors. However, he also said if an employee "without good reason bypassed an internal complaint procedure she knew to be effective, a court may be reluctant to find constructive termination and thus to award reinstatement or back pay." In other words, if the company has a legitimate grievance procedure, the sexually harassed employee should try to solve her problems inside the company before going to the EEOC. Also, both opinions suggest that if an employee is being harassed by co-workers instead of her supervisor, she should tell the supervisor before making a federal case out of it.

Taking Concerted Action

There is more than one way to deal with sexual harassment. In one case the company hired a new supervisor, David Jamison, on September 13, 1976. "By

Monday, September 20, 1976, Jamison had requested the sexual favors of six female employees" (*Downslope*). On Wednesday morning, September 22, 1976, several women refused to start work until Mr. Lane, the plant manager, agreed to listen to their complaints. When Lane arrived at the factory, he told the women either to work for Jamison or to "hit the clock." Jamison left town. The women complained to the National Labor Relations Board, which ordered the company to give them back their jobs. The NLRB ruled that these women had a right under federal labor law to "engage in concerted action" for their "mutual aid and protection" (see Chapter 14).

Collecting Real Damages

Title VII allows discharged employees to collect up to two years' back pay, be reinstated in their old job, and have their attorney's fees paid. The problem with this is that many employees who have undergone sexual harassment either do not want their old jobs back or did not quit and thus cannot collect back pay or be reinstated. About all they really get under Title VII is a court order telling the harassers to stop harassing people. While victims of racial harassment may be able to sue under the Reconstruction Civil Rights Act (we await a decision by the Supreme Court) and receive real monetary damages, federal courts have ruled that victims of sexual harassment cannot. This has caused more and more women to combine their Title VII lawsuits with claims under state law. If a supervisor has engaged in sexual harassment, he may also have committed the kind of wrong that state courts allow people to sue for. The federal courts will allow the employee to sue in federal court under both the federal civil rights law and the state common law.

In one case Ray Smalley fired Brenda Phillips because she refused to have sex with him (*Phillips*). The federal judge awarded her $2,666 in back pay. She also sued under Alabama state law for invasion of privacy. Smalley had asked her how often she and her husband had sex, what positions they used, and if she engaged in oral sex. The federal circuit court asked the Alabama Supreme Court if this was something people can sue for under Alabama common law. The Alabama Supreme Court said it was. Phillips was awarded an additional $25,000 to compensate her for the invasion of her privacy and for mental anguish.

In another case Romona Arnold, a police officer in Seminole, Oklahoma, was subjected to sexual harassment by her fellow police officers for several years. This consisted of lewd and vulgar sexual comments and innuendos communicated by sexually graphic and explicit pictures and photographs placed in various rooms in the police department (*Arnold*). She finally quit. For the Title VII violation the federal judge awarded her back pay and ordered her reinstated in the police department. Because he also determined she had suffered from intentional infliction of emotional distress under Oklahoma law, he awarded her an additional $150,000 to compensate her for mental anguish.

Evelyn Priest, a waitress, sued under Title VII and under California common law for intentional infliction of emotional distress, false imprisonment, invasion of privacy, and battery (unwanted touching). The federal district judge found that her employer

> touched intimate parts of her body, tried to kiss her, rubbed his body on hers, picked her up and carried her across the bar room, made sexually suggestive comments to and about her in the presence of others which violated her right to privacy, exposed his genitals to her, and subjected other female waitresses to similar treatment. . . .

The judge awarded $12,563 for back pay under Title VII, along with $95,000 compensatory damages and $15,000 punitive damages for the violation of California common law (*Priest*).

SUING UNDER STATE CIVIL RIGHTS LAWS

During the 1980s many attorneys have decided to take sex-discrimination and sexual-harassment cases to state rather than federal court. Many state statutes provide more damages than Title VII. Washington state's civil rights act allows women to sue for mental anguish as well as back pay (*Cagle*). In a 1986 sexual harassment case filed under Michigan's civil rights act the court awarded $240,000 in compensatory damages and $32,000 in punitive damages (*Eide*).

The Massachusetts Supreme Court and an Illinois Appeals Court have both ruled that victims of sexual harassment by supervisors do not have to complain to higher management in order to sue the company under the state civil rights acts (*College-Town, Green Hills*).

There is another reason attorneys are taking their cases to state rather than federal court. Under many state civil rights acts a woman can get a jury trial, something she cannot get in federal court under Title VII.

PREGNANCY AND PARENTING

In 1976 the U.S. Supreme Court ruled than an employer could provide disability and sick-leave benefits and at the same time exclude pregnancy (*Gilbert*). Congress then amended Title VII to make it clear that discrimination based on pregnancy is sex discrimination (42 U.S.C. sec. 2000e(k). In 1983 the U.S. Supreme Court acknowledged that Congress had overruled the *Gilbert* decision (*Newport*). This case involved a company that allowed its female employees to have pregnancy benefits under the health-insurance plan but gave lesser benefits to the wives of male employees. The U.S. Supreme Court said this was sex discrimination against the male employees and a violation of Title VII.

Over the years Congress has considered requiring employers to give employees who are new parents some time off without fear of losing their jobs. So far these proposals have not become federal law.

Several states have not waited for the federal government to act. California's statute requires employers to provide pregnant employees with an unpaid pregnancy leave of up to four months (Cal. Gov. Code sec. 12945(b)(2)). The California Fair Employment and Housing Commission has interpreted this statute to require employers to reinstate returning employees unless the position had to be filled because of a business necessity. If the position was filled, the employer must make a reasonable effort to place the employee in a substantially similar job when she returns.

The California Federal Savings and Loan Association did not want to do that for Lillian Garland so she took her case to the U.S. Supreme Court (*Cal. Fed.*). California Federal argued that California's law protecting pregnant women was in conflict with Title VII. The Supreme Court disagreed. If the purpose of Title VII is to put female employees on an equal footing with male employees, then the California law does just that by trying to minimize the negative effect of pregnancy on a woman's career.

Many states have statutes that allow public employees to take pregnancy leave and require the agency or school district to give them a comparable job when they return.

Several states have passed laws that allow new parents, male and female, to take time off from work without being penalized by their employer. The Minnesota statute requires employers with over 20 employees to give up to six weeks' unpaid leave "in conjunction with the birth or adoption of a child" (Minn. 181.940 to 943). The Rhode Island statute requires employers with over 49 employees to give up to 13 consecutive weeks' leave in any two-year period to parents who must take leave because of the birth, adoption, or severe illness of a child (R.I. 50-1-501 to 505). Both statutes require the employer to reinstate the employee to a comparable position after the leave and to continue the employee's health-insurance benefits.

9

Age and Handicap Discrimination

THE AGE DISCRIMINATION IN EMPLOYMENT ACT OF 1967

In 1967 Congress passed the Age Discrimination in Employment Act (ADEA). In 1974 it was amended to include government employees at the state, local, and federal levels. The act originally protected people between the ages of 40 and 65. In 1978 the upper age was raised to 70 and in 1987 the upper age was eliminated. Today an employer cannot discriminate against anyone 40 years of age or older because of age (29 U.S.C. sec. 631). Many states also have laws that protect against age discrimination, but most protect only people between the ages of 40 and 65 or 70. The federal law applies only to employers with 20 or more employees. Most state statutes apply to employers with many fewer employees (see Table 7–1 in Chapter 7).

The ADEA protects only people 40 years of age or older. If an employer fires a 39-year-old and hires and 18-year-old, that is not a violation of the federal act, even if the employer fires the 39-year-old simply because of age. The same is true in most states. The Oregon statute is different. It protects anyone 18 years of age or older from age discrimination (Or. Ch. 659).

It is a violation of the ADEA and most state civil rights statutes to discriminate because of age not only in hiring and firing but also in wages, hours, and working conditions. Employers cannot retaliate against workers who file charges against them, testify against them, or oppose age discrimination in the workplace (29 U.S.C. sec. 623(d)).

Defenses

The ADEA provides the employer with a number of defenses. First, employers can discriminate if age is a "bona fide occupational qualification reasonably necessary to the normal operation of the particular business" (29 U.S.C. sec. 623(f)(1)). The federal regulations acknowledge two legitimate BFOQs: when a federal law or regulation requires age discrimination (airline pilots), or when an actor of a particular age is needed to play a part (29 C.F.R. sec. 860.102(d)). The U.S. Supreme Court and federal circuit courts have struck down mandatory retirement policies for police, firefighters, and airline flight engineers (*EEOC, Johnson #5, Western Airlines*). The ADEA does allow mandatory retirement of executives who are at least 65 years old and who will receive a pension of at least $44,000 a year (29 U.S.C. sec. 631(c)(1)).

It is not a BFOQ just because it would cost more to train older employees or because the employer has some stereotyped belief about older employees (they cannot lift things). Even if most older employees would not be able to do the work, each employee has to be given a chance to prove he or she is capable of doing the work (29 C.F.R. sec. 860.103(d)(f)). The ADEA allows age discrimination in apprenticeship programs if the programs meet federal guidelines.

The ADEA allows employers to discriminate as part of a "bona fide employee benefit plan" (29 U.S.C. sec. 623(f)(2)). It is easier to explain what that means by first explaining what it does not mean. It does not mean employers can use an employee benefit plan as an excuse not to hire someone because of age ("If I hired you, my insurance premiums would go up"). It also does not mean employers can use an employee benefit plan as an excuse to fire someone ("Your higher age caused my insurance premiums to go up").

It does mean employers may reduce benefits because of age if the reduction is justified because the older employees cost more. However, employers may not require older employees to make larger contributions to employee benefit plans because they cost more (29 C.F.R. sec. 120(d)(4)(i)). For example, employers who provide life insurance can reduce the amount of life insurance for older employees so that the premiums stay the same, but they cannot keep the amount of insurance the same and force the older employees to pay the higher premiums.

If an employee benefit plan is voluntary, the older employees can be asked to pay more if higher costs justify this, but employers cannot provide older employees with less coverage under the group health-insurance plan than that provided to other employees (29 U.S.C. sec. 623(g)).

The ADEA allows employers to discriminate because of a "bona fide seniority system" or because of "reasonable factors other than age" (29 U.S.C. sec. 632(f)(1)).

Procedure

A victim of age discrimination must file a complaint with the EEOC within 180 days of the incident and wait 60 days while the EEOC tries to negotiate a settlement. Generally victims should also file a complaint with the state human rights commission at the same time (*Cahoon, Sullivan*). Victims of age discrimination do not have to get a right-to-sue letter but they must file a lawsuit within two years of the incident. Generally, victims of age discrimination should discuss the proper procedure with their own attorney before doing anything. Unlike Title VII cases, victims of age discrimination get a jury trial in federal court.

Proving Age Discrimination

There are two ways to prove age discrimination. First, the employee can prove the employer intentionally discriminated because of age. Generally the employer does not send a letter saying, "Because of your age I am letting you go," but there is other evidence of intent. In one case the employer refused to let the older employee bump less-senior employees during the reduction in force and then hired younger workers when new jobs opened up. The Seventh Circuit Court said that was proof of intentional age discrimination (*Ayala*).

In most cases employees prove age discrimination the same way they prove race discrimination: (1) they are a member of the protected group (over 39), (2) they were qualified for the job when they applied (or doing a good job when they were fired), (3) they were fired or not hired, and (4) they were replaced by a younger worker (*Rodriquez, Loeb*). Then the employer has a chance to prove there was a legitimate reason to fire or not hire this employee, and the employee has a chance to prove that this reason is just a pretext for age discrimination.

Three 1987 circuit court cases help make this clear. One executive was fired at 53 and replaced by a 36-year-old. This executive was able to prove that he had done a good job (received the highest bonus available) and that the average age of senior executives at the company went down significantly after a new vice president came to the company. The Eleventh Circuit Court said he had proved age discrimination (*Rosenfield*). In another case there was no prior warning that the employee was not performing up to expectations even though a warning was required by the company discipline policy. He was told to take early retirement and when he refused, they fired him. The Eighth Circuit Court said that was enough to prove age discrimination (*Washburn*). In a third case the company fired a 54-year-old employee who had 27 years with the company because they did not want to continue to pay his high salary ($26,000 a year). They said they fired him so that they could hire a younger worker who would work for less. The Seventh Circuit Court said this was age discrimination. The company should have offered the older worker a chance to take a cut in pay before firing him (*Metz*).

Damages

The ADEA allows the judge to grant "such legal or equitable relief as may be appropriate" (29 U.S.C. sec. 626(b)). The usual damages are back pay, reinstatement, and attorney's fees. The judges can award double the amount of back pay if they decide the employer acted "willfully" (*Laffey, Coston*).

Some courts have awarded money to compensate for pain, suffering, and mental anguish, and some have even awarded punitive damages (*Kennedy*).

Some judges have awarded "front pay" instead of reinstatement. In one case the judge decided reinstatement would be inappropriate because the employer-employee relationship had been irreversibly damaged by the animosity growing out of the lawsuit. Instead, the judge ordered the employer to pay back pay and front pay (what the employee would have earned in the future) totaling $242,659 (*Whittlesey*). In another case the judge awarded $88,000 in front pay. The employee had six years to go until retirement, and the judge did not feel it made sense to order the employee back to work for a few years, given the hostile environment he would have to work in (*Davis*).

HANDICAP DISCRIMINATION

Until two decades ago the law did not try to provide handicapped people with **rights**. It tried to provide them with financial and rehabilitative **assistance**. The Social Security Act of 1935 provided handicapped people with financial assistance. The LaFollette–Barden Act of 1943 provided funds for rehabilitation. At the end of the 1960s the law began to move on three fronts: reducing architectural barriers, improving educational opportunities, and increasing employment opportunities.

In 1968 Congress passed the Federal Architectural Barriers Act (42 U.S.C. sec. 4151). This law requires buildings built or leased by the federal government to be accessible to the handicapped. State and local governments have followed this lead and changed building codes to make new buildings more accessible to the handicapped.

The Urban Mass Transportation Act of 1970 requires local transit systems to be accessible to the handicapped (49 U.S.C. 1601).

In 1975 Congress passed the Education for All Handicapped Children Act (20 U.S.C. sec. 1401). This has done a great deal to bring handicapped children into the mainstream of American education.

THE REHABILITATION ACT OF 1973

While the federal government has done much to remove architectural barriers and improve educational opportunities for the handicapped, the same cannot be said for federal efforts to improve employment opportunities for the handicapped. The major effort in this area is the Rehabilitation Act of 1973. Section 501 requires federal agencies to take affirmative action to hire handicapped employees. Section 503 requires federal contractors to implement affirmative action plans to hire and promote handicapped employees. Section 504 prohibits discrimination against the handicapped in programs that receive federal funds (29 U.S.C. sec. 791).

Before we discuss what the federal law is, it is important to realize what it is not. It is not a Title VII-type law outlawing discrimination against the handicapped.

The Rehabilitation Act defines a handicapped person to be "any person who (a) has a physical or mental impairment, which substantially limits one or more of such person's major life activities, (b) has a record of such an impairment, or (c) is regarded as having such an impairment" (29 U.S.C. sec. 706(6)).

This is a very broad definition. Major life activities include walking, seeing, hearing, and socializing. According to federal regulations, the act covers people with diseases such as epilepsy and cancer as well as people suffering from mental retardation, emotional disorders, and learning disabilities. Even obesity is covered (45 C.F.R. sec. 85.31(b)(1)).

The main thrust of the federal Rehabilitation Act is to require affirmative action from federal agencies and federal contractors. A broad definition like this one is exactly what you do not want in a law designed to encourage affirmative action because too many people are included in the definition. If an agency or contractor can hire a shy person or a fat person instead of a really handicapped person, then affirmative action becomes meaningless. That is exactly what has happened with the Rehabilitation Act of 1973. The Fifth Circuit Court has ruled that left-handed people are not "handicapped" under the Rehabilitation Act but it was a close call (*Torres*).

Section 503

Section 503 requires companies that do work for the federal government (contractors) to develop affirmative action plans to hire the handicapped. Anyone who feels a company that contracts with the federal government is not doing what it should to hire the handicapped can call the Office of Federal Contract Compliance in the U.S. Labor Department and complain. However, individuals do not have the right to sue these companies under Section 503 to force them to develop affirmative action plans. Only the Secretary of Labor can do that.

Section 504

Individuals can sue in federal court under Section 504 of the Rehabilitation Act. Section 504 requires entities that receive federal grants (generally state and local governments) not to discriminate against the handicapped. The act says: "No otherwise qualified handicapped individual . . . shall, solely by reason of his handicap, be excluded from the participation in, be denied the benefits of, or be subjected to discrimination under any program or activity receiving federal financial assistance" (29 U.S.C. sec. 794).

The U.S. Supreme Court has held that an employee can sue for handicap discrimination even if the federal funds were not given to the state or local government specifically to help it increase employment of the handicapped. (*Darrone*).

In 1984 the U.S. Supreme Court said that only the particular activity receiving federal funds had to obey the dictates of the Rehabilitation Act, not the entire city or school district (*Grove City*). In 1988 Congress overruled this decision requiring the entire entity to obey the Rehabilitation Act (and all federal civil rights laws) if it receives any federal funds.

Section 504 requires that a reasonable attempt be made to accommodate the needs of handicapped employees. Generally if the accommodation costs anything, the entity does not have do it (*Southeastern, Gardner, Jasany*).

VOCATIONAL REHABILITATION SERVICES

A major function of the Rehabilitation Act was to provide funds for state rehabilitation programs (29 U.S.C. sec. 720). This is the familiar federal-grants-to-states type of program that began with the Social Security Act of 1935. The federal money supports vocational education, research, training, construction, and independent-living centers. In 1986 amendments continued this funding for another five years.

TAX INCENTIVES

Recent amendments to the Internal Revenue Code provide tax incentives to employers who hire the handicapped. These tax deductions are supposed to help defray the costs of accommodation.

STATE LAWS

Federal law does not outlaw employment discrimination against the handicapped except for entities that receive federal grants. The District of Columbia and most states do have laws that actually prohibit discrimination against handicapped people by private employers. These laws have different definitions of what it means to be "handicapped" and different procedures that victims must follow. Many states that require employers to have a minimum number of employees before the state civil rights law applies do not require that when it comes to handicap discrimination. If handicap discrimination is involved, employees should assume their employer is covered by the state law unless an attorney tells them otherwise.

Many states use the same definition of handicapped that is contained in the federal Rehabilitation Act of 1973. This means they have a very broad definition that covers many people. Under this definition, obesity is a handicap in New York, nearsightedness is a handicap in Wisconsin, and being colorblind is a handicap in Oregon (*Xerox, Brown County, Quinn*). In many states whether or not someone is handicapped may depend on what the employer "thinks." In one Illinois case the employee was fired after having a heart attack. The court decided the employer "perceived" the employee to be handicapped, even though he was not, and therefore the employee was protected by the law (*Kenall*). In a similar Wisconsin case, a police officer was told after a physical exam that he had weak back muscles. Because the city thought this made him handicapped, he was handicapped for the purposes of the state law (*LaCrosse*).

Other states do not use the Rehabilitation Act definition and have a much more restrictive definition of handicap. Texas may have the most restrictive definition. In a 1987 decision the Texas Supreme Court interpreted the Texas statute to apply only to people with handicaps that "severely limit" the persons' ability to perform "work-related functions" (Chevron). The case involved a woman who was not hired because one eye could be corrected only to 20/60 and Chevron had a minimum of 20/40. In most states this would have been handicap discrimination.

Of course, employers do not have to hire or keep employees who cannot do the work. In most states if the employee becomes handicapped and can no longer do the work, the employer is not required to give the employee another job with the same company.

Many states require employers to do whatever is necessary to "reasonably accommodate" handicapped employees. While federal judges have not been willing to order employers to do anything that has more than a minimum cost, that is not the case in many states. A Pennsylvania Appeals Court has ruled that under Pennsylvania law if the employer can accommodate the employee by buying a mechanical device, then the employer has to buy the mechanical device (Jenks).

Alcoholics, Drug Addicts, and Cigarette Smokers

In most states the state civil rights commission has ruled that alcoholics and drug addicts are protected by the law as handicapped people (Hazlett). The ironic result is that employers who use drug tests may be able to fire employees who flunk the test and are not addicted to drugs (these employees may still sue for invasion of privacy, as we will discuss in Chapter 12), but employers may not be able to fire true drug addicts without violating the state handicap-discrimination statute.

The Texas statute specifically states in the definition of handicap that handicap "does not include a condition of addiction to any drug or illegal or federally controlled substance or a condition of addiction to the use of alcohol" (Tex. Art. 5221k sec. 2.01(7)(b)).

All this raises some interesting questions with regard to cigarette smokers. In 1986 C. Everett Koop, the Surgeon General, issued a report that found just being in the room with a cigarette smoker could be injurious to people's health. That resulted in a major effort to limit smoking in the workplace. Many companies have even begun to refuse to hire cigarette smokers or to cover them with the company health-insurance plan. In May 1988, the Surgeon General issued another report that says many smokers cannot quit smoking because they are addicted to nicotine. If that is true, then they may be protected by the handicap-discrimination statutes in most states. They would not be protected in Texas or other states that exclude addiction the way Texas does. Will we see a round of lawsuits in the 1990s by cigarette smokers who feel they have been discriminated against because of their handicap? Will states revise their statutes to exclude smokers from the protection of the handicap-discrimination act? If they do, will they also exclude other drug addicts, alcoholics, and people addicted to too much food?

PEOPLE WITH DISEASES ARE HANDICAPPED

In 1987 the U.S. Supreme Court came to the same conclusion most state civil rights commissions had come to, that people with diseases are handicapped as that is defined in the Rehabilitation Act and most state statutes. The case involved Gene Arline, an elementary-school teacher, who was fired in 1979 after suffering a third relapse of tuberculosis in two years (*Arline*). The school board fired Arline because of the "continued recurrence of tuberculosis." The U.S. Supreme Court ruled that people with contagious diseases are handicapped under the Rehabilitation Act definition. The court said a hearing must be held to determine how contagious an individual person really is, how likely it is that he or she will infect others, and whether the employer can "reasonably accommodate" the contagious employee (see also *Atascadero*).

AIDS

The news media made much of the effect of the *Arline* decision on people with AIDS. However, as you have seen, the federal law affects very few people. More important is whether state supreme courts will agree with the U.S. Supreme Court when they interpret their state handicap statutes. Most state civil rights agencies have already ruled that cancer patients are protected by the handicap-discrimination statute. If cancer patients are protected, AIDS patients will probably also be protected.

The Center for Disease Control has concluded that AIDS is a bloodborne, sexually transmitted disease that is not spread by casual contact. The center does not recommend routine AIDS testing by employers. While the center has recommended that health-care workers wear gloves, it has not recommended similar precautions for food-service workers. Of course everyone should avoid contact with blood and other body fluids whenever possible.

Employers might argue that they were refusing to hire applicants with AIDS not because of the handicap but because of the increased cost in insurance premiums such employees might cause. Courts have not allowed employers to get away with that argument when the job applicant was obese and they will probably not allow them to get away with it when the applicant has AIDS (*Xerox*).

An employer who fires an employee who contracts AIDS will probably be in violation of ERISA (see Chapter 17). ERISA forbids the firing of employees in order to keep the premiums on group health-insurance plans from going up.

Employers might argue that they were firing or refusing to hire people with AIDS in order to protect their other employees. However, courts have generally ruled that employers cannot discriminate against handicapped people who are perceived to be dangerous to others (for example, people with epilepsy who operate machinery) unless the employer can show a "reasonable probability of substantial harm" to others. Generally, given what we know about how AIDS is transmitted, employers are not going to be able to show that people with AIDS present a "reasonable probability of substantial harm" to others (*Mantolete*).

Employers might argue that they were discriminating against people with AIDS for their own good. Generally courts have not bought that argument either (pregnant women cannot be fired for their own good unless there is real scientific evidence of substantial risk of harm to the fetus—*Shelby Memorial*).

Employers might argue that they were discriminating against people with AIDS because their other employees did not want to work with them. That argument did not work when co-workers refused to work with blacks and it will probably not work in this case.

Some employers will be tempted to test job applicants or employees for AIDS. The testing of people for disease is controlled in most states by specific health statutes. In 1987 the Texas legislature amended its health statute to forbid AIDS testing by employers unless the employer could prove a "bona fide occupational" need for the test. Given the findings and recommendations of the Center for Disease Control, that is not going to be possible in most cases. The Texas statute allows people who have been tested to sue and also carries criminal penalties (Tex. Art. 4419b-1 sec. 9.02). The statute also forbids AIDS testing by insurance companies (no person or entity may require another person to undergo an AIDS test except for very limited purposes, insurance not being one of them). That did not stop the Texas Board of Insurance from issuing an emergency regulation authorizing AIDS testing by insurance companies. The general legal rule is that a state agency cannot issue a regulation that purports to override a state statute. Apparently in this case the general legal rule was overcome by the general political rule that insurance companies can afford the best lobbyists and the most powerful attorneys. Still, anyone in Texas who took an AIDS test at the request of an insurance company should talk to an attorney. The general legal rule is probably going to win in the end if the case is taken to the Texas Supreme Court.

Part Four
Constitutional Rights

10

The Right of Free Speech

FREE SPEECH FOR PUBLIC EMPLOYEES

The Basic Free Speech Right

In 1968 the U.S. Supreme Court handed down the first decision holding that governments could not fire or take any other adverse action against their employees simply because the government employer did not like something the employee said (*Pickering*). The case involved a teacher who was fired for sending a letter to the local newspaper criticizing the school board. In deciding that the school board had violated the teacher's constitutional rights, the U.S. Supreme Court said:

> Free and open debate is vital to informed decision-making by the electorate. Teachers are, as a class, the members of a community most likely to have informed and definite opinions as to how funds allotted to the operation of the school should be spent. Accordingly, it is essential that they be able to speak out freely on such questions without fear of retaliatory dismissal.

The Supreme Court ruled that a government employer cannot fire an employee in retaliation for the employee's exercise of the right of free speech.

At the same time, the Supreme Court recognized that a balance would have to be struck between the right of employees to speak out on "matters of public concern" and government's need to conduct business in an efficient manner. The court said that if the things said had interfered with the employee's ability to teach or get along with co-workers, the decision might have been different.

In 1972 the Supreme Court reaffirmed this principle in a case involving

125

Professor Perry from Odessa Junior College (Perry). As president of the Texas Junior College Teachers Association, Perry often testified before the Texas Legislature. The Board of Regents of Odessa Junior College did not like what Perry was saying to the legislature, so they fired him (technically they did not renew his contract for another year). Their main disagreement was over whether Odessa Junior College should become a four-year college. Perry supported this change while the Board of Regents opposed it. The U.S. Supreme Court held that the Board of Regents could not fire Perry as "a reprisal for the exercise of constitutionally protected rights."

After these decisions some judges feared that public employees who felt they were about to be fired would run to the newspaper to criticize their supervisors, hoping to be able to sue for a free-speech violation if they were actually fired. In 1977 the Supreme Court addressed this problem in the Mt. Healthy case. A teacher called a radio station to criticize the teacher dress code. These comments were broadcast over the air, and this teacher's contract was not renewed for the coming school year. The school district said that it had good reasons to fire this teacher, which included fighting with other teachers and using obscene gestures with students. The Supreme Court imposed what has come to be called the Mt. Healthy procedure. First, the dismissed employee must prove that he or she was fired for exercising the right of free speech. Then the employer has a chance to prove that he would have fired the employee anyway, even if the employee had not exercised his or her right of free speech. Then the employee can come back and try to prove that these "good reasons" are only pretext.

Comments on "matters of public concern" do not have to be made in "public." In a 1979 case a teacher was fired after she criticized the school's lack of racial integration in a private discussion with the school principal (Givhan). The Supreme Court said that even her "private expression" of opinion was protected.

However, only speech about "matters of public concern" is protected by the U.S. Constitution. A 1983 U.S. Supreme Court case involved an assistant district attorney who circulated a questionnaire among her co-workers. The questionnaire dealt with transfer policies, office morale, and the need for an employee grievance committee. The district attorney fired her for insubordination and the Supreme Court refused to reinstate her. The court said:

> when a public employee speaks not as a citizen upon matters of public concern, but instead as an employee upon matters only of personal interest, absent the most unusual circumstances, a federal court is not the appropriate forum in which to review the wisdom of a personnel decision taken by a public agency allegedly in reaction to the employee's behavior.

The court did not feel the questionnaire dealt with "matters of public concern" but only with "matters of personal interest" (Connick).

Adverse Action

A government employer is not supposed to take any "adverse action" against a public employee because of something the employee says. Of course, that means the employee cannot be fired. What else can a government employer not do in retaliation for an employee's exercise of free speech? One teacher was transferred to another school while another teacher was reassigned to different teaching duties. In each case the federal judge ordered the school district to put the teacher back where she had been before she exercised her right of free speech (*Bernasconi, Childers*). In other cases just placing a letter of reprimand in the employee's file was enough to bring in a federal judge with a court order to remove the letter of reprimand (*Swilley, Aebisher, Columbus Ed. Assoc.*). In other words, a government employer is not supposed to do anything to retaliate against an employee who has exercised his or her right of free speech.

Matters of Public Concern

If government employees have a constitutional right to speak out on "matters of public concern," but not on "matters of personal interest," whether the topic of their conversation qualifies as a "matter of public concern" becomes of special importance. In one case a teacher felt that students were being placed in classes for the mentally retarded because they were being tested in English rather than Spanish, the language they grew up with. When the teacher advised parents to seek legal advice, she was transferred to another school. The Ninth Circuit Court ruled that she could not be transferred for speaking to the parents about a matter of public concern (*Bernasconi*).

In another case a teacher in Mississippi appeared on television and criticized the school superintendent, saying: "We'll either have to discipline the superintendent or put him back on one of those long midnight trains to Georgia" (*Jordan*). The federal judges found this to be a statement on a matter of public concern.

Several cases involved government employees who have been fired or mistreated because of their union activity. The courts have ruled that the right of free speech includes the right to engage in union activity as long as it is not disruptive (*Durango, Childers*).

Other comments that have been found to be comments on "matters of public concern" include: editorials critical of school-district policies broadcast from the school district's own radio station; picketing by teachers to protest the layoff of fellow teachers; comments to newspapers about being assaulted at work; and comments by teachers about how the school's funds were being spent (*Trotman, Aebisher, Glanville*).

One case involved a coach who was relieved of his coaching duties because he wrote a letter to the school board making suggestions on how the athletic program could be improved (*Central Point*). The superintendent was particularly upset because the coach had not followed the "channel rule," which required advance notice to the superintendent of any communication with the school board. The federal judge said the "channel rule" was unconstitutional. The coach had a right to communicate with his elected representatives on the school board, and the superintendent could not require him to report to the superintendent first. In a 1987 case, a group of Arkansas teachers wrote a letter to the state department of education complaining about the way programs for handicapped children were being run in their school district. The Eighth Circuit Court said the firing of these teachers was clearly a violation of their First Amendment rights, and these teachers could not be required to follow a similar "channel rule" (*Southside*).

Government employees do not have a right to make a nuisance of themselves over matters of personal interest. For example, one college professor kept complaining about his individual salary and his position on the organizational chart (*Mahaffey*). The judge said these were "private concerns," not "public concerns," and therefore not protected. In general, if the speech is about the individual employee's working conditions, it is not protected by the First Amendment (*Ballard, Renfroe, Callaway*).

Harmony among Co-workers

The right of government employees to speak out, even on matters of public concern, may be limited if the speech interferes with the efficient operation of government. This problem was explored in an early decision handed down by the Seventh Circuit Court (*Donahue*). The case involved a chaplain at a state mental hospital who was fired for criticizing the hospital's policies in the local newspaper. The circuit court ruled that a government employer might be justified in taking action against an employee if the statements:

1. interfered with harmony among co-workers;
2. interfered with the need for confidentiality;
3. interfered with the employee's ability to perform his or her duties;
4. were totally untrue and suggested that the employee was totally incompetent; or
5. interfered with a close working relationship between the employee and the supervisor in a situation that called for personal loyalty and confidence.

Since the judges did not feel the chaplain's situation fit any of these situations, the chaplain got his job back.

In a few cases the animosity among co-workers has been so great it outweighed the right of the individual employee to make comments about matters of public concern. In one case a teacher made a speech at the annual teacher's association dinner in which she insulted many of her fellow teachers (*Moore*). The judge refused to reinstate her. In another case a teacher made false charges against the principal and distributed leaflets inciting the students to violence (*Gilbertson*). The need to run an efficient school outweighed the free-speech right of this teacher.

Employees who occupy confidential or administrative positions do not have the same right to speak out on matters of public concern that other employees have. Phyllis Hamm was hired to assist the university administration in investigating charges of employment discrimination (*Hamm*). In several cases, Hamm released information to the newspaper before she had even reported to the administration. The judges felt that, because Hamm had been placed in a confidential position, the "interests of discipline and harmony outweighed the rights of the employee."

The right of free speech is not a license to be abusive. The speech of a junior-college administrator in Arkansas was not protected because it was accompanied by "abuse and threats" (*Russ*).

While a government employee has a right to speak out, a government employer has a right to run an efficient operation and avoid disruption. It is often difficult to see where the line should be drawn between these two worthwhile goals. In 1987 the U.S. Supreme Court handed down a 5-to-4 decision. The case involved a 19-year-old black woman who performed data entry in the constable's office in Harris County, Texas. On March 30, 1981, when she heard a radio announcement of the attempted assassination of President Reagan, she turned to a co-worker and said: "If they go for him again, I hope they get him." She was fired on the spot. The Supreme Court ruled that this was a comment on a matter of public concern and that it did not impair discipline in the office. Justice Powell, who cast the deciding vote, said, "The risk that a single, off-hand comment directed to only one other worker will lower morale, disrupt the work force, or otherwise undermine the mission of the office borders on the fanciful" (*Rankin*).

Whistleblower Laws

Congress and many state legislatures have passed whistleblower laws to protect civil servants. The federal law is part of the Civil Service Reform Act of 1978 (5 U.S.C. sec. 2302(b)(8)(A)). The act protects federal employees from adverse action if they disclose information regarding a violation of law or mismanagement, unless national security requires that the illegal activity or mismanagement be kept secret.

A number of states have passed similar laws. In some states the manager who wrongly fires a civil servant may even go to jail (see Chapter 6).

A government employee fired for whistleblowing should discuss with an attorney whether to sue in federal court for violations of the First Amendment or follow the whistleblowing statute.

Hatch Acts: The Right to Engage in Political Activity

A Hatch Act is a law that limits the kind of political activity government employees can engage in. These laws usually prevent government employees from campaigning for the people that will ultimately be their bosses. For example, federal employees can engage in local politics but not national. City employees can engage in national politics but not local.

Some people wonder how to reconcile the fact that public employees have the right to speak out about matters of public concern with the fact that they do not have the right to speak out about the matter of most public concern—who should be elected to public office. To understand how these laws came about and why they are constitutional requires a brief look at history.

Until the twentieth century the federal bureaucracy was small in comparison to state and local bureaucracies. That began to change in the 1930s as New Deal programs required civil servants to make them a reality. There was a fear that Franklin D. Roosevelt would turn the federal bureaucracy into a giant Democratic Party machine, like the big-city machines that held power in cities throughout America.

In 1940 Congress passed the federal Hatch Act. The act prevents federal civil servants from taking an active part in partisan political activities. Today there are two types of federal laws: criminal laws that make some kinds of political activities a crime (18 U.S.C. ch. 29) and other laws that result in dismissal (5 U.S.C. ch. 73).

The criminal laws carry fines of up to $10,000 and jail terms of up to five years. It is a crime for military officers to station troops near polling places or to interfere with the voting in any way. It is even a crime to take a public-opinion poll of members of the armed forces, asking them how they voted or if they voted. The law also prohibits using threats or coercion to try to influence the way people vote in federal elections.

Candidates for federal office are not allowed to promise jobs or other benefits in exchange for political activity or to threaten to take jobs away if someone does not engage in political activity. It is also a crime if candidates for federal office solicit campaign contributions from federal employees or for federal employees to make campaign contributions to federal candidates.

The noncriminal laws basically outlaw taking an active part in political campaigns. The law does allow federal civil servants to participate in nonpartisan politics as well as local politics in and around Washington D.C.

In 1947 the U.S. Supreme Court declared the federal Hatch Act to be constitutional (*United Public*). The vote was four justices for, three against, with two abstentions. The four justices who voted for the act felt that Congress had a right to control the excesses of machine politics and to prevent a "one-party system." The three dissenters felt the act was too vague. This question of vagueness came up again in 1973, and again the law was upheld (*Civil Service*).

Many states and large cities have their own Hatch acts, which generally have been found to be constitutional (*Broadrick, Wachsman*). In a few cases the laws have been struck down because of vagueness (*Barrett*).

Some state and local laws have run into trouble because of the need to allow union activity on the one hand and prevent political activity on the other hand. For example, in one case, the president of the St. Louis Firefighters Union criticized the vote of the city council and suggested that people should not vote for a particular city councilman in the next election (*Blackwell*). He was suspended for a month without pay for violating the city's Hatch act. The Missouri Appeals Court overturned the suspension, holding that he was speaking as a union president, not a city employee, and therefore his speech was protected by the First Amendment and did not violate the city Hatch Act.

While a government employee has a constitutional right to speak out on matters of public concern, he or she does not have a constitutional right to engage in political campaign activity if that activity is outlawed by statute.

The Right to Belong to a Political Party

Do government employees have the right to belong to the political party of their choice? That seems like a simple question, but it is one of the most difficult questions ever asked. Is belonging to a political party like speaking out on matters of public concern—in which case it is protected by the constitution—or is it like engaging in political activity—in which case it is not protected?

Until June 1976, the answer seemed simple. Government employees were divided into two groups: those protected by civil service laws who could not be fired because of their political-party affiliation because that was not "good cause" for dismissal; and the rest, at-will employees (often political appointees) who could be fired for any reason, including their political-party affiliation.

In June 1976, the U.S. Supreme Court handed down its decision in the *Elrod* case and everything changed. When Sheriff Elrod, a Democrat, was elected sheriff of Cook County, Illinois, in 1970, he fired all the non-civil service employees, who were Republicans, and replaced them with Democrats. These fired Republicans sued, arguing that they could not be fired simply because of their political-party affiliation.

The case raised the most difficult kind of problem the Supreme Court ever has to face. The United States political system is based on two fundamental beliefs: a belief in democracy and a belief in individual rights. The greatest legal problems come about when these two fundamental beliefs conflict. In this case they were in conflict because, it could be argued, our democratic system depends for its very survival on patronage (appointing members of the winning political party to positions of power). If candidates cannot hold out the possibility of jobs to campaign volunteers, there would be no campaign volunteers. On the other hand, surely people have a right to belong to whatever political party they want to without interference from government.

Justice Brennan, in a decision joined by Marshall and White, recognized this dilemma. He felt that policy-making employees could be replaced because of their political-party affiliation. Justice Brennan recognized that when the people elect a President or a sheriff they expect new policies to be carried out. These elected officials could not do that without the help of trusted assistants who were politically and personally loyal to them. However, he felt this power to replace because of political-party affiliation should not extend to low-level employees who perform routine tasks. Brennan believed their right to belong to the political party of their choice is protected by the First Amendment.

Justices Stewart and Blackmun agreed with Brennan's decision, but they wrote their own opinion to emphasize that both confidential and policy-making employees can be fired because of their political-party affiliation.

Justice Powell wrote an impassioned dissent. He pointed out that the patronage system is basic to the American political system because the patronage system is the backbone of the political-party system. The political-party system makes elected officials accountable to the voters, and without accountability there is no democracy. With patronage, a candidate who is not rich still has a chance. Without patronage, only the rich would be able to buy the campaign workers and campaign advertisements that are necessary to win political campaigns in America.

The Supreme Court has dealt with this problem in only one other case (*Branti*). A newly appointed public defender in Rockland County, New York, fired the Republican assistant public defenders and replaced them with Democrats. A majority of the Supreme Court felt this violated the constitution. Justice Stevens wrote the opinion for a majority that included Chief Justice Burger. Justice Stevens said that the question is: Is party affiliation an appropriate requirement for the effective performance of the office? In this case he did not think it was.

Federal judges, some of whom became federal judges through the political patronage system, have had great difficulty making decisions that apply the standards laid out in *Elrod* and *Branti*.

What jobs can be a part of the patronage system? The city attorney and his or her assistants can be patronage appointments because they give legal advice to elected officials (*Ness*). Assistant district attorneys can also be replaced because of their political-party affiliation (*Mummau, Livas*). Confidential secretaries for elected officials and high-level administrators can also be patronage appointments (*Hodge #2, Shakman*).

Jobs that are obviously protected from patronage politics are low-level road workers (*Bever*), administrative assistants (*Gannon*), city clerks (*Visser*), and town bookkeepers (*Grossart*).

While it is clear that employees who occupy policy-making or confidential positions can be fired for patronage reasons, it is less clear whether administrators who do not have any input into policy making can be fired. For example, Donald Tomczak held the second-highest post in the Chicago Water Department. The district judge ruled that he could not be fired because he did not have any input into policy making. The Seventh Circuit Court disagreed, finding that Tomczak occupied a position "where his political affiliation could affect the ability of a new administration to implement new policies" (*Tomczak*).

In another case, a court bailiff in Gary, Indiana, was fired. He did not occupy a "confidential" or "policy-making" position, but he did work closely with elected officials. The Seventh Circuit Court upheld his dismissal. The court felt that it would "strain credulity to read the First Amendment or *Elrod* to require an elected official to work in constant direct contact with a person viewed as a political enemy" (*Meeks*). While the Seventh Circuit Court has ruled that employees who occupy administrative positions, or have jobs in which they must work closely with elected officials, can be fired because of their party affiliation, other circuit courts do not agree.

The Eighth Circuit Court ruled that a newly elected court clerk in St. Louis could not replace his four deputy clerks (*Barnes #2*). The four deputies help the clerk run an office with over 200 employees. Efficient management of the clerk's office was a central theme of his political campaign, yet he could not appoint assistants to help him carry out those campaign promises.

Several circuit court decisions have tried to limit the impact of *Elrod* and *Branti*, and in so doing they have created the worst of all possible worlds. How they have accomplished this is best illustrated by a case from New Jersey (*Horn*).

New Jersey had a group of people known as "motor vehicle agents" when Thomas Kean, a Republican, was elected governor. These agents registered cars and issued driver's licenses. They were independent contractors, not state employees. They received a fee for every car they registered and every license they issued. In New Jersey, as in many other states, these agents were political patronage appointments. The Third Circuit Court held that these agents were independent contractors, not employees, and therefore they could be hired and fired for political reasons. Never mind that these agents performed a routine task that had nothing to do with policy making. The dissenting judges thought this decision was outrageous. It meant, first, that patronage lives on for those who have a lot of money to give to a candidate. They can give their money and get government contracts in return. But the little person, who has only labor to give, cannot give that labor and expect a low-level government job in return.

The Third Circuit Court is not alone in deciding that the principles of *Elrod* and *Branti* do not apply to independent contractors who perform government services. The Seventh and Eighth Circuit Courts have ruled the same way (*LaFalce, Sweeney #2*).

These decisions create a giant loophole in the Elrod–Branti rule. Any government official who wants to get around this rule can simply contract-out the work.

The people of New Jersey were incensed by this case. The New Jersey Legislature, in response to public pressure, instituted a system of competitive bidding for the motor vehicle agent positions (*The New York Times*, June 12, 1985, p. B4).

The bottom line is that most government employees cannot be fired simply to be replaced by members of a different political party or political faction. They can be replaced if they occupy high-level positions, or positions in which they have to work closely with elected officials. But, while employees cannot be replaced for political reasons, their jobs can be abolished for political reasons so that an independent contractor can take over.

Entities That Act as if They Were Governments

Private entities that perform government functions or accept financial support from government may also have to respect the free-speech rights of their employees. In 1988 a Texas Appeals Court ruled that an employee could sue a private hospital for violating the right of free speech protected by Article One, Section Eight of the Texas Constitution (*Jones #3*).

FREE SPEECH FOR PRIVATE EMPLOYEES

Some states have very broad civil rights laws, as Vanessa Redgrave proved in Massachusetts (*Redgrave*). Vanessa Redgrave had a contract with the Boston Symphony to narrate a series of concerts. When the public found out, they called the Symphony to protest her appearance. Apparently people objected to her stand on the Palestinian issue. The Boston Symphony canceled the contract, and

Vanessa Redgrave sued. The case took 16 days in a federal district court. The jury decided that the Boston Symphony had broken her contract without good cause so she got the money she had been promised in the contract. Redgrave also argued that her rights had been violated under the Massachusetts Civil Rights Act because the Symphony had fired her because of what she said on an important public issue. The Symphony argued that it was only doing what the patrons asked it to do. The federal judges sent a question to the Massachusetts Supreme Court: Is bowing to the wishes of someone else a defense in a civil rights case under Massachusetts law? The answer from the Massachusetts Supreme Court was NO. If that were true, people who interfered with someone's civil rights would say they did it because they had been asked to.

This case stands for the general proposition that in Massachusetts a private employer cannot fire an employee because he does not agree with that employee's "comments on matters of public concern." Private employees have the same protection public employees have because of the Massachusetts Civil Rights Act. Whether other state supreme courts will interpret their state civil rights acts the same way remains to be seen.

In 1983 the Connecticut legislature passed a special statute dealing with this issue. The statute reads:

> Any employers including the state and any instrumentality or political subdivision thereof, who subjects any employee to discipline or discharge on account of the exercise of such employee of rights guaranteed by the first amendment of the United States Constitution or section 3, 4, and 14 article first of the constitution of the state, provided such activity does not substantially or materially interfere with the employee's bona fide job performance or the working relationship between the employee and the employer, shall be liable to such employee for damages caused by such discipline or discharge, including the costs of any such action for damages. If the court determines that such action was brought without substantial justification, the court may award costs and reasonable attorney's fees to the employer.

In other words, in Connecticut, the right of free speech applies to everyone, not just to public employees. At the same time the Connecticut statute recognizes the same kind of "harmony among co-workers" defense that applies in public-employee cases. No other state has such a general statute.

California, Louisiana, and Ohio have statutes that keep employers from influencing the "political activities" of their employees. Pennsylvania has a statute that keeps employers from influencing the "political opinions" of their employees, while statutes in Indiana, New York, South Dakota, and Montana say employers may not influence employee "political opinions or actions." New Mexico and South Carolina have statutes that keep employers from discharging employees because of their "political opinions," while a Missouri statute says employers may not discriminate because of an employee's "political beliefs or opinions." Over half the states have statutes that keep employers from influencing how their employees vote (see Table 10–1).

TABLE 10–1. Statutes Protecting Free Speech or Voting Activity*

Alabama	Boss may not influence vote.	17-23-10, 11
Alaska	School teachers may speak out.	14.20.095, 100
Arizona	Boss may not influence vote.	16-1012
Arkansas	None	
California	Boss may not influence political activity.	Labor Code 1102
Colorado	Boss may not influence vote. Boss may not prevent political participation.	1-13-719 8-2-108
Connecticut	Boss may not influence vote. Boss may not discharge because of exercise of free-speech right.	9-365 31-51q
Delaware	Boss may not intimidate vote.	15-5162, 5163
District of Columbia	Boss may not discriminate because of political affiliation.	1-2512
Florida	Boss may not fire because employee did or did not vote for any candidate or measure.	104.081
Georgia	None	
Hawaii	None	
Idaho	None	
Illinois	None	
Indiana	Boss may not influence political opinions or actions.	3-14-3-21
Iowa	Boss may not influence vote.	49.110
Kansas	None	
Kentucky	Boss may not direct vote.	121.310
Louisiana	Boss may not influence political activity or discharge because of political opinions.	23:961, 962
Maine	None	
Maryland	None	
Massachusetts	Boss may not influence vote	Ch. 56, sec. 33
Michigan	None	
Minnesota	Boss may not influence vote.	210A.14
Mississippi	Boss may not direct or coerce vote.	23-15-871
Missouri	Boss may not coerce vote or discriminate because of political beliefs or opinions.	130.028
Montana	Boss may not influence political opinions or actions.	13-35-226
Nebraska	Boss may not influence vote.	32-1050, 1050.01, 1223
Nevada	Boss may not prevent employee from engaging in politics.	613.040
New Hampshire	None	

*The law is always changing. Consult an attorney about your situation.

TABLE 10–1. (Cont.)

New Jersey	Boss may not influence vote.	19:34-27
New Mexico	Boss may not coerce or discharge employees because of political opinions, beliefs, or vote.	1-20-13
New York	Boss may not influence political opinions or actions.	Election 17-150
North Carolina	None	
North Dakota	None	
Ohio	Boss may not influence political activity.	3599.05, 06
Oklahoma	No one may intimidate voters.	Title 26, sec. 16-113
Oregon	None	
Pennsylvania	Boss may not influence political opinions.	Title 25, sec. 3547
Rhode Island	Boss may not influence vote.	17-23-6
South Carolina	Boss may not intimidate or discharge because of political opinions.	16-17-560
South Dakota	Boss may not influence political opinions or actions.	12-26-13
Tennessee	Boss may not direct or coerce vote.	2-19-134
Texas	None	
Utah	Boss may not influence vote.	20-13-7
Vermont	None	
Virginia	None	
Washington	None	
West Virginia	Boss may not affect vote.	3-9-20
Wisconsin	Boss may not influence vote.	103.18
Wyoming	Boss may not interfere with political rights.	22-26-116

If your state does not have a special statute, and your state civil rights act does not cover this situation, then it becomes a question of wrongful discharge.

You saw in Chapter 6 that the judges in many states have decided people cannot be fired for "wrongful" reasons, such as refusing to do an illegal thing or reporting criminal activity to the authorities. Would it be wrongful for an employer to fire an employee because he did not like what the employee said about a "matter of public concern"? In many states it probably would be. The New Jersey Supreme Court said it is wrongful to discharge employees for reasons that violate public policy and that we find public policy expressed in constitutions and statutes. The New Jersey Constitution says "every person may freely speak, write, and publish his sentiments on all subjects" (N.J. Const. Art. I, para. 6). If a private employer fired an employee in New Jersey because he did not like what that employee had said, the New Jersey Supreme Court would probably find that to be a case of wrongful discharge.

In a recent New Jersey case a member of the Elks Lodge wrote a letter to the newspaper critical of the lodge's racial discrimination. The lodge kicked him out because he failed to clear the letter with the "Grand Exalted Ruler" before sending it to the newspaper. The New Jersey Appeals Court held that the Elks Lodge could not limit the free-speech rights of its members and ordered the member reinstated (*Zelenka*).

In a federal case an employee said he was fired because he refused to lobby the Pennsylvania legislature for his employer (*Novosel*). The Third Circuit Court held that if that were true it would be a violation of the right of free speech contained in both the U.S. and Pennsylvania constitutions and a case of wrongful discharge.

Administrators may not be as free to express their opinions as other private employees. In one case a General Motors executive said he had been fired because he refused to lie to a government agency (*Percival*). The Eighth Circuit Court refused to do anything about it. The court said that, even if true, this was not a case of wrongful discharge because employers should be free to hire and fire people in "high and sensitive managerial positions."

11

The Right to Due Process

DUE PROCESS RIGHTS FOR PUBLIC EMPLOYEES

The Fourteenth Amendment to the U.S. Constitution says governments cannot deprive people of "life, liberty, or property without due process of law." That means someone cannot have his or her home confiscated by government without a condemnation hearing or be thrown into prison without a trial. What does that have to do with public employees?

In 1972, the U.S. Supreme Court handed down decisions in the *Roth* and *Sindermann* cases. Roth, an assistant professor at Wisconsin University—Oshkosh, was hired with a one-year written contract. At the end of that year the university did not give him another contract. Roth sued, claiming he had been deprived of his property without due process of law. The Supreme Court held that if he had a property right in his job, then he was entitled to due process before being deprived of it. Persons could have a property right in their job either because a state civil service law gave them such a right or because they had a union or individual contract. In Roth's case, since his contract had run out and he was not protected by civil service, he did not have any "property" rights in his job. Roth lost.

There was no civil service statute or contract in Sindermann's case either, but Sindermann argued that there was an implied civil service system at his college, that people were given a kind of implied tenure, and that he had earned tenure under the implied rules. The court said that a property right could arise from such an implied contract, and sent the case back for trial.

In other words, the U.S. Supreme Court held that if a public employee has tenure under a civil service system, or works under an employment contract, he or she has a kind of property. The U.S. Constitution does not require governments to give this kind of property to its employees. All the employees could be at-will as far as the U.S. Constitution is concerned. But, once the government does give tenure or a contract to an employee, it cannot take it away without giving that employee the appropriate due process. The question then becomes: What kind of due process is appropriate?

The Supreme Court has answered that question in two cases. In the first, *Arnett*, in 1974, the employee was covered by the federal civil service system. Before his dismissal he was given the chance to respond in writing to the charges made against him. He was also given a trial-like hearing *after* his dismissal. Arnett argued that he should have been given a trial-like hearing *before* his dismissal. No more than three Supreme Court justices could agree.

Justice Rehnquist wrote an opinion joined by Chief Justice Burger and Justice Stewart. In his opinion, Justice Rehnquist argued that if the property right flows from a statute, then that same statute ought to be able to set up the procedure that is required to take the property away. Justice Rehnquist argued that the employee was entitled only to the process set out in the statute, in this case a chance to respond in writing before dismissal, followed by a trial-like hearing after dismissal.

Justice Powell, joined by Justice Blackmun, felt that only the Constitution, and the Supreme Court interpreting the Constitution, could say what procedure was due once a property right had been recognized. However, Powell felt that a trial-like hearing was not required by the Constitution before dismissal, provided the employee is given such a hearing soon after dismissal.

Justice Marshall, joined by Justices Brennan and Douglas, felt that the Constitution requires a trial-like hearing before dismissal.

These three different opinions in the *Arnett* case confused everyone until the Supreme Court handed down the *Loudermill* decision in 1985. This time Justice White wrote the majority opinion, which was signed by six other justices. Loudermill was a security guard with the Cleveland School District. When the school board discovered that he had failed to put on his job application that he had been convicted of a felony, they fired him. There was no hearing, and he was not even given a chance to tell his side of the story before being dismissed. The federal district judge ruled that Loudermill had all the the due process that was coming to him because "the very statute that created the property right in continuing employment also specified the procedures for discharge, and because those procedures were followed, Loudermill was, by definition, afforded all the process due." In other words the district judge read Justice Rehnquist's opinion and thought that was the majority opinion in *Arnett*.

The justices of the circuit court disagreed. They said Loudermill was entitled to a full trial-like hearing before being dismissed. The circuit court thought Justice Marshall's opinion was the majority opinion in *Arnett*.

They were both wrong. It turns out that Justice Powell's opinion was the real majority opinion in *Arnett*. Justice White said that Loudermill was "entitled to oral or written notice of the charges against him, an explanation of the employer's evidence, and an opportunity to present his side of the story" *before* dismissal. He could be allowed to respond in person or in writing. At some point *after* the dismissal, public employees who have a property interest in their jobs have to be given a trial-like hearing.

People have a property interest in their government job if they are non-probationary employees under a civil service law (which could be a local ordinance, regulation, or handbook) or have an employment contract that still has time to run (which could be a union or individual contract). If the employee is just an at-will employee, he or she does not have a property interest in the job and is not entitled to any due process (*Durepos*).

The next question is, what kind of process is required? As you have just seen, employees are entitled to know why they are being dismissed and must be given at least a chance to respond to the charges before being dismissed. Employees are also entitled to a trial-like hearing soon after dismissal if they were not given a hearing before dismissal. The hearing should be similar to a trial. Employees are entitled to have an attorney present (*Francis*); to have notice of what they are accused of (*Pickles*); and to cross-examine the witnesses who testify against them (*Tron*).

Above all, the employee is entitled to a fair and impartial judge. In some situations the school board or city council is not fit to be the judge. As the Pennsylvania Supreme Court said in reviewing a teacher-dismissal case, the "minimum requirements of due process demand that a litigant have, at some stage of a proceeding, a neutral fact finder" (*Belasco*). The court went on to say that most school boards act as both prosecutor and judge and therefore are by definition not neutral. However, in Pennsylvania, since the state secretary of education reviews the case and is considered an impartial judge, that provides dismissed teachers with due process.

Many situations depend on whether the employee can show that the board or council was biased before the hearing began. In one case the federal district judge said that the board should not be allowed to be the judge in a dismissal hearing if:

1. they have made up their minds that the employee is guilty before the hearing;
2. they have made up their minds on important facts before the hearing;
3. they have some personal interest in the outcome of the hearing; or
4. they have some personal animosity against the employee that would prevent an unbiased decision (*Salisbury*).

In those situations the school board or city council should hire an impartial hearing officer to hear the case and make a determination of the facts.

While the U.S. Constitution provides the minimum procedure that must be followed, if the state or local government has set up even stricter procedures, these stricter procedures must be followed. In one case in the city of St. Albans, Vermont, the employee handbook was not followed (*Furno*). The jury awarded

$31,000 in compensatory damages and $10,000 in punitive damages to compensate the employee for this violation of his right to due process.

In another case the city had rules that said probationary employees could be fired only for incompetence or disqualification (*Hayes*). The city was stuck with its own unique rules.

The U.S. Supreme Court has told us what the minimum procedure required by the U.S. Constitution is. Every state supreme court is free to decide that more is required by their state constitution's requirement that due process be given before property is taken. In 1987 the Supreme Court of Washington decided that the Washington Constitution did not require more than the U.S. Constitution (*Danielson*). The New Mexico Supreme Court decided in 1987 that the New Mexico Constitution required more. The court ruled that a civil servant is entitled to a trial-like hearing *before* being demoted (*Lovato*).

In some limited circumstances a government employee is entitled to a due process hearing even though the employee does not have a property interest in the job. If the supervisor has said bad things about the employee while firing him or her, then the supervisor has probably made it difficult for that employee to find another job. The judges say the supervisor has interfered with the employee's "liberty interest" because the employee is no longer at liberty to get another job (*Codd*).

In one U.S. Supreme Court case a police chief was fired one day after a city councilman, in open session, charged him with misappropriation of public funds. The police chief requested a hearing on the charges to clear his name, and the city council refused. The U.S. Supreme Court ruled that by "blackening" his reputation at about the same time the city fired him, the city had deprived the police chief of liberty without due process of law (*Owen*).

If the charges are told to the employee in private, there is no deprivation of liberty and no need for due process (*Ortwein*).

What happens if the court decides the government employee has had his or her liberty interest interfered with? Usually the judge will order the government involved to give the employee a name-clearing hearing. The employee may also be entitled to damages if he or she really had trouble getting a job and lost wages as a result (*White, Selcraig*).

DUE PROCESS RIGHTS FOR PRIVATE EMPLOYEES

Generally, private employers do not have to give a hearing to employees accused of wrongdoing. However, in many dismissal cases the employee has the option of suing because some right we have explained in this book was violated. Often, whether they sue or not depends on whether they believe they have been treated fairly. In other words, while the law does not require it, employers should consider giving employees a hearing if they have been charged with misconduct. The employer may even decide, after learning all the facts, to keep the employee.

GETTING A GOVERNMENT LICENSE

More and more jobs require a license. This puts great power into the hands of government. The purpose of the due process requirement is to make sure government exercises its power in a fair and impartial way. For many people this due process requirement comes into play in two situations: when they apply for a license and when that license is revoked.

People who are denied a license are generally not entitled to a full trial-like hearing, but they are entitled to know why they did not get the license (*Valdes*). They are also entitled to appeal the denial and to explain, in writing, why they should have been given the license (*Curran*).

People are also entitled to be treated in a way that is not arbitrary or capricious. This means that the board in charge of giving out licenses must have rules that spell out when someone is entitled to get the license. They must also tell people why they did not qualify under the rules.

When an adult-bookstore owner in New Jersey was denied a license to sell lottery tickets, he appealed. The New Jersey Appeals Court ruled that this denial was "arbitrary and capricious." The court said the agency must have rules that set standards on when someone will be given or denied a license. The court also said that the store owner had a right to a written statement explaining why he did not get the license. As the judge put it: "Administrative officers should articulate the standards and principles that govern their discretionary acts in as much detail as possible" (*Corp. 613*).

HAVING A GOVERNMENT LICENSE REVOKED

Once someone has a license from government, he or she has a piece of property that cannot be taken away without due process. Before the license is revoked, the person has a right to know why and should be given an opportunity to respond to the charges. At some reasonable time after the revocation, the person has a right to a trial-like hearing.

The agency should have regulations that are fair and reasonable. In one case Newton Tattrie appealed the revocation of his license to promote wrestling matches. When a deputy commissioner from the athletic commission asked Tattrie for a doctor's fee of $150 and a referee's fee of $100, he refused to pay because $100 and $60 are standard in the industry. The athletic commission revoked Tattrie's license, and the Pennsylvania Appeals Court overturned the revocation. The judges said the commission must set a fee schedule and put the schedule into a regulation, not make up things as it goes along (*Tattrie*).

In 1987 the Idaho Supreme Court overturned the revocation of an engineer's license because nothing in the regulations gave this engineer any warning that what he was doing could result in revocation of his license. The court said his right to due process was thus violated (*HV*).

People who work in highly regulated industries have a duty under the law to find out what those regulations say. Ignorance of the law (and the regulations) is no excuse. In one case a doctor was suspended from the Medicaid program for three years because he did not follow the proper record-keeping procedures. The doctor objected because the agency had never given him a copy of the regulations. The court did not care. It was his duty to get the regulations and follow them (*Del Borrello*).

ENTITIES THAT ACT AS IF THEY WERE GOVERNMENTS

In some cases a private group has great economic power and provides a kind of license without which it is almost impossible to practice some professions. The best example is hospitals. Doctors who are not admitted to practice at the local hospital can forget about practicing medicine in the community. Courts in many states have ruled that entities such as hospitals have to provide a kind of due process to applicants just as if they were a government agency. This means the hospital has to have reasonable rules concerning who is admitted to practice. In one recent New Jersey case a doctor was refused the right to practice at the local hospital. The hospital had a rule that a doctor would be admitted to practice at the hospital only if he or she was affiliated with a doctor who was already admitted to practice at the hospital. The New Jersey Supreme Court said the hospital could refuse to allow a doctor to practice at the hospital for good reasons, but this was not a good reason (*Desai*).

12

The Right to Privacy

Under both English and American law, invasions of privacy have always been taken very seriously. Under old English law a person's home was not to be violated and a person's body was not to be touched. The fact that the representatives of the English king did not accord "colonists" the same privilege was one of the major reasons for the American Revolution. That is why the Fourth Amendment to the U.S. Constitution says that the people have a right to be secure in their "persons, houses, papers, and effects" from "unreasonable searches and seizures." The question for the courts has been, when it is reasonable to invade someone's privacy? While the Fourth Amendment applies only to government invasions of privacy, American judges have interpreted the common law also to prevent private individuals from invading each other's privacy.

The judges have decided that the world is made up of zones of privacy (see Figure 12–1). The question is how much of an "expectation of privacy" do people have in each zone? The higher the expectation of privacy, the better the reason for invading that privacy needs to be. Public places fall in the outer ring. People do not have much of an expectation of privacy in public places. They might expect not to be overheard, but they do not expect not to be seen. Next come open fields. While an open field might be private property, most people do not expect much privacy there either, and if they do, they are not being reasonable in the eyes of the law. Next comes the front and back yards. To the extent someone has made those areas near the house private with fences and hedges, the law says that expectation of privacy should be respected. People have an even greater expectation of privacy in their purses, briefcases, and clothing. People have a very high expectation of privacy concerning what goes on inside their bodies and inside their homes. Finally people have the highest degree of privacy expectation concerning what goes on inside their minds. In

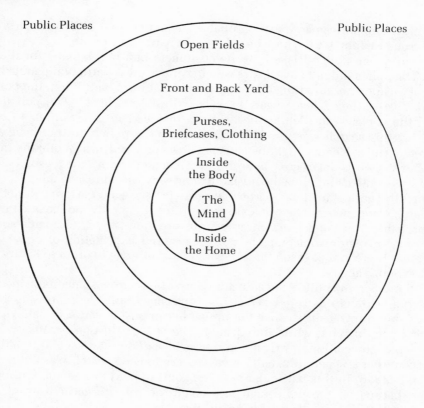

Public Places

Public Places

Open Fields

Front and Back Yard

Purses,
Briefcases, Clothing

Inside
the Body

The
Mind

Inside
the Home

Figure 12-1. Zones of privacy.

each case the reason for the privacy invasion has to be weighed against the zone that is being invaded. We can see how this works by looking briefly at the world of criminal law.

The U.S. Supreme Court has said that the police do not even need a reason to search a public place or an open field. However, they must have a pretty good reason to search the area immediately around a person's home (*Oliver*).

Generally, people expect their clothes and purses to be kept private and do not expect the contents of purses or pockets to be exposed to the world. This means that someone must have a good reason to invade those private areas. In *Terry*, a policeman in plain clothes observed two suspicious-looking characters in downtown Cleveland. They were obviously "casing" a store for a possible robbery, and he believed they might be armed. He confronted the men, grabbed Terry, and "patted down" the outside of his clothing. He felt a pistol under Terry's coat, which he removed. Terry was convicted of carrying a concealed weapon. The U.S. Supreme Court ruled that this search was reasonable. The court felt that the "frisk" of outer clothing was not that much of an intrusion into Terry's privacy and that the policeman had a very good reason to want to frisk Terry. The policeman had "reasonable suspicion" that Terry was carrying a dangerous weapon with which he might have harmed someone.

In *Ybarra*, the police frisked all the customers in a bar, looking for illegal drugs. The police did not have any reason to believe these particular people had drugs or weapons or anything else they should not have had. When the police frisked Ybarra, they felt a "cigarette pack with objects in it." The police removed the package and found illegal drugs inside. The U.S. Supreme Court ruled that this search was unreasonable because the police did not have any reason to suspect Ybarra might be carrying a weapon or drugs. While the invasion of privacy was not as great as searching someone's home, the reason for the search was nonexistent; thus the invasion of privacy was unreasonable.

Generally, police must have probable cause (a very good reason) before they can search someone's purse, briefcase, or clothing. Generally, police must have both probable cause and a search warrant before they can search inside someone's body or inside someone's home. Because our expectation of privacy in those areas is great, the reason for the search must be great in order to justify the invasion of privacy.

In *Schmerber*, the police had a doctor remove blood from someone suspected of driving while intoxicated. The U.S. Supreme Court found this to be a "search" but allowed it because the police had probable cause to believe the man had been driving while intoxicated. The court held that because we all have a high expectation of privacy in the insides of our bodies, and the fluids that reside there, it would usually be necessary to get a search warrant before removing blood. In this particular case the court upheld this search without a warrant because if the policeman had taken the time to get a warrant, the alcohol level in the blood would have dissipated.

In one case the U.S. Supreme Court held that the expectation of privacy in the inside of our bodies is so great that it would not allow the search, even though there was probable cause to believe evidence of a crime was contained inside the body. In this case the police wanted to operate on a suspect to remove a bullet. The police had a great deal of evidence and did not really need this bullet to prove their case. Because of this, and the high degree of privacy invasion involved in cutting someone open on an operating table, the Supreme Court would not allow the operation, even though the police had probable cause and a search warrant (*Winston*).

Finally, the Fifth Amendment to the U.S. Constitution says that the police cannot search our minds (ask us questions) unless we want them to. In 1966 the U.S. Supreme Court said police cannot even begin to search the mind (interrogate suspects) without warning them that they have the right to remain silent and that everything they say can be used against them (*Miranda*).

The same general principles apply to searches and other invasions of privacy by private individuals, even if that private individual is an employer. The further in toward the center of the circle, the better the reason for the search needs to be if the person doing the searching does not want to lose a lawsuit for invasion of privacy.

SURVEILLANCE

What if an employer, public or private, hires a private detective to follow employees around in order to find out where they go and whom they meet? If all the detective does is follow the employees to public places, their privacy has not been violated. If the detective uses electronic devices to listen in on conversations that the employees have every reason to believe are private, even if conducted in a public place, that is an invasion of privacy for which the employees can sue (*Pemberton*).

If the employer taps an employee's phone at home or at work or uses electronic devices to listen in on private conversations, the employee can do more than sue. Such activity is a crime under federal law and under many state penal codes (18 U.S.C. sec. 2510–2520). The question is whether or not the employee had a reasonable expectation of privacy in the conversation. If the employer told the employee all calls at work would be monitored, then the employee did not have a legitimate expectation of privacy and cannot sue or file criminal charges.

The Federal Fair Credit Reporting Act requires employers to inform an employee if the employee is being investigated in a way that will involve interviewing people (15 U.S.C. sec. 1681). If any adverse action results from the investigation, such as dismissal, the employee has a right to know the name and address of the company that made the investigation and what their file contains. If the employee disagrees with any of the information contained in the file, he or she has a right to have the information reinvestigated or to place a statement in the file containing the employee's side of the story.

SEARCHES OF LOCKERS AND DESKS AT WORK

Whether an employer, public or private, has the right to search lockers and desks at work depends on whether the employee has a legitimate expectation of privacy in those lockers and desks. In one Texas case a private employer provided the employee with a locker and told her she could use her own lock to keep things inside the locker private. In other words, the employer gave the employee an expectation of privacy in the locker. The employer then searched the locker. The jury awarded $100,000 in punitive damages for invasion of privacy and the Texas Appeals Court upheld that jury verdict (*Trotti*).

Whether an employee has a legitimate expectation of privacy in a locker or desk at work is going to depend on the individual circumstances. An employer who intends to search lockers and desks has a duty to tell the employees that is his intention (remove the employee's expectation of privacy). The same rule applies to government employers. In one case security guards at the U.S. Mint searched all the employee lockers and found one that contained a bag of freshly minted quarters. The regulations stated that "no mint lockers in mint institutions shall be considered to be private lockers." In other words, the regulations removed any expectation of privacy, and the court said this was not an invasion of privacy (*Donato*). In a similar case postal inspectors searched a post-office employee's locker. Since the Postal Manual stated that the lockers were "subject to search by supervisors and postal inspectors," the court found no invasion of privacy (*Bunkers*).

In 1987 the U.S. Supreme Court handed down its first decision in a desk-search case. The court said an employer could remove the expectation of privacy in the desk with notice or regulations just as these earlier courts had ruled. Since in this case the employer had not done this, the employee did have a reasonable expectation of privacy in his desk at work. The court ruled that the employer needed "reasonable suspicion" to believe he would find something in this employee's desk before he could invade this employee's privacy by searching it (*O'Connor*).

SEARCHES OF PURSES, BRIEFCASES, AND CLOTHING

People have more of an expectation of privacy in their own purses, briefcases, and clothing. Generally employers, public and private, must have a good reason to suspect that something is contained there before a search would be legitimate.

In one case a customs-service supervisor searched the jacket of an employee after a package containing $152,190 worth of emeralds disappeared. The jacket was hanging on a coat rack in the employee's office, and the package would have passed through this employee's hands. The customs officials did not conduct a random search of all the employees, only those they had reason to suspect. The Second Circuit Court said the search of the jacket was reasonable because the supervisor had good reason to suspect this individual employee of the wrongdoing (*Collins #2*).

It is not clear to what extent an employer can take away employees' expectation of privacy in their own purses, briefcases, and clothing. It will probably depend on the reason for doing so and the nature of work involved. If the employer is involved in national security matters, it would probably be reasonable to say to people, "if you take a job here we reserve the right to search you and your purses or briefcases at any time for no reason at all." The New Jersey Supreme Court has ruled that casinos, and the government officials who regulate casinos, can say this to casino employees and then search them at any time without violating their right to privacy under the New Jersey Constitution (*Martin #2*). Casinos and racetracks are highly regulated industries and considered to be a special case. It is not clear to what extent other employers can say this to their employees.

SEARCHING INSIDE THE BODY: DRUG TESTS

Drug Tests by Public Employers

When it comes to drug tests, we will have to discuss government and private employers separately. In what circumstances can a government employer force its employees, or employees in industries that it closely regulates, to submit to a urinalysis in an effort to find evidence of drug use? When the New Jersey Horse Racing Commission required jockeys to submit to random drug tests, five well-known jockeys sued, arguing that the tests violated their right to privacy. The jockeys argued that the tests should be used only when the commission has reason to suspect a particular individual of drug use. The commission argued that horse racing is highly regulated and people participating in horse racing know they are going to be subject to random searches because of the nature of the sport. The Third Circuit Court agreed with the commission. The court held that the need for the search was great, and the expectation of privacy of people involved in horse racing was low. The court upheld the random drug testing of jockeys (*Shoemaker*).

The Eighth Circuit Court faced the same issue when Iowa prison guards were subjected to random strip searches and drug tests (urinalysis). The court found that the need for security at the prison was very high, and the expectation of privacy of prison guards was very low because of the nature of the work. The court allowed the random use of drug tests on the prison guards (*McDonell*).

The District of Columbia Circuit Court has ruled that public employers may conduct drug tests as part of a routine physical examination (*McKenzie*).

There are other cases on appeal. In *Government Employees v. Weinberger*, a federal district judge ruled that the Defense Department may not conduct random drug tests on civilian security employees. The judge found the tests to be a "highly intrusive search" and held that there must be reason to suspect a particular employee before drug testing can take place (*Gov. Employees*).

A federal district judge in Tennessee has ruled that the city of Chattanooga must have reason to suspect a particular employee before it can conduct drug tests. The case involved the random drug testing of police (*Lovvorn*). After tests were conducted on 360 police officers, only two tested positive for marijuana. These two policemen were already suspected of drug use because of their behavior at work. In other words, nothing was gained by violating the privacy of the other 358 police officers. A federal district judge in New Jersey has ruled the same way (*Capua*).

In May 1988, the U.S. Supreme Court handed down a decision in the case of *California v. Greenwood* (*Greenwood*). The police searched Greenwood's garbage and arrested him on drug charges. Did they need a reason to search the garbage (such as probable cause to believe drug evidence would be found), or was the garbage the equivalent of an open field where people do not have a legitimate expectation of privacy? The court ruled that the garbage was like an open field. Justice White, writing for a majority of the court, said, "It is common knowledge that plastic garbage bags left on or at the side of a public street are readily accessible to animals, children, scavengers, snoops, and other members of the public." In other words, no one has a legitimate expectation of privacy in garbage once it is placed on the street. Some people believe this decision foretells what the court will decide in upcoming drug-testing cases, but the two situations are not at all similar. People do not urinate on the sidewalk; they urinate in a bathroom with the door closed. When people put their garbage on the sidewalk, they know it can be identified as theirs and that the city is going to take it away. When people urinate into a toilet and flush, they expect that their urine will be instantly mixed with everyone else's and that no one will be able to tell what it contains. People do not have a legitimate expectation of privacy in their garbage. They do have a legitimate expectation of privacy in their urine. In other words, the *Greenwood* case does not really tell us anything about how the U.S. Supreme Court will rule when it comes time to declare the constitutional limitations on drug tests by public employers.

While everyone is eagerly awaiting a decision from the U.S. Surpeme Court, it is important to keep in mind that the U.S. Supreme Court interprets only the U.S. Constitution. What it says will apply to federal employees and will set the minimum standards for state and local governments. However, state supreme courts are free to interpret their own state constitutions much more strictly than the U.S. Supreme Court interprets the U.S. Constitution. So far every state court that has been asked about drug tests of public employees has ruled against the tests because of state constitutional provisions that protect privacy.

In 1985, a Florida Appeals Court ruled that the random drug testing of police officers and fire fighters violated Article One, Section Twelve, of the Florida Constitution (*Bauman*).

In 1986 two New York courts ruled the same way. A New York District Court ruled that the city of New York could not conduct random drug tests of police officers who were members of the organized crime bureau because the testing would violate Article One, Section Twelve, of the New York Constitution (*Caruso*). A New York appeals-level court ruled that a school district could not drug-test teachers without reason to believe the particular teacher was using drugs. The court held that there must be some degree of individual suspicion "before the dignity and privacy of a teacher may be compromised by forcing him or her to undergo a urine test" (*Patchogue-Medford*).

In 1987, a New Jersey Appeals Court ruled that the Newark Police Department could not conduct random drug tests of members of the narcotics bureau (*Newark*). The court held that such random searches violated Article One, Section Seven, of the New Jersey Constitution.

In 1987, a Georgia Appeals Court ruled that random drug testing of government employees violated Article One, Section One, of the Georgia Constitution (*East Point*).

There is much confusion concerning drug tests because of a failure to distinguish between random drug tests and drug tests of individual employees when the supervisor has reason to believe that particular employee is using drugs. Courts have generally ruled that a government employer may require an individual employee to take a drug test if the employer reasonably believes that particular employee is using drugs (*Allen #1, Suscy, Krolick*). It is the invasion of the privacy of many employees on a random basis that bothers the judges.

Drug Tests by Private Employers

In 1987 states began passing statutes to regulate drug testing by private employers. The statutes fall into three categories.

First, there are statutes like Utah's (Utah 34-38-1 to 15). The Utah statute is a license for employers to test for alcohol and drugs. The statute allows employers to test all their employees for drugs and alcohol on a routine or random basis "as a condition of hiring or continued employment," but it also requires employers and management to "submit to the testing themselves on a periodic basis." The statute requires that any positive reading be validated by using one of the more reliable (and more expensive) methods of testing before any action is taken against the employee. The statute makes it difficult, if not impossible, for an employee to sue an employer because adverse action was taken based on a false drug test.

Second, there are statutes like Rhode Island's (R.I. 28-6.5-1). The Rhode Island statute prohibits urine and blood testing by employers unless the employer "has reasonable grounds to believe, based on specific objective facts, that the employee's use of controlled substances is impairing his ability to perform his job." If the employer does have "reasonable suspicion," he must follow the procedures required in the statute and must have a "bona fide rehabilitation program" for those who test positive. Violation of the statute is a crime, and employees may also sue for actual damages, punitive damages, and attorney's fees. Vermont has a similar statute (Vt. tit. 21 sec. 511 to 519).

Third, there are statutes like Minnesota's (Minn. 181.950 to 956). The Minnesota statute is a compromise between these two extreme positions. Employers may conduct random or routine drug tests of employees in "safety-sensitive positions." Employers may drug-test other employees if they have "reasonable suspicion" to believe the employee is under the influence of drugs or the employee has been injured or has caused an accident. The statute has many provisions to guarantee the reliability, fairness, and privacy of the tests. If the statute is violated the employee may sue "in a civil action for any damages allowable at law." The judge may also award attorney's fees. Montana has a similar statute (Mont. 39-2-304).

There are many unanswered questions even after the passage of drug-testing statutes. Alcoholism and drug addiction are considered handicaps in most states under the handicap statute. How do we reconcile this with the provisions of the drug-testing statute? The Utah drug-testing statute says that a person shall not be considered "handicapped" solely because he or she tested positive on a drug test. That seems to suggest that if persons can prove they are bona fide alcoholics or drug addicts with other evidence, they are still protected by the handicap discrimination statute.

Is flunking a drug test going to be "good cause" for dismissal under civil service laws and union contracts? Almost every drug-test case that has come before an arbitrator interpreting a union contract has been lost by the employer. The arbitrators do not consider flunking the drug test alone to be good cause for dismissal. That is because drug tests cannot tell us how "impaired" the employee is by the drug use. Also, arbitrators have generally held that if the employer wants to start drug testing, he has to negotiate with the union about it first (*At Work While "Under the Influence,"* 70 Marquette Law Review 88 (1986)).

Can employees who are fired because they flunked a drug test collect unemployment compensation? A Virginia Appeals Court has ruled that flunking a drug test is not evidence of misconduct and does not justify withholding unemployment compensation (*Hercules*). Pennsylvania and Texas Appeals Courts have ruled that flunking a drug test is misconduct and does justify withholding unemployment compensation (*Shaw #2, Hughes*).

SEARCHING THE MIND: POLYGRAPH TESTS

At least 25 states and the District of Columbia have statutes that regulate the use of polygraph (lie-detector) tests by employers. The Massachusetts, New York, Oregon, Rhode Island, Vermont, and District of Columbia statutes completely prohibit the use of polygraph tests by employers. Most of the other state statutes prevent employers from requiring employees to take a polygraph test but employees may voluntarily consent to the test (see Table 12–1). Congress is considering a statute that would limit polygraph use nationwide.

Some employers think the absence of a statute on this subject means they are free to use polygraph tests on their employees. That is not true. The West Virginia Supreme Court ruled, before West Virginia had a statute on this subject, that it was wrongful discharge to fire an employee who refused to take a polygraph test (*Cordle*).

Some employers think if their state has a statute regulating the use of polygraphs by employers, their employees can no longer sue under the common law for wrongful discharge. That is not true. In 1985 a Maryland Appeals Court allowed employees to sue for common-law wrongful discharge, even though Maryland had a statute regulating employer use of polygraphs. The court upheld a jury verdict of one million dollars in punitive damages for each of the four employees (*Moniodis*). The Nebraska Supreme Court ruled the same way in 1987 (*Ambroz*).

Several states allow police departments to require police officers to take polygraph tests. These special rules for police officers have been upheld by the courts (*Fichera, Coursey*).

Texas does not have a special statute dealing with employer polygraph tests. That did not keep the Texas Supreme Court, in 1987, from ruling that the state of Texas could not require its employees to take polygraph tests (*TSEU*). While the court recognized that "unique circumstances" might justify requiring police officers to take polygraph tests, the court did not believe any circumstances justified the use of polygraphs on other government employees.

No one should ever submit to a polygraph examination. No one should ever think that the result of a polygraph examination proves anything. There is no scientific basis for polygraph examinations, and there is a great deal of scientific evidence that they have no validity. Today's polygraph examiners are the modern equivalent of ancient witch doctors. The examiner wears a white lab coat (the modern equivalent of a ceremonial mask) and sits at a machine (because we believe machines have magic powers). If anyone wants to give you a polygraph examination, say you would rather have some bones tossed

TABLE 12–1. Polygraph Statutes*

Alabama	None	
Alaska	Boss cannot request, suggest, or require. Employee may volunteer. Police must take the test.	23.10.37
Arizona	None	
Arkansas	None	
California	Boss cannot demand or require. Governments may require.	Labor Code 432.2
Colorado	None	
Connecticut	Boss cannot request or require. Police must take the test.	31-51g
Delaware	Boss cannot require, request, or suggest (includes voice stress).	19-704
District of Columbia	Boss cannot administer test, or accept or use the results. Police must take the test.	36-801 to 803
Florida	None	
Georgia	None	
Hawaii	Boss cannot require. Police must take the test.	378-26.5
Idaho	Boss cannot require. Police must take the test.	44-903
Illinois	None	
Indiana	None	
Iowa	Boss cannot require. Police must take the test.	730.4
Kansas	None	
Kentucky	None	
Louisiana	None	
Maine	Boss cannot require, request, or suggest. Police must take the test.	32-7166
Maryland	Boss cannot demand or require. Police must take the test.	Art. 100, sec. 95
Massachusetts	Boss cannot "subject employee to the test."	Ch. 149 sec. 19B
Michigan	Boss cannot request, require, or administer. Employee may volunteer.	37.203
Minnesota	Boss cannot solicit or require.	181.75
Mississippi	None	
Missouri	None	
Montana	Boss cannot require.	39-2-304
Nebraska	Boss cannot require. Police must take the test.	81-1932
Nevada	Employee must consent to test in writing.	648.189

*The law is constantly changing. Consult an attorney about your situation.

TABLE 12–1. (Cont.)

New Hampshire	None	
New Jersey	Boss cannot influence, request, or require unless the employee makes or distributes drugs.	2C:40A-1
New Mexico	None	
New York	Boss cannot require, request, suggest, or permit test or utilize the results.	Labor 733 to 739
North Carolina	None	
North Dakota	None	
Ohio	None	
Oklahoma	None	
Oregon	Boss cannot require or subject.	659.225 to 227
Pennsylvania	Boss cannot require. Police and employees who make or distribute drugs must take the test.	Title 18 sec. 7321
Rhode Island	Boss cannot request, require, or subject.	28-6.1-1
South Carolina	None	
South Dakota	None	
Tennessee	Boss cannot take any action based solely on result of test.	62-27-128
Texas	None	
Utah	None	
Vermont	Boss cannot request, require, or administer test. Police and employees who work with jewelry or make or distribute drugs must take the test.	Title 21 sec. 494a,b
Virginia	None	
Washington	Boss cannot require. Police and employees who make or distribute drugs must take the test.	49.44.120 to 135
West Virginia	Boss cannot require or request. Police and employees who make or distribute drugs must take the test.	21-5-5b
Wisconsin	Employee must consent to test in writing.	111.37; 942.06
Wyoming	None	

on the ground and read by a witch doctor. It really does amount to the same thing.

Judges in pro-boss northern states have generally taken the position that private employers are free to invade their employee's privacy at work unless the legislature passes a law that prevents such an invasion. Judges in fair states have generally taken the position that private employers are not free to invade their employee's privacy at work unless the legislature passes a law that allows such an invasion. Judges in pro-boss southern states may well end up agreeing with the fair states because in southern culture privacy is considered to be a quintessential part of southern society. Protecting employee privacy will be a fundamental legal issue in the 1990s at both the state and federal levels.

Part Five
Rights under Wage, Hour, and Labor Laws

13
Wages and Hours

THE PAST

When millions were killed by the Black Plague, the demand for workers increased, driving wages up. In 1350 King Edward of England enacted the Statute of Laborers, which required all ablebodied men to work and kept workers from charging more than a "reasonable" wage. In 1875 the English Parliament repealed the statute. By that time workers were so abundant that there was no longer any need to control their wages. In fact, some politicians worried that workers were being paid so little they could not survive.

There was also a concern about the long hours employees were expected to work and the use of children in mines and factories. A number of American states and the U.S. Congress tried to pass laws to prohibit child labor and control the number of hours people could work in a week. In 1905 the U.S. Supreme Court declared a New York statute that limited the hours bakers could work to 60 hours a week and 10 hours a day to be unconstitutional. The justices said the law interfered with "the freedom of master and employee to contract with each other in relation to their employment" (*Lochner*). In 1918 the Supreme Court overturned a law in which Congress tried to prohibit the interstate transportation of products made with child labor (*Hammer*).

In 1932 Franklin Delano Roosevelt was elected President. From 1934 to 1936 the Supreme Court declared most of the New Deal legislation unconstitutional. In 1936 Roosevelt won a landslide victory, and in 1937 one member of the court changed his mind. That year the court upheld a state law that set a minimum wage for women, even though several years before they had declared a similar law to be unconstitutional (*West Coast Hotel*). In 1941 the court upheld the federal Fair Labor Standards Act of 1938 (*Darby*).

THE LAW OF SUPPLY AND DEMAND

Under the law of supply and demand, if there is an abundance of workers, the supply of workers will be high in relation to demand, and wages will be low. If the supply could be reduced or the demand increased, the price of workers (wages) would go up. With low unemployment workers would be able to demand higher wages and better working conditions. This principle seems still to apply. In 1986 the two states with the lowest unemployment rates were Massachusetts and New Hampshire. They were also the two states with the highest average increase in wages.

If the problem is how to get more people working, one solution is to limit the number of hours workers are allowed to work. Suppose a country has 100 workers, 25 of whom are out of work, and the average worker is working 60 hours a week. What happens if a law is passed that limits the number of hours to 40 hours a week? There are 75 workers times 60 hours of work to be done a week ($75 \times 60 = 4500$) or 4500 hours of work a week. If a worker can work only 40 hours a week, then 112 workers will be needed to do the work ($4500/40 = 112$). If the demand for workers is greater than the supply, wages will go up.

There is also a recognition that there will always be an abundance of unskilled workers who will be exploited if government does not step in. The idea is, by setting a minimum wage, the government is requiring employers to pay at least a subsistence wage. If there is a specific number of unskilled jobs in the society and employers will pay only the minimum required for this kind of labor, the minimum should provide at least the necessities of life.

THE FAIR LABOR STANDARDS ACT OF 1938

Overtime Pay

The Fair Labor Standards Act was passed in 1938 to help achieve full employment. One weapon in the fight for full employment is to control the number of hours worked in a week. The target is 40. The Fair Labor Standards Act tries to enforce this goal with overtime pay. Workers are supposed to be paid one and a half times their usual hourly wage for every hour over 40 worked in a week. (The Fair Labor Standards Act is encoded at 29 U.S.C. section 201.)

Does it work? Not very well. Studies show that in 1975 the average full-time worker spent 43.1 hours a week at work. In 1984 this had increased to 47.3 hours a week. If one goal of the 40-hour week is to increase employment, another goal is to protect the mental and physical health of the workers by making sure they have a certain amount of leisure time every week. If leisure time is considered hours devoted to things other than sleeping, eating, and working, average leisure hours decreased from 24.3 a week in 1975 to 18.1 a week in 1984 (*The New York Times*, Sept. 22, 1985).

Why is the 40-hour week disappearing? There are many reasons. More and more jobs require special training. The employer often finds it cheaper to work the existing work force a little more rather than pay the cost of training more workers. Employees today have more fringe benefits compared to workers of half a century ago. This makes each new employee more expensive and encourages employers to work their existing work force harder rather than add new workers. Also, the wage-and-hour provisions of the Fair Labor Standards Act do not apply to professional employees. As our economy has advanced, a larger percentage of the work force simply is not covered by the act. Also, if the minimum wage is low, the time-and-a-half provision is easy to overcome. Instead of paying $8.00 an hour and $12.00 for overtime, the employer pays $6.00 an hour and $9.00 for overtime. The employee works 50 hours and makes what he or she would have made working 40 hours. The time-and-a-half provision works only if the minimum wage is set at a reasonable level.

Minimum Wage

The minimum-wage provision recognizes that there will always be more unskilled workers than there are jobs. The minimum wage is supposed to guarantee that the unskilled worker makes at least a subsistence wage. During the 1980s the federal minimum wage remained at $3.35 an hour. Should the minimum wage be increased? Economists point out that the minimum wage prevents some people from working at all because they are so unproductive they are just not worth the minimum. That may be true, but with the minimum wage, society is saying that if someone cannot earn at least that, he or she should be in a training program, not working in an unproductive job. Also, every time Congress has raised the minimum wage, the employment level has gone up. The fact that a few workers are fired because they are not productive enough to receive the new minimum wage is more than offset by the increase in employment caused by the spending of the new money these workers have in their pockets.

Child Labor

The Fair Labor Standards Act also prohibits child labor. The minimum age is 14 for most nonmanufacturing nonmining jobs that do not interfere with school or threaten the child's health. The minimum age for most purposes is 16, but 18 is the minimum age for jobs declared hazardous by the Secretary of Labor. The major exceptions are for farm work, newspaper delivery, and the making of wreaths. Most states also have child-labor laws that apply if they are more restrictive than the federal law.

Coverage

In the beginning the Fair Labor Standards Act applied only to workers directly involved in interstate commerce. Over the years it has been amended to cover almost every private and government employee in the United States. For a while the U.S. Supreme Court could not make up its mind whether the law applied to employees of state and local governments, but in 1987 it decided that these employees are also covered by the federal law (*Garcia*).

There are exceptions. Professionals are not covered, nor are workers on small farms, babysitters, fishermen, and amusement-park employees. There are additional exceptions from the 40-hour-a-week provision for cab drivers, live-in domestic help, and car salesmen. There are also special provisions for seasonal workers, hospital employees, firemen, and retail salespeople on commission.

Enforcement

Persons who think the Fair Labor Standards Act has been violated, or just want to know how the law applies to them, should call the Wage and Hour Division of the U.S. Labor Department. Usually, a complaint to the Labor Department will take care of the problem. Of course, sometimes the employee has to sue. He or she can sue in either state or federal court to enforce this federal law. If the employer has violated the time-and-a-half or minimum-wage provisions in bad faith, he or she can be ordered to pay double the wages owed and will also have to pay for the employee's attorney. In one case the employee, Martin Cuevas, sued his employer for violations of the act. Cuevas was a busboy at Junction Eating Place in DeKalb, Illinois. After being fired, he filed a complaint under both the Illinois and the federal law. Cuevas testified that he worked from 7 a.m. to 5 p.m. seven days a week with half an hour each day for lunch. While Cuevas did live in an apartment provided by the employer and ate meals provided by the employer, the Illinois Appeals Court did not allow any credit for this because the employer failed to keep the records required by the Labor Department. The appeals court also held that Cuevas was entitled to twice the wages owed to him because the employer did not try in good faith to comply with the act (it takes only a phone call to the Labor Department). The appeals court also ordered the employer to pay for Cuevas's attorney. Finally, the appeals court sent the case back to see if Cuevas should be allowed three years' back wages. While employees can usually recover only two years' back wages, the federal act allows the court to award damages covering the last three years if the judge finds that the employer willfully disregarded the act (*Cuevas*).

In 1988 the U.S. Supreme Court decided that an employer will not be considered to have willfully violated the act unless the employer "knew or showed reckless disregard for the matter of whether its conduct was prohibited by the statute." Simply not bothering to find out whether or not he or she is in compliance will not qualify as a "willful" violation (*Richland Shoe*).

Both employers and employees should call the U.S. Labor Department and the state labor commissioner if they have any questions about these statutes.

WAGE ASSIGNMENT OR GARNISHMENT

In many states an employee can voluntarily assign part of his or her wages to someone else. Different states have different procedures that must be followed (call the state labor commissioner).

When a person gets a court order telling the employer to pay him or her part of the worker's wages directly, it is called garnishment. While assignment is voluntary, garnishment is not. It means the person has sued the worker and gotten a judgment against him or her. This judgment is then enforced by getting a court to order the employer to hold back part of the employee's wages and pay it to the person with the judgment. The Federal Consumer Credit Protection Act of 1968 (15 U.S.C. sec. 1671) sets a maximum on how much can be garnished from a worker's wages. A creditor cannot take more than 25% of the worker's disposable income (meaning the money left over after taxes and minimum living expenses have been subtracted). The federal law allows up to 60 percent of disposable income to be garnished if it is for child-support payments. Most states also have laws on this subject. If there is a conflict between the state and federal law, the one that allows the smallest amount to be garnished controls. Since the federal law does not set up any priority list concerning which debts get paid first, the state priority list applies. In many states child-support payments have priority (*Com. Edison*).

For a century, any kind of wage garnishment was illegal in Texas. The Texas Constitution was recently amended to allow for garnishment to pay for child support (Texas Const. Art. 16 sec. 28).

If you have any questions about wage assignment and garnishment, call the state labor commissioner.

STATE WAGE-PAYMENT PROVISIONS

Different states have different provisions regarding when wages must be paid. Some states require a paycheck every two weeks, which means, as one Ohio court said, 26 checks a year, not 24 (*Ohio Council 8*). Other states, such as Indiana, require biweekly paychecks only if the individual employee asks to be paid biweekly (*Pope*). Some states have a wage-assurance fund that pays employees up to two weeks' wages if the employer goes out of business and cannot meet the payroll (*Seeley*).

Many states also have statutes that control when wages must be paid if an employee is discharged. In New Hampshire the employer has three days to pay. If he does not pay, he has to pay an additional 10 percent of the wages owed for every business day he delays up to the amount of wages owed (*Ives*). As you can see from Table 13–1, different states allow the employee to collect different penalties if forced to sue to collect back wages. In Arizona the judge can award up to three times the amount of wages owed and order the employer to pay the employee's attorney's fees (*Patton*). In Colorado the penalty is 50 percent of the wages owed and attorney fees. In one Colorado case the employee collected $93,740 in back wages, $46,870 in penalties, plus attorney fees (*Mulei*).

On the other hand, many states have little or no penalty. The employee can sue for back wages, but without an award for attorney fees many employees cannot afford to sue. In these states the employee should contact the state labor department for help in collecting wages.

TABLE 13–1. Wage Collection Statutes*

†Alabama 37-8-270	Public-service corporations must pay wages every two weeks or semimonthly.
Alaska 23.05.140 to 280 23.10.040 to 047	Terminated‡—must be paid within 3 working days. Penalty—up to 90 days' wages. Labor Dept. will help collect wages owed.
Arizona 23-350 to 361	Wages must be paid semimonthly. Penalty—up to triple the wages owed. Labor Dept. will help collect owed wages if less than $2,500.
Arkansas 81-301 to 334	Corporations must pay wages semimonthly. Terminated—must be paid within 7 days. Penalty—go back on the payroll until paid. Must sue within 60 days.
California Labor Code 200 to 272	Wages must be paid semimonthly. Professionals and executives may be paid monthly. Terminated—must pay wages immediately. Penalty—go back on the payroll for up to 30 days. Refusal to pay wages may be a crime.
Colorado 8-4-104,105,114	Wages must be paid monthly. Penalty—50% of wages owed and atty. fees.
Connecticut 31-71,72,73	Wages must be paid weekly (exceptions may be granted). Quit—must be paid by next payday. Fired—must be paid by next business day. Laid off—must be paid by next payday. Penalty—double the wages owed and atty. fees. Labor Dept. will help collect owed wages.
†Delaware 19-1101 to 1115	Wages must be paid monthly. Terminated—must be paid by next payday. Penalty—10% of wages owed per day up to amount owed. Labor Dept. will help collect owed wages.
District of Columbia 36-101 to 110	Wages must be paid semimonthly. Fired—must be paid by next working day. Penalty—pay atty. fees. Mayor will help collect owed wages. Refusal to pay wages may be a crime.
†Florida	None
†Georgia	None
Hawaii 388-1 to 42	Wages must be paid semimonthly. Quit—must be paid by next payday. Fired or laid off—must be paid by next working day. Penalty—double amount of wages owed and atty. fees. Labor Dept. will help collect owed wages. Refusal to pay wages may be a crime.
Idaho 45-601 to 615	Wages must be paid monthly. Fired or laid off—pay within 48 hours. Penalty—go back on the payroll for up to 30 days and atty. fees.

*The law is always changing. Consult an attorney about your situation.
†Pro-boss state.
‡Terminated means the employee quit, was fired, or was laid off. Employers may pay sooner than required.

TABLE 13–1. (Cont.)

	Labor Dept. will help collect owed wages if less than $1,000. Must demand wages in writing before suing.
Illinois Ch. 48, sec. 39m-1 to 39m-15	Wages must be paid semimonthly or every two weeks. Terminated—must be paid next payday. Must be paid for earned vacation. Labor Dept. will help collect owed wages. Refusal to pay wages may be a crime.
†Indiana 22-2-4-1; 22-2-5-1 to 3 22-2-9-1 to 7	Wages in mining and manufacturing must be paid every two weeks. Other workers must be paid semimonthly or every two weeks if the worker requests it. Terminated—must be paid by next payday. Penalty—10% of wages owed per day up to double the amount owed and atty. fees. Labor Dept. will help collect owed wages. Farmers are exempt from most of this.
Iowa 91A.1 to 91A.13	Wages must be paid monthly. Terminated—must be paid next payday. Penalty—atty. fees. Labor Dept. will help collect owed wages.
Kansas 44-314 to 327	Wages must be paid monthly. Terminated—must be paid next payday. Penalty—1% of wages owed per day. Human Resources Dept. will help collect owed wages.
Kentucky 337.020 to .385	Wages must be paid semimonthly. Penalty—double the amount of wages owed and atty. fees.
†Louisiana 23:631 to 653	Wages for some employees must be paid semimonthly or every two weeks. Terminated—must be paid within 3 days. Penalty—go back on the payroll for up to 90 days and atty. fees.
Maine 26-625B to 626B	Penalty—double the wages owed and atty. fees. Labor Dept. will help collect owed wages. Special severance provisions for some workers.
Maryland Art. 100, sec. 94	Wages must be paid semimonthly or every two weeks, except for executives and professionals. Terminated—must be paid next payday. Penalty—up to triple the wages owed. Labor Dept. will help collect owed wages. Refusal to pay wages may be a crime.
Massachusetts Ch. 149, sec. 148	Wages must be paid weekly for most workers. Wages must be paid semimonthly or every two weeks for salaried employees. Quit—must be paid next day. Fired—must be paid the same day. Labor Dept. will help collect owed wages. Refusal to pay wages may be a crime.
Michigan 408.472 to .489	Wages must be paid semimonthly. Penalty—triple the wages owed and atty. fees.

TABLE 13–1. (Cont.)

	Workers must take their complaints to Labor Dept. Refusal to pay wages may be a crime.
Minnesota 181.08 to .17	Wages must be paid monthly. Quit—must be paid in 5 days. Fired—must be paid in 24 hours. Penalty—15 days' wages. Labor Dept. will help collect owed wages.
†Mississippi 71-1-35	Large manufacturers must pay wages semimonthly or every two weeks.
Missouri 290.080 to 120	Corporations and manufacturers must pay wages semimonthly. Executives and professionals may be paid monthly. Fired—must be paid in 7 days. Penalty—go back on the payroll for up to 60 days.
Montana 39-39-101 to 706	Wages must be paid every two weeks except for professionals, supervisors, technicians. Terminated—must be paid in 3 days. Fired for cause—must be paid immediately. Penalty—5% of wages owed per day for up to 20 days and atty. fees. Labor Dept. will help collect owed wages.
Nebraska 48-1230 to 1232	Terminated—must be paid in two weeks or by the next payday if sooner. Penalty—atty. fees.
Nevada 613.030 to 170 607.170 608.020 to 195 608.300 to 330	Wages must be paid semimonthly. Quit—must be paid in 7 days or by the next payday if sooner. Fired—must be paid immediately. Penalty—go back on the payroll for up to 30 days and atty. fees. Labor Dept. will help collect owed wages. Employee has a lien on employer's property for owed wages. Refusal to pay wages may be a crime.
New Hampshire 275:43 to 56	Wages must be paid weekly (exceptions may be granted). Quit—must be paid next payday. Fired—must be paid in 3 days. Penalty—10% of wages owed per day up to the amount owed and atty. fees. Labor Dept. will help collect owed wages.
New Jersey 34:11	Has a very elaborate wage collection process. See an attorney or call the Labor Dept.
New Mexico 50-4-2 to 12	Wages must be paid semimonthly. Some workers may be paid monthly. Quit—must be paid next payday. Fired—must be paid in 10 days. Labor Dept. will help collect owed wages.
†New York Labor secs. 190 to 199	Penalty—25% of wages owed and atty. fees. Labor Dept. will help collect owed wages.
†North Carolina 95-25.6 to 25.22	Wages must be paid monthly. Terminated—must be paid next payday. Penalty—up to double the wages owed.

North Dakota 34-14	Quit—must be paid next payday. Fired—must be paid next payday or in 15 days if sooner. Labor Dept. will help collect owed wages.
†Ohio 4113.15	Wages must be paid semimonthly.
Oklahoma Title 40, secs. 165.1 to 165.4	Wages must be paid semimonthly. Public employees may be paid monthly. Terminated—must be paid next payday. Penalty—2% of wages owed up to the amount owed and atty. fees.
Oregon 652.110 to 445	Quit—must be paid in 48 hours. Fired—must be paid immediately. Penalty—go back on the payroll for up to 30 days and atty. fees. Labor Dept. will help collect owed wages.
†Pennsylvania Title 43, sec. 251; Title 43, sec. 260.1 to 292	Wages must be paid semimonthly. Terminated—must be paid by next payday. Penalty—25% of wages owed up to $500 and atty. fees. Labor Dept. will help collect owed wages. Refusal to pay wages may be a crime.
†Rhode Island 28-14	Terminated—must be paid next payday. Labor Dept. will help collect owed wages.
South Carolina 41-11	Terminated—must be paid next payday. Penalty—go back on the payroll until wages paid. Labor Dept. will help collect owed wages. Must sue within 60 days.
South Dakota 60-11	Quit—must be paid next payday. Fired—must be paid within 5 days. Penalty—double the wages owed and atty. fees. Labor Dept. will help collect owed wages. Refusal to pay wages may be a crime.
Tennessee 50-2-103	Wages must be paid semimonthly. Labor Dept. will help collect owed wages.
Texas Art. 5155 to 5159; Civil Prac. & Rem. Code 38.001	Wages must be paid semimonthly or monthly depending on the type of work. Terminated—must be paid within 6 days after demand for wages is made by employee. Penalty—$50 and atty. fees.
Utah 34-27-1 34-28	Wages must be paid semimonthly. Wages may be paid monthly for salaried employees. Quit—must be paid in 72 hours. Fired—must be paid in 24 hours. Penalty—go back on the payroll for up to 60 days and atty. fees. Labor Dept. will help collect owed wages. Must sue within 60 days.
Vermont Title 21, secs. 342 to 347	Wages must be paid semimonthly or every two weeks. Quit—must be paid next payday. Fired—must be paid in 72 hours. Penalty—double the wages owed and atty. fees. Labor Dept. will help collect owed wages. Refusal to pay wages may be a crime.
Virginia 40.1-29	Wages must be paid semimonthly or every two weeks. Salaried employees may be paid monthly. Terminated—must be paid next payday.

TABLE 13–1. (Cont.)

	Labor Dept. will help collect owed wages.
	Refusal to pay wages may be a crime.
Washington	Terminated—must be paid next payday.
49.48.010 to .090	Penalty—atty. fees.
	Labor Dept. will help collect owed wages.
	Refusal to pay wages may be a crime.
West Virginia	Quit—must be paid next payday.
21-5	Fired—must be paid in 72 hours.
	Penalty—go back on the payroll for up to 30 days and atty. fees.
	Labor Dept. will help collect owed wages.
Wisconsin	Wages must be paid monthly.
109.03 to .11	Quit—must be paid in 15 days.
	Fired—must be paid in 3 days.
	Penalty—the penalty goes up depending on the length of time wages are not paid.
	Labor Dept. will help collect owed wages.
	Refusal to pay wages may be a crime.
Wyoming	Wages must be paid semimonthly by some employers.
27-4	Quit—must be paid in 72 hours.
	Fired—must be paid in 24 hours.
	Penalty—18% interest and atty. fees.
	Labor Dept. will help collect owed wages.
	Refusal to pay wages may be a crime.

Most states say everything the employee is owed counts as wages for the purposes of these statutes. That includes bonuses and deferred compensation, as well as payments for accrued vacation and sick leave. These provisions apply to government as well as private employers (*Figgie, O'Hollaren, Golden Bear, Hammond, Matson*).

Maine has a statute that requires an employer to pay severance pay if 100 or more employees are laid off because of a plant closing. The employees get one week's pay for each year they worked for the employer. In 1987 the U.S. Supreme Court was asked whether this state statute had been preempted by federal law. The court, in a 5 to 4 decision, ruled that the statute was not preempted by any federal law. While ERISA (see Chapter 17) controls employer benefit plans, wages and bonuses are "wages," not "benefit plans," and states can continue to control how and when they are paid as well as allow penalties for nonpayment (*Ft. Halifax*).

EMPLOYEES VERSUS INDEPENDENT CONTRACTORS

In some cases the question is whether someone is an employee, for whom the Fair Labor Standards Act and state wage statutes provide protection, or an independent contractor, who is not protected. Take the case of Cathy Adler, a dancer at the Lonely Lady Club. Her duties included working an eight-hour shift six days a week. During her working hours Adler was required to dance three times for about fifteen minutes each time. She was also expected to solicit private dances and drinks from the customers, for which she usually received tips. The tips were her main source of income. The Supreme Court of Alaska held that Cathy Adler was an employee, not an independent contractor, and was therefore protected by both the Federal Fair Labor Standards Act and the Alaska wage statutes (*Jeffcoat*).

Whether someone is an employee or an independent contractor is a difficult question. For example, two different federal circuit courts have ruled on pickle pickers. The Sixth Circuit ruled they were independent contractors, while the Seventh Circuit found them to be employees (*Lauritzen*). Some employers try to get around state and federal laws by having employees sign a contract saying they are independent contractors. The judges do not care what the piece of paper says; they make a decision based on the facts of each case. Generally, if there is any way persons can be called employees, the courts will call them employees.

THE FUTURE

Should the Fair Labor Standards Act be revised? If time and a half for overtime is not enough to encourage a 40-hour week, should the law require double pay for hours over 40? Today many professional employees are expected to work 70 or 80 hours a week to the detriment of their health and the wellbeing of their patients and clients. Should there be an absolute limit for everyone? Some companies want to pay blue-collar workers an annual salary instead of paying them by the hour. Should the federal government allow this change if the employer pays above a minimum annual salary and works the employees less than some set maximum per week? In 1987 France amended its fair labor act to require time and a half after an employee has worked 2000 hours during a year, rather than over 40 hours in a week. The purpose of this change is to allow employers and employees the flexibility to work more during peak periods and then take a long vacation when demand is slack. Should the United States make a similar change?

14

Labor Unions

THE PAST

The history of labor unions is a history of struggle. From the Civil War to the Great Depression unions had to contend not only with employers but also with the legal system. Judges put labor leaders in jail and used the power of injunction to stop strikes and picket lines.

Two centuries ago English judges found labor unions to be "criminal conspiracies" and put union leaders in jail. In 1836 the High Court of New York also found union leaders guilty of criminal conspiracy (Fisher). In 1842 the Supreme Court of Massachusetts began the movement to allow the existence of labor unions when it found that just forming a union was not "criminal conspiracy" (Hunt).

An injunction is a court order telling someone to stop doing something. This order was invented by the English judges to use against people who were in the process of injuring private property. During the Industrial Revolution, American judges reasoned that a business is private property; strikes and picket lines hurt business; therefore strikes and picket lines hurt private property.

In 1896 the Massachusetts Supreme Court upheld an injunction against peaceful union picketing. Justice Oliver Wendell Holmes wrote a famous dissenting opinion in which he said it was wrong to prohibit "organized persuasion" if it was free from the "threat of violence." He felt the majority of the justices of the Massachusetts Supreme Court made the unwarranted assumption that all union picketing leads to violence (Vagelahn). Most American judges made that assumption. One federal judge in 1905 said: "There is and can be no such thing as peaceful picketing, any more than there can be chaste

170

vulgarity, or peaceful mobbing, or lawful lynching. When men want to converse or persuade, they do not organize a picket line" (*Gee*).

In 1932 Congress passed the Norris-LaGuardia Act, which took away from federal judges the power to use injunctions to stop strikes and picket lines. Some leaders hoped that would be the end of it. Others felt that more would be required to end the conflict, not only between union and employer but also between union and union.

THE NATIONAL LABOR RELATIONS ACT: THE WAGNER ACT

Congress passed the Wagner Act in 1935. The act had two purposes: to end labor conflict (including the conflict among rival unions) and to set up a system under which fair collective bargaining could take place. To accomplish this, Congress created a new entity, the National Labor Relations Board (NLRB) to enforce and interpret the new law. The board also acts as a court and hears disputes that relate to the law.

The Wagner Act made it illegal to fire or not hire workers simply because of their union membership. If a worker feels that has happened, he or she must take the case to the NLRB within six months. The NLRB can order the employer to hire back the employees and pay them the wages they would have been paid if they had been hired, or not fired, in the first place.

The purpose of the Wagner Act was to end conflict not only between union and management but also between union and union. The staff at the NLRB oversees elections in which employees decide if they want to be represented by a union, and which union they want to represent them. Once a union wins that election, it becomes the workers' exclusive voice. The employer cannot bargain with another union.

The NLRB also determines what the appropriate "bargaining unit" will be. A bargaining unit is a group of workers who will be dealt with as a group for the purposes of collective bargaining. Bargaining units might be set up to differentiate between skilled and unskilled workers, blue-collar and white-collar workers, or workers in different parts of the country.

Section Seven of the act states that employees "shall have the right to self-organize, to form, join or assist labor organizations, to bargain collectively through representatives of their own choosing" and to do anything else necessary for their "mutual aid or protection." How are these rights enforced? By allowing the NLRB to punish employers who interfere with these rights.

The act also created a new concept in the law, the concept of an unfair labor practice. Section Eight explains what an unfair labor practice is. First, it is an unfair labor practice for an employer to interfere with the right to organize spelled out in Section Seven. It is unfair for employers to form company unions or to help one union win an election contest over another union. It is unfair to discriminate against union members in any way, or to discriminate against employees who file charges with, or testify before, the NLRB.

It is also an unfair labor practice for an employer to refuse to bargain. This means the employer cannot refuse to: (1) meet with the union, (2) sign a contract with the union that embodies the terms that have been agreed to, or (3) turn over information to the union. The employer also cannot change wages and working conditions during the negotiations unless the negotiations reach an impasse.

While the statute set out the broad outlines of this new concept of unfair labor practices, it has been up to the National Labor Relations Board and the U.S. Supreme Court to fill in the details.

Can an employer keep union members from talking about the union at lunch or on coffee breaks? No, but an employer can keep nonemployees (such as outside union organizers) off his or her property. He or she has to treat union organizers fairly. If the employer allows others to solicit on the premises, he or she has to let the union organizers do the same thing. That is why most factories have a big sign that forbids all nonemployees from coming onto the property (*Republic Aviation, Babcock & Wilcox*).

Does the employer have to let the union have a meeting in the company cafeteria? No, but he or she cannot discriminate against the union. If the employer rents the cafeteria to other groups, he or she has to rent it to the union as well (*Stowe Spinning*). Can the employer talk to the employees about unions and their disadvantages? Yes, as long as the employer is not trying to coerce them into not joining the union (*Va. Electric*).

If the employees go on strike, can the employer hire workers to keep the business going? Yes. When the strike is over and the strikers ask for their jobs back, can the employer refuse to rehire them? It depends on why the workers went on strike. If they went on strike to protest unfair labor practices by the employer, the employer has to take them back and fire the replacement workers (*Mastro Plastics*). If the workers went on strike for economic reasons (wages and working conditions), then the employer can refuse to hire them back immediately. However, when new job openings occur, the employer cannot discriminate against the former strikers (*Mackay Radio*).

The employer can refuse to hire back workers who engaged in criminal activity during the strike. In one case, the Supreme Court ruled that the NLRB could not order an employer to hire back the strikers. While on strike, the workers had engaged in a sit-down strike in the factory. The Supreme Court felt the employer should not have to hire back employees who trespassed on private property during the strike (*Fansteel*).

Workers also have the right to take "concerted action" for their "mutual aid and protection." Workers have this right even if they do not belong to a union or work for a unionized company. The classic example of this is a group of workers who walked off the job because they believed in good faith that it was too cold to work. The NLRB ordered the employer to hire them back (they were fired because of the walkout), and the U.S. Supreme Court enforced the NLRB's order (*Washington Aluminum*). There is a great deal of disagreement about just what kinds of situations this right applies to. It does not protect employees who are insubordinate, but it does protect them if they legitimately feel compelled to protect their own safety.

If employees feel their safety is threatened, they should consider taking concerted action. In some situations this may mean walking off the job and going to an agency such as OSHA (which we will discuss in Chapter 17). In other situations it may mean just banding together and asking to speak to higher management. In one case the company hired a new supervisor who, during his first week on the job, requested the sexual favors of six different female employees. When the women refused to start work one morning until the plant manager agreed to listen to their complaints, he fired them (the new supervisor left town and was never seen again). The NLRB ruled that these women had engaged in "concerted action" for their "mutual aid and protection" and ordered them reinstated with back pay (*Downslope*).

With the passage of the Wagner Act a new chapter of American employment law began. Union membership grew from three to fifteen million. Unions finally had a way of establishing that they really did represent the workers through NLRB elections. Unions could also go to the NLRB with complaints about unfair labor practices.

THE TAFT-HARTLEY ACT OF 1947

By 1947 Congress felt that the labor statutes needed to be revised. The Wagner Act had allowed the closed shop. The Taft-Hartley Act outlawed the closed shop. It appeared to allow the union shop, but after the Supreme Court interpreted the act, what it really allowed is the agency shop. A **closed shop** is an agreement between the employer and the union that the employer will hire only union members. In a closed shop, persons cannot get a job unless the union first accepts them as members. This kind of agreement is now forbidden by federal law. The act appeared to allow the **union shop,** which is an agreement that within a certain period of time new employees must join the union. They do not have to belong to the union to get the job in the first place, but they must join if they want to keep their jobs. The act says the employer cannot make them join the union until they have worked for thirty days.

An **agency shop** is an agreement that within a certain period of time new employees must start paying union dues. They do not have to actually join the union, but they must pay the dues. While Taft-Hartley appears to allow a union shop, the Supreme Court has decided that people have a right not to belong to organizations they do not want to belong to. Congress cannot pass a law that requires people to join a union, but Congress can require people to pay union dues, and that is what Taft-Hartley really does. In other words, while the language of the statute appears to allow union shops, it really allows only agency shops. States are allowed to pass right-to-work laws that outlaw even the agency shop (*General Motors*).

In one case employees resigned from the union during a strike and went back to work. The union tried to fine them, but the U.S. Supreme Court said the union could not fine people who were no longer members of the union. While these workers were still required to pay dues under the agency-shop agreement, they could not be fined by an organization they no longer belonged to (*Pattern Makers*).

People who are forced to pay union dues because of an agency-shop agreement do not have to pay to support political causes they do not agree with. Unions must refund that portion of union dues that goes to support political causes. The U.S. Supreme Court has ruled that unions must provide a reasonably prompt opportunity for nonmembers to challenge the amount of dues the union collects, and the decision on the amount of dues to be refunded must be made by an impartial decision maker (*Chicago Teachers*).

The other major change brought about by the Taft-Hartley Act was the addition of unfair labor practices that unions could commit. Unions cannot coerce employees or employers, refuse to bargain, charge excessive dues, or insist on featherbedding (requiring employers to pay people who do not work). It is not always easy to tell what constitutes featherbedding. In one case the Supreme Court allowed a union to demand that newspaper type be set twice a day even though the second set was not used. In another case the court allowed a union to demand that a theater hire a local orchestra to play at intermission, even though the traveling road shows brought their own orchestras to play during the performances. In other words, the U.S. Supreme Court has interpreted featherbedding narrowly to mean having workers standing idly by and not doing any kind of work. That is something a union cannot ask an employer to do. Unions can ask employers to pay workers who do useless work. Of course, the employer is free to refuse to agree to that kind of clause in the union contract (and face a strike or picket line that might destroy the company). Many employers think Congress should amend the law to include useless work in the definition of featherbedding. So far Congress has not responded (*American Newspaper, Gamble*).

The Taft-Hartley Act also allows the President to stop a strike if he or she determines health and safety are threatened. The President can order the workers back to work for up to 80 days (a cooling-off period), during which time the two sides must work to try to settle the dispute. The act also requires either side to give the other side 60 days' notice before asking to negotiate a new contract. They must also notify the Federal Mediation and Conciliation Service that they intend to negotiate a new contract. Some legal scholars believe requiring union members to go back to work violates the Thirteenth Amendment's prohibition against "involuntary servitude," but the U.S. Supreme Court has never ruled on this question.

THE LANDRUM-GRIFFIN ACT OF 1959

In 1935 the Wagner Act was passed to protect unions from employers. In 1947 the Taft-Hartley Act was passed to protect employers from unions. In 1959 the

Landrum-Griffin Act was passed to protect workers from unions. The part of the act we are concerned with is called the Labor-Management Reporting and Disclosure Act (LMRDA). It set out a Bill of Rights for union members.

Equal Rights within the Union

The first right listed is the right to be treated equally. All members of the union have the same right to nominate candidates, vote in elections, and attend meetings. All union members also have the right to vote on dues increases.

The Right of Free Speech and Assembly

The LMRDA guarantees the right of free speech and assembly to all union members. This includes the right to speak at union meetings. If one group of union members shouts down another group of union members, they have violated this right (*Scovile*).

This also includes the right to criticize union leaders. In one case, the secretary of a painter's union in New York accused other union officials of getting excessive reimbursement checks for attending a union convention. A union court found him guilty of making false statements and suspended him from all union activity for five years. The Second Circuit Court ordered the union to reinstate him. The court said the other union officials could sue him for defamation, but the union could not discipline him for exercising his right of free speech, even if what he said was defamatory and untrue (*Salzhandler*).

This right of free speech also includes the right of free assembly, which means that union members can get together in groups to discuss union business without fear of retaliation from the union leadership (*Kuebler*).

The Right to Sue the Union

The LMRDA allows union members to sue the union. At the same time, it allows unions to require members to bring problems to the union before they file a lawsuit. The act says a member "may be required to exhaust reasonable hearing procedures" (not to exceed a four-month lapse of time) within the union. The U.S. Supreme Court has ruled that, because the statute says "may be required" instead of "shall be required," it is up to the district judge to decide if he or she will delay the trial in order to give the union a chance to solve the problem internally. The judge does not have to do this. Also, the judge may award attorney's fees to union members who have to sue their own union (*Marine*).

The Right to Fair Discipline Hearings

It is common for union constitutions to contain provisions that allow members to be disciplined for doing things not considered in the best interest of the union. Discipline might include a fine or expulsion from the union. The

LMRDA guarantees union members the right to a fair hearing before being disciplined. The union member must be "(a) served with written specific charges; (b) given a reasonable time to prepare; (c) afforded a full and fair hearing." Courts have said that a full and fair hearing includes the right to cross-examine witnesses; the right to have a lawyer if the union has a lawyer; and the right to an unbiased judge and jury (*Kiepura, Cornelio, Semancik*).

The Right to Fair and Open Elections

The LMRDA guarantees free and open elections. Local union officers must be elected at least every three years, national officials at least every five years. A secret ballot is required in local elections. Higher officials may be elected at a convention. Unions are allowed to set "reasonable" qualifications for candidates. In one case a union required candidates for major office to have served in a lower office. The Supreme Court declared this rule invalid because it disqualified 93 percent of the union members (*Wirtz*). In another case the Supreme Court declared invalid a rule that required candidates to have attended at least half the union meetings during the three years preceding the election. This rule disqualified 96 percent of the members (*Steelworker's #2*).

Unions have to treat all candidates equally and distribute their campaign literature to the members at the candidate's expense. A union cannot use union funds to support a particular candidate. The union must provide members with a reasonable opportunity to nominate candidates and notify members at least 15 days before an election. Union members who are unhappy with a union election cannot sue directly. They have to get the Secretary of Labor to sue for them to set aside the union election.

The Right to Review Financial Information

Unions are required to file annual financial reports with the Secretary of Labor. Union members have a right to examine these reports. Union officials have a fiduciary duty to use great care in handling union funds.

The Right to Fair Representation

Once a union is certified as representing a bargaining unit, it represents all employees in the unit, even those who refuse to join the union. The certified union is the only entity that can negotiate a group contract for these employees. The union has a duty to represent all the employees fairly, even those who do not belong to the union but are covered by the union contract. In one case a union tried to negotiate different benefits for black and white employees. The Supreme Court held that this violated the union's duty to represent all the workers fairly (*Steele*). The union must also treat all employees fairly in grievance and arbitration procedures and may not act in bad faith or arbitrarily to exclude any employee (*Anchor Motor*).

The union has a duty to "make an honest effort to serve the interests of all its members without hostility to any" (*Ford Motor Co.*). If the union breaches this duty, the injured employee can sue. If the union has done a bad job of representing the employee at the arbitration hearing, the employee is usually stuck with the arbitrator's decision unless the union was "dishonest," acted in "bad faith," or was "discriminatory." On the other hand, the union should have a good reason for not taking the case to arbitration and has a duty to follow up on leads provided by the employee (*Anchor Motor*).

An employee who feels the union has breached the duty of fair representation must sue both the employer and the union together. The employee has to prove two things: that the employer violated the union contract, and that the union did not live up to its duty to represent the employee fairly in the grievance and arbitration proceedings. If an employee does prove both these things, the judge can order both the employer and the union to pay damages (*Vaca*).

ARBITRATION

Over the last century more and more disputes in the area of labor relations have come to be settled by arbitration. Arbitration is used for two purposes: contract formation and contract interpretation.

Contract Formation

Because a strike can be costly to both sides, labor and management have an incentive to find better ways to settle disputes over what the union contract should contain. One approach is **mediation.** With mediation a neutral third party is chosen by both sides to help them come to an agreement. A mediator does not have the power to impose an agreement, only to help the parties achieve the result they want, a fair contract. In some situations the federal government will provide a mediator.

Another approach is **fact finding.** A fact finder looks at the company books or the market for the product and presents both sides with a set of facts. These facts might relate to the profitability of the company or the effects of competition on the company.

In some situations mediation and fact finding do not help, and both sides agree to abide by what an **arbitrator** decides. Several industries, including the coal and apparel industries, have used arbitrators over the last half century in order to reach agreements and avoid strikes.

Contract Interpretation

While arbitration is not a common way of making union contracts, it is a very common way of interpreting union contracts. Many union contracts require both sides to submit a dispute about the interpretation of the contract to an arbitrator. Most disputes over the contract involve whether or not the employer had a right under the contract to fire a particular employee. Many union contracts require the employer to have good cause before firing an employee protected by the union contract. The contract may define good cause in great detail or leave it up to the arbitrator to decide what constitutes good cause. Some contracts recognize two types of good cause. Heavy-duty good cause consists of those things for which the employee can be fired without a warning and a chance to improve. Dishonesty, insubordination, being drunk on the job, or fighting at work are often considered heavy-duty sins for which the employee can be fired immediately. Lesser infractions and plain old incompetence require a warning and a chance for the employee to improve. In most situations an employee who wants to have his or her case heard by an arbitrator must first file a grievance with the employer. This gives the employer a chance to change his or her mind. If the employer does not, the case is presented to an arbitrator. Both sides present evidence and the arbitrator makes a decision. While the arbitrator can award back pay and order the employer to reinstate the employee, arbitrators usually will not award punitive damages or attorney fees. Arbitration is supposed to be a quicker and easier way of settling disputes than going through a court battle.

Labor arbitrators have developed a set of principles that they live by. The arbitrator is supposed to determine whether the employee actually did what he or she was accused of doing, and if so, what the appropriate penalty should be. The arbitrator is more likely to go along with the punishment decided on by the employer if the employer conducted a fair investigation. More and more arbitrators are ordering employers to take back employees who are alcoholics or drug addicts if the employee promises to get treatment in a rehabilitation program. Arbitrators will usually not allow employees to be disciplined or dismissed because of conduct that takes place off the job unless there is a clear relationship between the off-the-job conduct and the interests of the employer.

The U.S. Supreme Court has ruled that an employee protected by a union contract has a right to be represented by a union representative at the earliest stage in the process where discipline might result (*Weingarten*). If the employee gets no satisfaction from the grievance procedure, then the union can take the case to an arbitrator. Usually the union represents the employee at the arbitration hearing, and the employee is not allowed to bring his or her own attorney to the hearing. The hearing is informal. Witnesses testify and are cross-examined just the way they are at a trial. The arbitrator is not bound by the normal rules of evidence and can hear any testimony he or she feels might be helpful. Generally, if the employee does not testify on his or her own behalf, the arbitrator is going to consider that a black mark against the employee (criminal defendants have a constitutional right not to testify at their own trial but the same does not apply in a labor arbitration hearing).

The award of the arbitrator can be enforced in court. In 1960, in a series of decisions involving the Steelworkers Union, the U.S. Supreme Court laid down the fundamental principle that the award of the arbitrator is to be enforced in almost all situations. The court said it was the intent of Congress that disputes over the interpretation of union contracts be handled by arbitration whenever possible and that the arbitrator's decision should not be overturned except in extraordinary circumstances (*Steelworkers Trilogy*).

Generally, courts will overturn an arbitrator's decision only if the decision does not follow the contract, if it violates public policy, or if there were gross defects in procedure. Of course, courts can disagree about what violates public policy. In one case the Fifth Circuit Court overturned the arbitrator's decision. The arbitrator had found that the employee had not used marijuana at work as alleged. The circuit court believed that he had and that to allow him to work around heavy machines under the influence of marijuana was a violation of public policy. The U.S. Supreme Court overturned the circuit court's decision and reinstated the arbitrator's decision. The Supreme Court said that the whole purpose of arbitration is to have a quick and final decision. Courts cannot second-guess the arbitrator in most situations (*Misco*).

FEDERAL PREEMPTION

Federal labor law preempts state law. This means if workers have a complaint that falls within the jurisdiction of federal labor law, they have to file a complaint with the NLRB or the Secretary of Labor, not in state court. In many situations the workers must file the complaint within six months. If the employer mistreats or discharges them because they are union members, it is a matter for the NLRB. If they have a complaint about the way the union has treated them, they should call the U.S. Labor Department.

In one case a worker felt he had been fired for "passing out petitions and voicing complaints." He wanted to sue under California law but the federal circuit court held that he was dismissed for activities that constituted "concerted activity" under federal labor law so he had to go to the NLRB instead (*Buscemi*).

While federal law has generally preempted the field, there are some employers the federal law does not reach. This is because, while there is no size limit written into the federal statute, the NLRB has decided it will not deal with small employers. It is often unclear how small is too small. Generally, any employer or employee in the private sector should assume federal labor law applies to them until an attorney tells them otherwise.

Federal labor law does not cover state and local government employees.

There are many state statutes that were passed decades ago and are still on the books, even though federal law has preempted this area. It will be up to your attorney to decide if they still apply. For example, many states have criminal laws that prohibit blacklisting. If the workers are being blacklisted because of their union membership, that is a matter for the NLRB, not the local police. Many states have laws that purport to control strikes, picketing, and boycotts by unions. Many of these state statutes either violate the U.S. Constitution or have been preempted by federal labor law. Many states also have laws against rioting that were designed to be used against strikers. Some of these criminal laws have been declared unconstitutional by the U.S. Supreme Court (*Medrano*).

SUING THE BOSS

What if the employee is covered by an agreement that calls for arbitration but he or she wants to sue the employer instead? The U.S. Supreme Court has ruled that it depends on what the agreement says. In one recent case Kenneth Thomas tried to sue his former employer, Kidder Peabody Inc., because of a dispute over commissions Thomas felt he was owed. Kidder Peabody Inc. argued that the case had to be handled by arbitration. It seems that when Thomas applied for his job as a stockbroker, he signed a job application that said he would abide by New York Stock Exchange rules. Those rules say that any and all disputes between employees and member stockbrokerage firms must be settled by arbitration. The California labor code specifically says that a suit for wages can be brought without regard to any private agreement to arbitrate. The U.S. Supreme Court found that this state statute had been preempted by a 1925 federal statute that declared arbitration agreements to be enforceable (9 U.S.C. sec. 1). Thomas was stuck with arbitration (*Thomas*).

That is fine if the contract says every dispute of every kind will be handled by arbitration. What if the contract is a union contract and says only that disputes about the interpretation of the contract will be handled by arbitration? What effect should the arbitrator's decision have on a suit by that employee against the employer?

Federal courts have made it clear that if the lawsuit involves a federal statute, the employee is not stuck with an arbitrator's decision. In one case the U.S. Supreme Court allowed the employee to sue under the Civil Rights Act of 1964 for race discrimination even though he had lost his arbitration case (*Gardner-Denver*). In another case the Supreme Court allowed the employee to bring his lawsuit under the Fair Labor Standards Act, even though he had lost his arbitration case (*Barrentine*). Federal circuit courts have ruled that employees can file complaints with the NLRB or the Secretary of Labor even if the arbitrator ruled against them (*Roadway Express, Grand Rapids Die*).

UNIONS AND THE RIGHT OF FREE SPEECH

In the early 1900s the American Federation of Labor published a list of companies that refused to bargain with the AFL, hoping consumers would stop buying products made by the companies on the list. Bucks Stove and Range Co. was on the list because it refused to bargain with the stove worker's union. A federal judge issued an injunction against publishing the list. The head of the AFL, Samuel Gompers, argued that he had a right of free speech which included the right to publish a list like this, but the U.S. Supreme Court disagreed. While it struck down this particular injunction on a technicality, it declared that these kinds of lists could be enjoined by judges concerned with protecting private property (*Gompers*).

Unions argued that they had a right of free speech under the First Amendment that protected their right to picket and boycott. In 1940 the Supreme Court finally agreed, holding that peaceful picketing against employers with whom the union has a direct labor dispute is protected by the First Amendment and cannot be prevented by statutes. The case involved an Alabama statute that made peaceful picketing by unions a criminal offense (Thornhill). The next year, the court applied the same logic to strike down an injunction by a state court that tried to prevent a union picket line (Swing).

In 1959 federal labor law was amended to outlaw picket lines against people who are not directly involved in a labor dispute. This means unions cannot put a full union picket line around a company in an attempt to get the picketed company to stop doing business with the employer the union has a dispute with. In 1964 the Supreme Court made a distinction between a full picket line and an informational picket line. The case involved union picket lines around supermarkets. The union asked consumers not to buy apples from Washington state. The union did not ask employees to refuse to work, and it did not ask customers to boycott the store. It asked consumers only to boycott Washington apples. The Supreme Court said the union had a right to do that. The court felt this kind of informational activity was not the kind of coercive picket line that may not be used against parties not directly involved in a labor dispute (Tree Fruits).

It is generally believed that a union can use other methods of speech, short of a full picket line, to inform consumers about a labor dispute and ask them to boycott in support of the union. The federal labor laws specifically allow "publicity, other than picketing, for the purpose of truthfully informing the public, including consumers," about a labor dispute. The U.S. Supreme Court had to interpret this provision in 1988. The case involved a dispute between construction unions and the owner of a shopping mall in Florida. The construction unions passed out handbills at the entrances to the shopping mall urging consumers not to shop there because a department store was being added to the mall and the construction company was paying, in the union's opinion, substandard wages and benefits. The U.S. Supreme Court upheld the right of the union to pass out handbills. The court made much of the fact that the union did not form a picket line, and did not ask anyone to stop work or refuse to make deliveries to the mall. The court allowed this kind of informational activity and made it clear that any other interpretation of the statute would raise "serious constitutional problems" (DeBartolo).

State supreme courts are also protecting the free-speech rights of union members. One 1987 case involved union members in Connecticut who were arrested for picketing in front of the home of the president of the company against which they were on strike. Connecticut had a statute that made it a crime to picket in a residential neighborhood. The Connecticut Supreme Court struck down the statute as an unconstitutional infringement on the right of free speech. The attorney trying to save the statute argued that it did not infringe the right of free speech because the statute was used only against union members (presumably this attorney assumed union members do not have the same rights as everyone else). The Connecticut Supreme Court ruled that union members do have constitutional rights and struck down the statute (French).

There are still many unanswered questions concerning the extent to which the First Amendment's right of free speech protects union members. However, some things are fairly well settled. People have a right under the First Amendment to form groups including labor unions (while states and the federal government may be able to prevent public employees from going on strike, they cannot prevent them from joining a union). People have a right to picket employers with whom they have a direct conflict. Judges can limit the use of full picket lines against businesses that are not directly involved in a labor dispute because these kinds of picket lines involve more than just speech (the law still believes that full picket lines are coercive). Finally, people have the right to form informational picket lines or pass out leaflets to inform their fellow consumers about a business and its practices.

THE FUTURE

Over the last fifty years American labor law has become more and more complex. Many labor leaders have asked Congress to write a comprehensive new federal labor code. Public administrators have pointed out that federal agencies run by boards are inefficient, and that the National Labor Relations Board is no exception. Perhaps fifty years ago there was a need to provide a board to make decisions that would overcome the antiunion bias of the federal judges. That is no longer true. Most federal judges have spent their professional lives in a world in which everyone took for granted the right of unions to organize and make use of their legitimate weapons of strike and picket line. The tasks of holding union elections could be turned over to the Labor Department. The task of holding hearings to determine whether unfair labor practices have occurred could be turned over to the federal district judges.

Part Six
Rights after Injury

15

Accidental Injury and Worker's Compensation

THE PAST

A century ago English and American judges ruled that employers owed several duties to workers (they still do). The major duties were (and still are):

1. the duty to provide and maintain a safe workplace;
2. the duty to provide safe tools and machines;
3. the duty to provide a competent group of co-workers;
4. the duty to promulgate and enforce safety rules;
5. the duty to warn of known dangers.

If an employer breached one of these duties and a worker was injured as a result, the worker could sue. Of course, to recover, the worker had to prove the employer was negligent (breached one of these duties). In major-injury cases workers managed to prove that about 20 percent of the time. This meant two things. First, 80 percent of seriously injured workers received nothing. Second, the 20 percent who did win received a lot of money, so much money that people were afraid the Industrial Revolution would come to a halt.

In 1837 the case of *Priestly v. Fowler* came before the English House of Lords (in England the House of Lords is the Supreme Court) (*Priestly*). Lord Abinger wrote an opinion that denied the worker a recovery for two reasons. The first reason was that a fellow servant had been partly responsible for the injury. Lord Abinger said the injured worker should sue the person really responsible for the injuries, the fellow servant, not the employer. Lord Abinger also said that when a worker goes to work in a dangerous industry, the worker assumes the risk of injury. If workers do not want to assume that risk, they should get some other kind of job.

In 1842 the Massachusetts Supreme Court adopted these ideas (*Farwell*). Eventually every state supreme court agreed, and Lord Abinger's opinion evolved into the three defenses that came to be called the unholy trinity. The first, **contributory negligence,** said that if the worker was the least bit at fault, he or she could not recover anything in damages. The **fellow servant doctrine** said that if a fellow servant was the least bit responsible, the injured worker could not recover from the employer. The **assumption of the risk doctrine** said that anyone taking a job in a dangerous industry knew at the time that it was dangerous and thus assumed the risk of injury.

The English legal system had been built on the idea of fault. They believed making the person at fault pay for the damages prevented injuries, as well as providing damage awards to injured people. Of course, if no one was at fault, there was no compensation. With the invention of the unholy trinity, it was even less likely that an injured worker was going to recover anything from an employer, even if the employer was at fault (negligent). Stories appeared of mine owners who saved mules rather than men in flooding mines because mules cost money to replace. In 1897 the English responded by passing a Worker's Compensation Act that required the employer to compensate the injured worker (or his widow) regardless of fault. No longer was the concept of negligence to be used, or the three defenses. English economists believed the consumers of a product should pay the full cost of the product, including the cost of lost arms and lost lives. The English also felt that employers would have an incentive to save the workers rather than the mules because the workers would now cost more than the mules. American states followed the English model requiring compensation for "injury by accident arising out of and in the course of employment."

THE WORKER'S COMPENSATION SYSTEM

The easiest way to think about the worker's compensation system is that it replaced a system based on fault with a no-fault system. The employee gives up the right to sue and perhaps win a big award in exchange for quick but low compensation and the employer passes along the cost to the consumers.

Employees Covered

Most employees are covered by worker's compensation. The major exceptions in most states are domestic servants and farm workers. Also, partners and business owners are usually not covered (or have the option in most states not to be covered). Some states have a separate system for state and local government employees, while the federal government has its own federal employee's compensation act (5 U.S.C. sec. 810).

Independent contractors are also not covered. The distinction between employees and independent contractors is obvious in most cases. If there is any doubt, judges look at two basic factors: (1) the degree of control over the worker, and (2) whether the worker is helping this employer engage in his or her regular business. In deciding on the degree of control, courts look at things such as whether the employee comes fully trained for the job, supplies his or her own tools, and is paid by the hour or by the job. The more the worker is helping the employer engage in his or her regular business, the more likely courts are to find that worker to be an employee rather than an independent contractor. Many employers have workers sign contracts in which they agree to be independent contractors so that the employer can avoid having to pay worker's compensation. These agreements have no legal effect. What counts are the facts.

Injury by Accident

The first requirement is that there be an "injury by accident." Early in the twentieth century most courts required an "impact" before they would find that an accident had occurred. If the worker had a heart attack or a hernia or slipped a disk, there was no impact and no recovery.

Over time, courts moved away from this impact requirement. Still, to be an accident, some judges felt the injury should be sudden. Also, many judges felt the injury should be unexpected. In one case the District of Columbia court held that a bus driver who strained his back when he turned around quickly to tell passengers they could not smoke on the bus had had an "accident." The judges said it was an accident because something "unexpectedly" went wrong with the human frame (*Wash. Metro.*).

Some courts hold that before they will find "something gone wrong with the human frame" to be an accident, the worker must be doing something other than routine work. Over the years more and more courts have dropped this "other than routine work" requirement. Recently Indiana did just that when a worker suffered a herniated disk while picking up planks. Under the old interpretation this injury would not have been covered by worker's compensation because this worker routinely picked up planks, but under the new interpretation the appeals court found this to be an "accident" covered by worker's compensation (*Savich*). Today most back problems and hernias are found to be "accidents."

What if problems develop slowly over many months or years and are caused by doing the routine tasks of the job? Under the old interpretation this would not be an accident either because it was not "sudden" enough, or because it was caused by "routine work." More and more state supreme courts are allowing recovery for these types of injuries. The Illinois Supreme Court recently held that a laundry-room employee who suffered from "carpal tunnel syndrome" (compressed nerves caused by repetitive trauma to the hands) was suffering from an "accident." The court held that there should not be any requirement of "sudden mishap." The key should be whether the injury was work-related or not (*Belwood Nursing*). Supreme courts in North Dakota and Utah have recently found arthritis in the shoulder and back pain caused by years of lifting to be "accidents" covered by worker's compensation (*Syverson, Specialty Cabinet*).

Three areas that cause a great many problems are heart attacks, occupational diseases, and mental illness.

Heart Attacks

Heart attacks are something employers bring up as an example of how unfair the law is. If you look at the cases, it seems persons are covered by worker's compensation if they have the heart attack at work and are not covered if they have the heart attack at home, even though heart attacks are caused by years of improper diet and lack of exercise.

The New York High Court developed the "greater than ordinary wear and tear of life" test for heart attacks. If the worker is doing something similar to what he or she would be doing if he or she had stayed home and has a heart attack, the New York court will not allow worker's compensation to pay benefits. In 1979 the New Jersey Legislature added this requirement to the New Jersey Worker's Compensation Act. In New Jersey a heart attack is not covered unless it was caused by work stress greater than what most people experience during the "wear and tear of daily living." In 1988 the New Jersey Supreme Court ruled that a heart attack caused by moving heavy doors in the heat of summer met this test (*Hellwig*).

Some states, such as North and South Carolina, require the heart attack to be the result of "sudden, unusual exertion" at work (*Dillingham, Cline*). North Dakota requires the worker to have the heart attack as the result of "unusual" work stress, and the North Dakota Supreme Court found working for a long time in 120-degree heat was not "unusual" enough to qualify (*Grace*).

Occupational Diseases

Occupational diseases were a problem for a long time. How can a disease be an accident? Most states have now amended their statutes to include occupational diseases if they meet certain requirements. Also, over time, more and more courts have come to regard illness as an "accident."

Mental Illness

Since most state legislatures did not deal with mental illness when they wrote their statutes, the courts have had to come up with some way of dealing with claims that work stress caused mental illness.

Some courts require the mental problems to be the result of "abnormal" working conditions. A Pennsylvania court held that a worker who got anxiety depression after being transferred to the night shift was just reacting to "normal working conditions" and could not receive worker's compensation (*Andracki*). The Arizona Legislature amended the statute to deal with this problem (something every state legislature could do). In Arizona a worker must prove the mental illness was caused by "unexpected, unusual, or extraordinary stress" related to the job (*Lapare*).

Pennsylvania and Minnesota courts have divided mental-illness cases into three types: (1) mental illness caused by physical injury, (2) physical injury caused by mental illness, and (3) mental illness without physical injury. Workers get compensation in the first two situations. In the third situation, where there is no physical injury, the Pennsylvania courts will allow recovery if the worker can prove "abnormal" working conditions existed that could have caused the mental illness (*Boeing Vertol*). The Minnesota Supreme Court simply does not allow workers in the third situation to receive compensation, no matter how stressful the working environment (*Paul's Auto*).

Other state courts do not require a physical injury or abnormal working conditions. In 1986 New Mexico had its first case where a worker asked for compensation because of mental illness unrelated to a physical injury. The worker's mental problems began when he was transferred to the day shift, where he had to work for a supervisor he did not get along with. The worker finally had a nervous breakdown. The New Mexico Appeals Court held that this was an injury caused by work stress and was covered by worker's compensation. The worker did not have to prove "out of the ordinary stress" in order to get compensation (*Candelaria*).

In 1987 courts in Alaska, Oregon, and Indiana agreed that neither physical injury nor "abnormal stress" would be required in mental-illness cases (*Wade, Duran*). The Indiana case involved a woman who suffered from severe anxiety depression after her supervisor walked up behind her and stuck his finger in her ribs as if it were a gun. She had a terrible fear of guns. The Indiana Supreme Court rejected the "abnormal stress" requirement and found that she had suffered an "accidental injury" (*Hansen*).

Arising Out of

The second requirement is that the injury "arise out of" the employment. This means the job must in some way "cause" the injury. At the beginning of the twentieth century many judges felt that the injury did not arise out of the job unless it was the kind of injury that was "peculiar" to that particular job. This is best illustrated by two early cases. In 1935 a workman suffered from frozen feet because his job required him to be outside all night in the Boston cold. The Massachusetts Supreme Court said that everyone had to accept the risk of bad weather and it did not let him receive worker's-compensation benefits (*Robinson's Case*). In 1938 a Texas judge saw things differently:

> In the case before us the very work which the deceased was doing for his employer exposed him to a greater hazard from heat stroke than the general public was exposed to for the simple reason that the general public were not pushing wheelbarrow loads of sand in the hot sun on that day (*Webster #1*).

Over time most judges came to agree with the Texas judge. Most modern judges ask if a particular job increased the probability of a particular injury.

In a recent New Jersey case a worker was lighting a cigarette during the lunch break when her hair caught on fire. The New Jersey Supreme Court found this to be a risk she took every time she lighted a cigarette and being at work did not increase the probability of this injury, so she did not receive compensation (*Coleman*).

Cases involving assaults at work demonstrate the logic of "arising out of." In one case a worker was shot at work by her estranged husband. The Maine Supreme Court said that while her husband happened to catch up with her at work, being at work did not increase the probability of her being shot so she did not receive compensation (*Johnson #4*). The Connecticut Supreme Court ruled the same way in a similar case (*Fair*). On the other hand, an off-duty bartender was stabbed to death while trying to break up a fight at his employer's bar. The Pennsylvania Appeals Court felt the widow should receive compensation because this worker would probably not have tried to break up the fight if he had not been an employee of the bar (*Webster #2*).

Sherman Black and Allen Aylsworth were co-owners of a small furniture factory in Georgia and both were covered by worker's compensation. When Aylsworth murdered Black, Black's widow sued for her worker's-compensation death benefits. The insurance company argued that Aylsworth killed Black for personal reasons (he may have been in love with Black's wife) which did not arise out of the job. Aylsworth testified that he killed Black for business reasons (he was tired of Black coming to work late). The judges believed him. Aylsworth got a life sentence and Mrs. Black got the compensation (*Black*).

In the Course of

The third requirement is that the injury occur "in the course of" employment. This refers to the location of the worker and the activity the worker was engaged in when the injury occurred. Generally, the worker has to be working to receive worker's compensation.

One difficult type of case is when the employee is injured while engaging in horseplay. Some courts simply hold that when employees engage in horseplay, they are not working and are not covered by worker's compensation. In one case the Colorado Appeals Court refused to allow the worker to receive compensation. She had injured herself showing a fellow employee a new dance step (*Kater*).

Other courts take a more generous view. The North Carolina Appeals Court said horseplay was simply a "reality of human conduct" and should be covered (*McGraw*).

Injuries that occur commuting to work are another problem. The general rule is that workers are not covered by worker's compensation when they are commuting to work, but there are several exceptions to that rule. A Pennsylvania Appeals Court listed four major exceptions to the rule. The employee is covered by worker's compensation commuting to and from work: (1) if the employment contract includes transportation to and from work, (2) if there is no fixed place of work, (3) if the worker is on a special mission for the employer, and (4) if the worker is doing something that is furthering the employer's business (*Kear*).

Generally, once the employee reaches the employer's parking lot the commute is over and the employee is considered to be at work and "in the course of" employment.

Many cases involve workers who are engaged in recreational activities. Generally, employees who are hurt playing on the "company team" get compensation. The team provides advertising and benefits the employer.

The 1979 changes in the New Jersey statute prevent recovery in most recreation cases. In a recent case the employee was injured playing paddle ball during the lunch break. The New Jersey Supreme Court said he did not meet the new test. The statute requires the recreational activity to be a "regular incident of employment" and "a benefit to the employer beyond just improving the health and morale of the employees" (*Sarzillo*).

The question in other recreation cases is: When did the benefits to the employer end and the benefits to the employee begin? In one case the employee was told to dispose of the office plants. She took them home and hurt herself when she fell off a chair trying to hang one of the plants on her porch. The North Carolina Supreme Court said when she got the plants home, the benefit to the employer ended and the benefit to her began. She did not get compensation (*Fortner*).

In a Connecticut case, Caryn Luddie drove to New London to meet with a client. After transacting their business, she was driving him to Hartford so he could catch a train. Along the way they went to the Plainfield dog track to watch the races, and then they headed for her house so she could take a shower. They were involved in a car wreck at 3:00 a.m. The Connecticut Appeals Court said the trip to the dog track and to her house were not benefiting her employer and therefore were not "in the course of" her employment. She did not receive compensation (*Luddie*).

The Modern Approach

Many modern judges are no longer trapped by the phrase "injury by accident arising out of and in the course of" employment. These judges believe the law should be interpreted liberally to achieve the purposes for which it was passed. The two main purposes were to provide compensation for injured workers and to transfer the cost of compensation to the consumers of a particular product instead of to the society in general. Today "injury by accident" means any kind of injury, mental or physical, caused by impact, work stress, or disease. "Arise out of and in the course of employment" means that the job increased the probability of getting this particular injury or illness. If the worker was more likely to suffer this injury at work than at home, he or she is going to receive worker's compensation.

Death

Worker's-compensation laws provide benefits to the dependents of workers who die on the job. Death benefits are usually limited to the maximum amount the worker would have been entitled to if he or she had lived and been totally and permanently disabled.

Under modern interpretations of the equal-protection clause, people cannot be treated differently because of sex. This means if a statute provides benefits to widows, the same benefits must also be provided to widowers. Many statutes contained the assumption that widows were dependent on their husbands. A Michigan Appeals Court in 1987 declared that part of the Michigan statute to be unconstitutional. The question of dependence is a fact to be determined in each case regardless of the sex of the dependent (*Williams #2*).

Most statutes require someone to be both a relative and one actually dependent on the worker for support before he or she can receive benefits. Many statutes cut off widow's benefits if the widow (or widower) remarries—this encourages a lot of people to "live in sin." The Illinois act tries to avoid this by giving the widow(er) a lump sum equal to two years' benefits if he or she remarries (*Stewart*). The New Jersey act says children between the ages of 18 and 40 cannot be dependent on the worker, even if in reality they actually were (*Piscopo*).

The fact that more and more people in our society choose to live together rather than get married causes problems. Under most statutes live-in boyfriends or girlfriends cannot collect benefits, even if they were dependent on the worker for their support at the time of the death, because they are not "relatives."

In one case Rita Stone had lived with the worker for six years before his death, but during that time she was married to someone else. She filed for death benefits as a "concubine." Specifically, she asked the Rhode Island Supreme Court if a "concubine" who had been financially dependent on the worker for six years before his death is a "member of the family" for the purposes of the worker's-compensation statute. The court held that she was not a member of the family because she was not related by "blood or marriage" (*Stone*).

A few states have amended their statutes to deal with this problem. The Oregon statute allows a person who has "cohabited" with the worker for at least one year before the worker's death, and who had a child with the worker, to collect death benefits. In a recent Oregon case the couple cohabited for three years and had a child. However, one month before his death, the worker had moved out. The Oregon Supreme Court ruled that his girlfriend could not get death benefits because they were not cohabiting at the time of his death (*Cottrell*).

Disqualification

Most statutes have a list of things that will disqualify a worker from receiving compensation. Many states disqualify workers who are injured because of their own "willful misconduct." About half the states disqualify workers who "willfully disobey safety rules." Many states will not allow a worker to collect if he or she was intoxicated at the time of the injury. However, some courts say the intoxication must be the sole cause of the injury. If the injury would have happened regardless of the intoxication, the worker can still receive compensation and the burden is on the employer to prove the accident was caused solely by the intoxication (*Bama Tran., Poole*).

Many states will not allow dependents to collect death benefits if the worker committed suicide. There are two main exceptions to that rule: (1) if the worker was driven crazy by the job before the suicide, or (2) if the worker received an injury on the job, which caused insanity, which in turn caused the suicide. In one case a security guard shot a robbery suspect and was so upset he then shot and killed himself. His widow received benefits (*Globe Sec.*). When a doctor, hospitalized for depression after being sued for malpractice, committed suicide, his widow received benefits (*McGill*).

Weekly Benefits

In most cases the worker receives a weekly payment equal to a percentage of his or her average weekly wages (up to a maximum set by law). This is another reason everyone should keep track of wages. This can include overtime pay if the worker regularly received overtime pay (*Bradley*). If the worker has two jobs, then the wages are added together to get the worker's average weekly wage (*Boles*). The value of fringe benefits may also be included (*Ragland*).

These statutes have complex rules concerning how much the worker's benefits are to be reduced if the worker is receiving a pension (*Baltimore*). The Social Security rules require that the combined worker's-compensation payments and Social Security disability payments add up to not more than 80 percent of what the worker was actually earning before he or she became disabled (*Larimer County*).

Second-Injury Fund

Most states have a second-injury fund. This fund pays if a worker who has already been injured is injured again, and the second injury is worse because of the prior injury. The idea is to encourage employers to hire disabled workers. Of course, in the real world, many employers will not hire workers if they know they have received worker's-compensation payments in the past. This fact causes most employees to lie about previous compensation if asked. Withholding this information is usually not going to keep the worker from getting compensation unless keeping the prior injury a secret "caused" the new injury (*McDaniel, Ledbetter*).

Medical Expenses

Besides paying money to the worker to compensate for lost wage-earning capacity, worker's compensation is also supposed to pay medical expenses. Different states have different rules on such issues as who chooses the doctor and what expenses are included. In some states, such as Virginia, the worker has to go to the employer's doctor, and if he or she does not go, the employer does not have to pay the doctor bills. Of course there are going to be times when employees should still go to a doctor of their own choosing. In one recent Virginia case the only reason the worker collected anything from worker's compensation was because the worker had a doctor at the hearing who contradicted the employer's doctor (*Richmond Memorial*).

In some states, such as Kansas, if the worker is unhappy with the employer's doctor, he or she can ask the Worker's Compensation Agency to pick a doctor (*IBP*). In many states the employee is free to choose any doctor. In Oregon the employee is even allowed to get a second opinion (*Welch*).

The employer, or the insurance company, also has to pay for other medical-type expenses that result from the injury. Recently the Pennsylvania Appeals Court ordered the employer to pay for hand controls on the worker's car and for remodeling his home to accommodate a wheelchair. The court said these expenses constituted "orthopedic appliances" and were therefore covered by worker's compensation (*Rieger*). Medical expenses can include the cost of home care (*Bello*).

Temporary or Permanent; Partial or Total

Worker's-compensation insurance is really several different kinds of insurance in one. First, it is life insurance. If the worker dies from a work-related injury or illness, his or her dependents are taken care of. Second, it is medical insurance. It pays the hospital and doctor bills for a work-related injury or illness. Third, it provides short-term disability payments for temporarily disabled workers. Fourth and finally, it provides compensation for the *loss* the worker has suffered. The worker may have lost a hand or an eye or been disfigured. Also, the worker may have suffered a loss in wage-earning capacity. In most states worker's compensation does not provide long-term income-replacement payments to disabled workers. Social Security does, and we will discuss that in Chapter 17. What worker's compensation does provide is an amount of money intended to compensate the disabled worker for the physical loss and the loss in wage-earning capacity caused by the accident. This loss is figured in terms of number of weeks times the worker's average weekly wage. In most states a totally and permanently disabled worker receives between 300 and 500 times his or her average weekly wage.

Most statutes have four basic kinds of coverage for workers who survive the accident. The worker can receive payment from any one of the four sources, and can receive payment from all four over time, but he or she can receive only one type of payment at a time. The four categories are Partial Temporary, Total Temporary, Partial Permanent, and Total Permanent. Throughout this system, the payments are based on a percentage (between 50 and 70 percent) of the worker's average weekly wage (up to a maximum).

Temporary Partial pays the worker who is injured, but can still work, for a temporary physical loss. Someone who can work only a limited number of hours a week, or cannot use a hand or leg temporarily, would qualify for this.

Total Temporary disability means the worker is injured and cannot work at all for a while. In some systems a totally disabled worker goes on Total Temporary disability first to see if he or she is going to recover.

Partial Permanent disability means the worker can still work at some jobs but either has suffered a permanent loss (such as a lost arm or leg) or has suffered a permanent reduction in wage-earning capacity (can no longer do high-paying work).

Total Permanent disability means the worker is so disabled he or she cannot do any kind of work.

Many worker's-compensation statutes also contain a Scheduled Injury section. This part of the law spells out what a lost hand or eye is worth. A lost thumb might be worth 60 weeks of wages. A lost eye might be worth 300 weeks of wages. Remember, the payment is to compensate for the *physical loss*, and whether or not the worker is still able to work is irrelevant (*Bethlehem Mines*).

In some states if the worker has a "scheduled loss," he or she gets whatever the schedule says and that is the end of it. In other states the schedule is only a minimum. If the worker is entitled to more through one of the four types of coverage, then he or she gets that instead. In a few states the worker can recover from both the schedule and the other four types of coverage.

Recently the Tennessee and Arkansas Supreme Courts said that a worker must stop getting Total Temporary payments when either of two events occur: when the worker is able to go back to work or when the worker attains the maximum level of recovery. At that point the worker gets either some kind of permanent-disability payment or a payment from the schedule (*Roberson, Guffey*).

The question of whether someone is stuck with the scheduled amount often depends on the full extent of the injury. If the impact was to the leg, but the injury extends beyond the leg, then the worker has more than a scheduled injury. Recently the Kansas Supreme Court made this point in a case that involved injury to the left elbow (*Bryant*). The award of permanent partial disability instead of the scheduled amount for an arm was correct because the pain went up into the shoulder. The court said the key is the location of the disability, not the impact. Generally, it is to the worker's advantage to have more than a scheduled injury and to find pain in the shoulder or hip if the arm or leg is injured. A total and permanent disability can "arise out of" a scheduled injury (*Mendez #2, Alva*).

In some cases the award is for lost earning capacity even if the physical symptoms have disappeared. In a recent Rhode Island case the worker was a cook who suffered a back injury. The doctor testified that the worker could no longer be a cook because doing the things required of a cook would cause the injury to recur. Even though the worker no longer had any physical symptoms, he was entitled to Partial Permanent compensation because he had suffered a loss in wage-earning capacity (*Herley*).

The largest award is for Total and Permanent disability. There is a big difference between the legal definition of "disability" and the medical definition of "incapacity." A worker can be partially incapacitated and still be totally and permanently disabled. To illustrate, in a recent Utah case the worker had been a coal miner for 39 years before a heavy cable fell on him. The doctors testified that before the accident the coal miner had a 14 percent impairment to the whole body as a result of previous injuries, and after the accident he had a 31 percent impairment to the whole body. As the Utah Supreme Court pointed out, the degree of impairment is a medical finding, the degree of disability is a legal finding. The court said we must look at the individual's work history, educational level, age, and past injuries as well as the injury resulting from this particular accident. In this case the miner managed to continue to work for several years after the injury, but he had to go to the hospital often for traction and he never recovered. The court found him to be totally and permanently disabled (*Norton*).

If an injured worker, because of age, education, and work history, is not able to get a job, then he or she is totally and permanently disabled (*Swan*). This is true even though a younger, better-educated worker might be able to get a job and would not be disabled. In a recent Arkansas case a man who worked with his hands suffered torn biceps tendons. He was 50 years old and had a high-school education. The court awarded total and permanent disability (*Atchley*).

One of the things that is hard to understand is that a worker can receive compensation for Total and Permanent disability more than once. A worker can be totally and permanently disabled, get another job, have another injury, and be totally and permanently disabled again. Or, a worker can receive partial benefits for one injury and then total benefits for another injury. In a South Carolina case the worker received 248 weeks of compensation for his first back injury. He received 500 weeks (the maximum for Total and Permanent) for his second back injury. In a sense, he was now one and a half times totally disabled (*Wyndham*).

Claims Procedure

Worker's compensation is controlled by a state agency. While different states have different names for this agency, many call it the Industrial Accident Commission. In many states this commission has three members: one represents employers, one represents workers, and one is neutral.

Notice

The statutes require two kinds of notice when a worker feels he or she has had a work-related injury: notice to the employer and notice to the commission.

TABLE 15–1. Worker's Compensation Statutes*

State	Notice Requirement	Citation
Alabama	5 days to notify boss.	25-5-1 to 231
Alaska	30 days to notify boss.	23.30.005 to 270
Arizona	Notify boss forthwith. Optional for employee. No fellow-servant doctrine. Jury decides risk assumption.	23-901 to 1073; Const. Art. 18, sec. 4,5,8
Arkansas	60 days to notify boss.	81-1301 to 1367
California	Unclear.	Labor Code 3201 to 6149
Colorado	2 days to notify boss.	8-40-101 to 8-66-112
Connecticut	Notify boss forthwith.	31-275 to 355a
Delaware	90 days to notify boss.	19-2101 to 2397
District of Columbia	30 days to notify boss and Mayor.	36-301 to 345
Florida	30 days to notify boss.	440
Georgia	Unclear.	34-9-1 to 367
Hawaii	Notify boss as soon as practicable. Temp. disability ins. provided. Health ins. provided.	386–1 to 174 392-1 to 101 393-1 to 51
Idaho	Notify boss as soon as practicable (60-day max.).	72-101 to 1429S
Illinois	Notify boss as soon as practicable (45 day max.). Optional for employee.	Ch. 48
Indiana	Unclear.	22-3-1-1 to 22-3-11-5
Iowa	90 days to notify boss.	85.1 to 87.22
Kansas	Unclear.	44-501 to 5a22
Kentucky	Notify boss as soon as practicable. Optional for employee.	342.001 to 990
Louisiana	30 days to notify boss.	23:1021 to 1379
Maine	30 days to notify boss.	39-1 to 195
Maryland	10 days to notify boss.	Art. 101, secs. 1 to 102
Massachusetts	Notify boss as soon as practicable. Optional for employee.	Ch. 152
Michigan	90 days to notify boss.	Ch. 418
Minnesota	14 days to notify boss (notice within 180 days may be all right).	176.001 to .85
Mississippi	30 days to notify boss.	71-3-1 to 119
Missouri	30 days to notify boss.	287.010 to 810
Montana	30 days to notify boss.	39-71-101 to 2914
Nebraska	Notify boss as soon as practicable.	48-101 to 1109
Nevada	30 days to notify boss.	616.010 to 680
New Hampshire	2 years to notify boss.	281
New Jersey	14 days to notify boss (notice	34:15-1 to 128

*The law is always changing. Consult an attorney about your situation.

TABLE 15–1. (Cont.)

	within 90 days may be all right). Optional for boss and employee.	
New Mexico	30 days to notify boss.	Ch. 52
New York	30 days to notify boss.	Worker's Comp.
North Carolina	Notify boss as soon as practicable (30-day max.).	Ch. 97
North Dakota	Unclear.	Title 65
Ohio	Unclear.	4123
Oklahoma	60 days to notify boss.	Title 85
Oregon	30 days to notify boss.	Ch. 656
Pennsylvania	21 days to notify boss (notice within 120 days may be all right).	Title 77
Rhode Island	30 days to notify boss. Optional for employee.	28-29-1 to 28-37-31
South Carolina	Notify boss as soon as practicable (90-day max.). Optional for boss and employee.	Title 42
South Dakota	Notify boss as soon as practicable (30-day max.).	Title 62
Tennessee	Notify boss as soon as practicable (30-day max.).	50-6
Texas	30 days to notify boss. Optional for boss and employee.	Art. 8306 to 8309-1
	May sue for punitive damages if death resulted from gross negligence or willful act or omission.	Const. Art. 16, sec. 26
Utah	48 hours to notify boss (notice within one year may be all right).	Title 35
Vermont	Notify boss as soon as practicable.	Title 21, secs. 601 to 710
Virginia	Notify boss as soon as practicable (30-day max.).	65.1
Washington	Notify boss forthwith.	Title 51
West Virginia	Notify boss as soon as practicable.	Ch. 23
Wisconsin	30 days to notify boss.	102
Wyoming	72 hours to notify boss. Notify county clerk within 10 days.	27–14

Usually the worker must notify the employer quickly (see Table 15–1). In some situations the worker knows about the injury but does not realize the injury is work-related. Generally, the worker's obligation to give everyone notice does not begin until he or she knows, or a reasonable person would have known, that the injury was work-related.

Recently the Tennessee Supreme Court had to tell Linda Sue Puckett she could not receive worker's compensation (*Puckett*). The doctor told her in January 1984 that her arthritis-like symptoms were caused by her job. At that point, under Tennessee law, she had 30 days to notify her employer of a work-related injury. She did not and lost any chance of getting worker's compensation.

The worker also has to notify the commission before the deadline. In a recent Virginia case Patricia Garcia was injured on February 25, 1982, and notified the commission on March 19, 1984. Since Virginia worker's have two years to notify the commission, Patricia Garcia could not receive worker's compensation (*Mantech*).

There is something to consider before filing a claim for worker's compensation. We will discuss in Chapter 16 when a worker can sue the employer for a physical injury. In many states if the worker files for worker's compensation, he or she cannot sue the employer later for the same injury. Workers who think they might want to sue their employer for an injury should consult an attorney right away.

Settlements and Releases

The goal is for the injured worker and the worker's-compensation insurance company or state insurance fund to come to an agreed settlement. This happens in 90 percent of the cases. This is a dangerous time for the worker. Workers should not settle with an insurance company until they have discussed their case with an attorney. In some states the Industrial Accident Commission has to approve the settlement. In other states the worker can go to the commission and have the settlement overturned if it turns out to have been unfair.

In one case the employer told the worker if he would sign a little piece of paper, he would be put back on the payroll. The worker signed and was fired. The little piece of paper was a settlement agreement ending his worker's-compensation claim. The Pennsylvania court overturned this agreement because the employer had induced the worker to sign the agreement by misrepresentation and because the worker was still disabled. The worker had to prove both things to get out of the agreement (*Exxon #2*).

Reductions, Increases, Discontinuation, Reinstatement

In most lawsuits there is a final end to the case. This is not true of worker's compensation in many states. If something changes, either the employer or the worker can go back to the commission to ask for more or less compensation or to ask to stop or restart compensation payments. What either side has to prove in order to accomplish this differs from state to state.

In Pennsylvania, if the employer wants to reduce the compensation, he has to prove not only that the worker is physically capable of doing work but also that there actually are jobs available for this particular worker (*Kachinski*).

In most states the employer cannot just stop paying compensation when he or she hears the worker has gotten a job. The employer has to go to the commission and get permission. In a recent case the Rhode Island Supreme Court made the employer pay the worker 20 percent extra because the employer had stopped compensation payments without permission (*Lavey*).

Generally, for a worker to get increased compensation, he or she has to prove his or her physical condition has gotten worse and that the worsened condition resulted from the original injury.

There is a big difference between "recurrence" of an old injury and "aggravation" of an old injury. In a recent Rhode Island case, the court found that the worker had a recurrence of an old injury. He got compensation again, but at the old compensation rate. If it had been an aggravation (meaning his present job increased his old injury), then he would have been entitled to a higher rate based on his new, higher wages (*Mignowe*).

On Appeal

Different states have different appeal procedures. Once the hearing officer has made a decision, either side can appeal to the full commission. After that, in most states, the appeal goes to a district judge, then an appeals court, and finally to the state supreme court.

In most states, if either side wants to appeal the decision of the commission, they have to act quickly (usually within 30 days). Most courts use the "substantial evidence test." If the decision of the commission is supported by substantial evidence, then the court will uphold it. Of course, the courts are free to tell the commission how to interpret the statute. They are also free to decide what kind of procedure is acceptable. In other words, if you (employer or worker) feel there was not substantial evidence to support the decision against you, or your constitutional or procedural rights were violated, or the statute was not interpreted correctly, you should appeal your case to a court. In Texas and Maryland neither side is stuck with the facts as found by the commission and each can get a whole new trial in front of a judge and jury. In every other state that is not possible. Once the commission decides the facts, those are the facts and no judge can change them.

Generally, the worker is going to need the help of an attorney. In Wyoming the county attorney will help. In Minnesota the attorneys at the state department of labor will help workers with worker's-compensation claims.

FEDERAL LAWS

Over the course of the last century Congress has passed a number of special statutes for special groups of workers. Three groups of workers benefit from these laws: sailors, railroad workers, and longshoremen.

Sailors

There are three things a sailor can sue the employer for when injured. The first is **maintenance and cure**. In medieval law a master had to care for an injured apprentice regardless of how the apprentice became injured. American judges did away with that duty for everyone except ship owners. The judges felt that many sailors are far from home when injured, and therefore the employer has a special responsibility to care for an injured sailor.

Secondly, the employer has a duty to provide a **seaworthy vessel.** Because of the obvious risks that result from being on an unseaworthy vessel, judges require ship owners to provide a safe ship. This is an absolute duty. If the ship is unseaworthy and an injury results, the employer pays regardless of "fault" in the usual sense.

Finally, Congress passed a statute many years ago called the **Jones Act** (46 U.S.C. sec. 688). This act allows an injured sailor to sue the employer for negligence and takes the unholy trinity of defenses away from the employer.

Anyone who works on a boat in a navigable waterway is a sailor, even if it is on a river or a lake. A sailor not only gets money to pay for his doctor bills and basic living expenses while injured (maintenance and cure) but he or she is also allowed to sue if the boat was unsafe in any way, or the employer was negligent. In a sense, sailors have the best of all worlds. In a recent Illinois case the jury awarded $1,250,000 to the injured sailor, far more than any worker would receive from worker's compensation (*Ruffiner*).

Longshoremen and Harbor Workers

For longshoremen and harbor workers there is a special federal worker's compensation statute that is administered by the U.S. Labor Department called the Longshoremen and Harbor Workers Compensation Act (LHWCA). It pays higher benefits than most state worker's-compensation statutes. Many workers who would be entitled to these payments do not get them because they do not realize they are harbor workers under the law. The federal government has jurisdiction over any navigable waterway. That means people who work along most rivers and lakes in the United States are harbor workers and are covered by the act. In 1980 the U.S. Supreme Court held that a worker is entitled to receive the best of both worlds: if the state act is better in any way, the injured worker can recover under the state as well as the federal act (*Sun Ship*).

Railroad Workers

There are two federal laws for railroad workers. The first is the Federal Safety Appliance Act of 1893 (45 U.S.C. sec. 1). This law says that if a railroad employee is injured by a piece of railroad equipment, the railroad company pays the costs. The worker does not have to prove the employer was negligent. In a recent case the automatic coupling system failed to work and the switchman got hurt when he tried to couple the cars manually. The railroad had to pay. The court did not want to know if anyone, either the worker or the company, was at fault (*Leveck*). In another case the worker hurt his back trying to release the handbrake. The jury awarded $470,000 in damages (*Geiser*).

Another federal law is the Federal Employers Liability Act (FELA) (45 U.S.C.

sec. 51). This act allows an injured railroad worker to sue if the employer is negligent, just as all workers could do under the common law a century ago. In 1939 Congress amended the law and removed the unholy trinity of defenses from the railroads. Cases that are tried under this act give us an idea of what the world would be like if the judges had not invented the unholy trinity of defenses in the first place and the states had not responded with worker's-compensation insurance. First of all, the injured worker has to prove the employer was negligent. That means the employer breached one of the duties employers owe to employees.

For example, in a recent Georgia case the injured railroad worker was hit by a piece of metal protruding from the side of a boxcar. The worker sued the railroad company for breach of the duty to provide a safe place to work and breach of the duty to warn workers about hazardous conditions. The jury awarded $561,282 in damages (*Seaboard*). In a recent Texas case the worker hurt his shoulder when he was forced to jump off a runaway train. The jury awarded $400,000 for future physical impairment; $900,000 for lost future earning capacity; $343,000 for pain, suffering, and medical expenses; and $150,000 for punitive damages (finding the railroad company to be grossly negligent) (*Southern Pacific*).

Of course, the injured railroad workers do not always recover. They have to prove negligence or that the equipment caused the injury. In one case the worker suffered a heart attack at the railyard in a situation where he would probably have collected under worker's compensation. The jury found that the railroad company was not negligent, and the worker got nothing (*Greenfield*).

THIRD-PARTY DEFENDANTS

In many cases the worker is hurt on the job and worker's compensation pays. At the same time there is a third party whom the worker could sue and recover from. In these situations it is in everyone's interest for the worker to sue that third party. In most states the employer or his insurance company has a **right of subrogation.** That means if the worker recovers from the third party, he or she has to pay back the worker's-compensation benefits. This is an ideal system for the injured worker. He or she has a sure, if small, recovery from worker's compensation helping to pay basic living expenses. The worker also has a chance at a really big recovery in a court of law. The employer has an incentive to cooperate because if the worker wins, the employer is off the hook for worker's compensation.

Manufacturers

Whom are we suing? Anybody other than the employer who had something to do with the injury. Often we are suing the maker of some piece of equipment that was defective and caused the injury. In one case the worker lost a thumb and three fingers on his left hand while operating a radial saw that the jury decided was defective. The jury awarded $792,000 (*Bussell*). In another case the worker lost an arm and received $35,000 from worker's compensation. He sued the machine's Italian manufacturer and received $800,000 from an American jury (*Mason*).

Medical Malpractice

Some injured workers die in the hospital because of medical malpractice. If the widow(er) sues and proves malpractice, then the worker's-compensation company is off the hook. If there is no malpractice, and the worker dies in the hospital, then worker's compensation pays just as if the worker had died instantly at the job (*Powell*).

The Landlord

In some cases the employee sues the owner of the property the employer leases. Even if the property owner is a parent company or subsidiary of the employer, it is a different entity and can be sued (*Kiehl*).

On the Streets

The streets of America are very dangerous. Many workers are hurt or killed in car accidents in circumstances where worker's compensation must pay off. If the worker can sue and recover from the driver of the other car, everyone stands to gain.

Co-workers

Generally, if a co-worker causes the worker's injury, the co-worker cannot be sued. He or she is protected by the worker's-compensation statute just as the employer is. However, there are times when the co-worker can be sued. The Arkansas Supreme Court recently said an injured worker can sue the co-worker if the co-worker's actions were willful or intentional (*Fore*). The Connecticut statute allows a worker to sue a co-worker if the case involves the use of a motor vehicle (*Kiriaka*).

A recent Indiana case illustrates how a co-worker might be sued even in a case involving simple negligence. Karen Seiler's supervisor was showing her how to use a pistol when it went off and injured her. The Indiana Appeals Court said whether or not Karen could sue this co-worker, the president of the company, depended on why he was showing her the gun. If he was showing her the gun so she could use it to defend herself at work (she was a bartender), then the co-worker could not be sued. On the other hand, if he was showing her the gun for personal reasons (to show it off), then she could sue him for her injuries (*Seiler*).

If the co-worker is the company doctor and has committed malpractice, some states will allow the worker to sue, even though the doctor is a co-worker (*Stover*).

Dual Capacity

On occasion the employer acts in a dual capacity, as both employer and product provider. What if the worker is hurt, not because of on-the-job negligence, but because the product is defective? In most states the injured worker can sue the employer, not as employer but as product maker. In one case a Uniroyal truck driver was injured when one of the Uniroyal tires on his truck blew out. The Ohio Appeals Court said he could sue Uniroyal as the maker of a defective product, just as any other consumer could (*Mercer*).

SUING THE INSURANCE COMPANY

There are many times when the worker feels more injured by the insurance company than by the original accident. In some states the worker is prevented, either by statute or by court decisions, from suing the worker's-compensation insurance company. That is not true of all states, and more courts are allowing these lawsuits.

Bad Faith

There is a general legal principle that says: Implied in every insurance policy is the promise from the insurance company that it will act with good faith toward both the person paying the premiums and the beneficiaries of the policy. While some state courts hold that this does not apply to worker's-compensation insurance, other states will allow such lawsuits. In 1987 the South Dakota Supreme Court allowed a worker to sue an insurance company for intentional, fraudulent, and bad-faith termination of worker's-compensation benefits (*Cert. Question*).

A number of states have deceptive trade-practice acts and special insurance statutes that allow insurance companies to be sued for up to triple the actual amount owed if they acted deceptively or in bad faith. Recently both the Minnesota and Texas Supreme Courts allowed this to happen to worker's-compensation insurance companies. In the Minnesota case the insurance company kept trying to terminate benefits. Finally, the worker's-compensation agency awarded a penalty to the worker under a special provision of the worker's-compensation statute. In addition the Minnesota Supreme Court allowed the worker also to sue for triple damages in court (*Kaluza*). In a recent Texas case, when the insurance company failed to live up to a settlement agreement, the Texas Supreme Court awarded triple the $30,355 owed by the insurance company, plus $50,000 in punitive damages, and made the insurance company pay the worker's attorney fees (*Aetna*; see also *Aranda*).

Intentional Injury

In other cases the worker has been allowed to sue the insurance company for things such as fraud or intentional infliction of emotional distress. In one case, Ms. Young was assaulted at work and suffered emotional trauma. The insurance company refused to pay the psychiatrist's bills. When she called the insurance company, the insurance agent told her that she was crazy and if it were up to him she "would not get a penny." Ms. Young then tried to kill herself. The Maryland Supreme Court said she could sue the insurance company for intentional infliction of emotional distress (*Hartford*).

Negligent Safety Inspections

Many worker's-compensation insurance companies perform safety inspections. If they do this negligently, should the injured workers be allowed to sue? Recently the Massachusetts Supreme Court held that the worker could not sue the insurance company for negligently performing safety inspections. The court expressed the fear that if they were held liable, the insurance companies would stop conducting safety inspections (*Swift*).

The Supreme Court of Vermont recently held that Vermont workers could sue for negligent safety inspections by insurance companies. The Vermont Supreme Court felt "no inspection is better than a negligent inspection" (*Derosia*).

SHOULD EMPLOYEES OPT OUT OF THE SYSTEM?

In New Jersey, South Carolina, Texas, Arizona, Kentucky, Rhode Island, Massachusetts, and Illinois (and possibly other states) workers can opt out of the system and take their chances with the common law. Should workers do this? That is a difficult question to answer. If workers could prove negligence, they would receive more than they would under worker's compensation. Take a recent case. Lorenzo Sanchez lost his right hand in a potato harvester and sued his employer. As a farm worker he was not covered by worker's compensation. The Idaho Supreme Court upheld an award of $1,350,000 (*Sanchez*).

What about the unholy trinity of defenses? In many states the concept of contributory negligence has been replaced by comparative negligence. Under contributory negligence, if a person is the least bit at fault, he or she receives nothing. Under comparative negligence, a person who is partly at fault can still recover some money from the other person. This would allow workers to receive some money even if they are partly responsible for the accident.

Several state supreme courts have done away with the idea that workers "assume the risk of injury" just by taking the job. The Texas Supreme Court did away with this concept in 1975 finding that once a system of comparative negligence is adopted, the concept of assumption of the risk no longer makes sense (*Farley*). The Nevada Supreme Court did the same thing in 1987 (*Central Telephone*).

What about the fellow-servant doctrine, which says if a co-worker is involved, the injured worker cannot sue the employer? This doctrine grew out of and was tied directly to the assumption-of-the-risk doctrine. Logically, if one goes, so does the other. The odds are that a modern court would eliminate both given half a chance.

Several states have statutes or constitutional provisions that eliminate or limit these defenses. The Arizona Constitution eliminates the fellow-servant doctrine and says the question of assumption of the risk is strictly up to the jury (Ariz. Const. Art. 18, sec. 4,5).

Of course injured workers have to prove the employer was negligent. Also, if workers opt out, they should make sure their medical insurance will pay for a work-related injury. Many exclude this.

Workers who wish to opt out of worker's compensation must follow the state's rules. Texas and Massachusetts allow the worker to opt out only when first hired. Rhode Island and Illinois give the worker a chance to opt out once a year.

THE FUTURE

John Doe was covered by a very good benefit package at work when he was hurt badly in a church softball game. The group medical insurance covered the doctor and hospital bills. The short-term disability insurance paid him almost what he had been earning to cover his living expenses. There was no hassle with the insurance company. A few months after returning to work he suffered a hernia on the job. The worker's-compensation insurance company took over. Even though the injury was clearly work-related, they refused to pay any benefits, including the doctor bills. Their attitude was "sue me."

What kind of system would an enlightened state create that would minimize the insurance hassle and reduce this gap between the benefit package and worker's compensation? First, a modern state would require the employer to provide some kind of major medical insurance that would pay whether the injury is work-related or not. The worker might be required to pay half the premiums. The employer would pay the rest, including the extra premium required because of the safety record of his company. Massachusetts has just implemented mandatory medical insurance. Hawaii has had it for several years (Ha. 393-1 to 51).

Second, a modern state would require some kind of short-term disability insurance that would pay for living expenses whether the injury was work-related or not. Again, the worker might pay part of the premiums with the employer picking up the rest of the bill. Several states have temporary-disability systems separate from worker's compensation. The federal Social Security system is supposed to take care of long-term disability payments. A modern state might leave that up to the federal government.

Third, a modern state might require every employer to offer every worker some kind of life-insurance policy that would pay off whether the death occurred at work or not. The premiums might be divided between the worker and the employer, with the employer paying any extra premium required because the company kills workers on a regular basis.

That leaves one kind of coverage that is provided by the present worker's-compensation system, the payment for the *loss* to the worker. The present system, through the schedule and awards for permanent disability, tries to compensate the worker for physical loss and lost earning capacity. What if we had a system that said every worker was worth a certain amount—let's say $100,000? A totally and permanently disabled worker would receive this for his or her *loss* on top of the disability payments under the short-term disability policy and the Social Security system. A lost eye might be worth $20,000. A total loss in wage-earning capacity would entitle the worker to the full $100,000. In no case would a worker receive more than a total of $100,000. With medical and short-term disability payments coming automatically, the only issue would be the amount of the loss, and whether or not the injury was work-related.

16
Intentional Injury and Suing the Boss

The law distinguishes between **intentional injury** and **negligence.** Someone is negligent if he or she has not been careful enough and an accident has resulted. If employees have been physically or emotionally injured at work because of negligence, worker's compensation is supposed to take care of them. They cannot sue.

If an employer or supervisor negligently causes injury other than physical or emotional injury, the employee can sue. If an employer or supervisor intentionally causes injury of any kind, even physical or emotional, the employee can sue (in most states).

There are four main reasons employees sue employers: the employer lied to the employee, the employer lied about the employee, the employer intentionally caused emotional injury, the employer intentionally caused physical injury.

LYING TO THE EMPLOYEE

If an employer tells an employee something that turns out to be untrue, the employee can sue. If the employer knew what he or she was saying was untrue (or was reckless regarding the truth), it is called **fraud.** If the employer did not know it was a lie but was negligent in not trying to find out before speaking, it is called **misrepresentation.**

Many cases are decided on summary judgment. That means there is no trial. The trial judge reads the petition of the employee and rules that, even if everything the employee said was true, he or she would still lose. If the petitioner is going to lose in the end, there is no need to bother with a trial.

This is illustrated by the *Shebar* case. Arthur Shebar sued Sanyo Corporation, and the trial judge ruled against him on summary judgment. Shebar appealed to the New Jersey Supreme Court, which ruled that if he could prove everything he alleged, he should win.

What did Shebar allege? Shebar was the national sales manager of Sanyo's U.S computer division. He was given awards by the company, but in September 1984 he decided to look for another job. He felt he would never be promoted because he was not Japanese. Shebar was offered a job with Sony as national sales manager, with the assurance that he would be made a vice president within a reasonable time. On October 1, 1984, he submitted his resignation to Sanyo. His Japanese supervisors ripped it up and told him they would "solve his problems." Shebar says they told him he would receive a raise in March, and that he had a job for the rest of his life. They told him Sanyo would never fire anyone with the rank of manager or above. Shebar stayed with Sanyo and was fired four months later. He sued for fraud.

To make out a case of fraud an employee has to prove the employer lied and knew it was a lie at the time (or was reckless); the employer intended the employee to rely on the lie; the employee did rely on the lie; and the employee was damaged as a result. The New Jersey Supreme Court sent the case back for a jury to decide if all that had happened.

Shebar accused his employer of intentionally lying to him (fraud). What if the lie was a result of negligence? Maria D'Ulisse-Cupo was a teacher at Notre Dame High School. Her supervisor told her several times in the spring that she would be rehired in the fall. She could have looked for another job if she had known she would not be rehired. She did not look for another job and she was not rehired after all. The Connecticut Supreme Court said she could sue for misrepresentation (*D'Ulisse-Cupo*).

In these cases whether or not the employee recovers often depends on whether the employer was making a promise or stating a fact. In one case the employer stated as a fact that the employees would work for the company for at least eight years and the jury awarded damages of $135,000 (*Bernoudy*). In a Utah case the employer said he was in the business of selling insurance, gold, and securities. It turned out the employer was only licensed to sell insurance. The employee had been induced to quit his old job because of these lies and was allowed to recover for his damages (*Conder*).

At the beginning of the twentieth century it was a common practice for employers to place ads in newspapers to recruit employees to move to another state. When the employees arrived, they often found that they had been hired to be strike breakers or that the working conditions were nothing like the advertisements. This was particularly true of employers in the western states. Several states passed statutes to deal with this problem. These statutes are still on the books in at least nine states: Alaska (23.10.015 to 030), California (Labor Code 970 to 977), Colorado (8-2-104 to 107), Minnesota (181.64 and 181.65), Montana (39-2-303), Nevada (613.010 to 030), Oklahoma (tit. 40 sec. 167, 170), Tennessee (50-1-102), and Wisconsin (103.43). These statutes are virtually identical. They generally say that if an employer induces an employee to move (either into the state or from one place to another within the state) by "means of false representations" concerning the "character of the work," the "compensation," the "conditions of employment," or the existence of a "strike or lockout," then the employee can sue the employer for "all damages" and attorney fees. The California statute allows the court to award double the amount of actual damages. Most of these statutes also make this activity a crime, for which the employer and the supervisor can be fined and put in jail for at least a year. Employers in these states should be particularly careful about what they say to prospective employees, particularly if the employees are going to have to move in order to accept the job.

Sometimes the worker can sue the employer not because the employer lied but because the employer did not tell the employee something. In a New Jersey case, a group of employees sued Du Pont alleging that the company doctors had known these employees were suffering from diseases caused by asbestos exposure and had deliberately kept it from them (*Millison*). In a Michigan case a research chemist alleged that Dow had hidden the potential dangers involved in working with "agent orange" (*Beauchamp*). Both cases involved **fraudulent concealment.** In some situations the law says people have a duty to tell what they know in order to prevent harm. The allegations in these two cases are classic examples of this. An employer or supervisor has a duty to tell employees that they are being exposed to dangerous chemicals or are already suffering from such exposure.

The lower courts in both these cases granted summary judgment for the companies. The supreme courts of New Jersey and Michigan sent the cases back for trial. They said that, if the employees could prove their allegations, they should be allowed to recover for their damages. Both companies argued that worker's compensation should take care of this and that the employees should not be allowed to sue. Both supreme courts held that worker's compensation was intended to deal with negligence, and if a worker could prove intentional conduct, he or she could sue in court to recover damages. Intentionally concealing a dangerous aspect of the working environment is something for which employees can sue their employers.

LYING ABOUT THE EMPLOYEE

If the employer lies about the employee, the law calls it **defamation.** If it is oral, it is called **slander.** If it is written, it is called **libel.** To prove defamation the employee has to prove that the employer said something untrue about the employee, that the employer "published" it, meaning the employer told it to someone other than the employee, and that the employee's reputation was damaged as a result. It is usually easy to prove that the employer said something that damaged the employee's reputation and that what was said was untrue. These cases usually come down to whether the employer abused the privilege and whether or not the defamatory statement was published.

The courts have always allowed some people to be privileged in our legal system. The idea is that a general good can be accomplished only if we allow people in certain situations to be free from the worry of being sued. There are two types of privileges: absolute and conditional.

An **absolute privilege** means someone cannot be sued. For example, judges have an absolute privilege relating to the decisions they make as judges. The law wants judges to do what they think is right without worrying about lawsuits.

A **conditional privilege** means the person has a privilege, but he or she can lose the privilege if it is abused. The law says that employers and supervisors have a privilege to speak about employees to people who need to know about the employees, such as other employers and supervisors. If the employer or supervisor happens to lie about the employee, that is usually acceptable. In other words, employers and supervisors have a privilege to defame their employees. However, this is a conditional privilege.

Employers and supervisors can lose the privilege if they know what they are saying about the employee is false at the time they say it; if they are reckless about whether or not it is true; or if they talk to someone they are not privileged to talk to, such as their customers (*Shannon*).

In one case a prospective employer called a school superintendent about a teacher. The superintendent said the teacher had been a bad teacher. In fact, the teacher had an excellent record. The superintendent had never observed the teacher in class and had never received any negative comments about the teacher from parents or fellow teachers. The jury found that this superintendent lost his privilege because he either knew what he was saying was untrue or showed a reckless disregard for the truth (*True*).

In another case an Exxon auditor tracked the employee down at a crowded restaurant in order to accuse him of stealing money from the company. The court held that, while the auditor had a privilege to talk to some people about this problem, he was not privileged to tell it to the people who happened to be in that restaurant. At one moment the auditor had both published the defamation (told it to people other than the worker) and violated his privilege (by telling it to people not covered by the privilege) (*Exxon #1*).

A 1986 decision by the Minnesota Supreme Court has made it even easier for employees to win defamation suits against supervisors and employers (*Equitable*). Carole Lewis and three other former employees sued the Equitable Life Assurance Society for breach of the employee handbook and defamation. These employees were dental-claim approvers in the St. Paul office. In the fall of 1980 the company's Pittsburgh office asked for help to deal with a heavy work load. Lewis and her colleagues were sent to Pittsburgh for two weeks to help out. They had never traveled on company business before. The St. Paul office manager was responsible for explaining company travel-expense policy to them before the trip but because he was out of the office at the time, this task fell to his secretary, who had never given these kinds of instructions before. The secretary did not tell them detailed expense reports would have to be filled out when they returned. The employees were each given a $1,400 travel advance, which they spent in full. When the four employees returned to St. Paul, they each received a personal letter from management commending them on their job performance in Pittsburgh. They were also told to fill out detailed daily expense reports. They did this, but management was not happy. Apparently upper management thought each employee should give back about $200 from the travel advance. Over the course of several months the employees were asked to revise the expense reports several times, and each time they were given a different set of guidelines to follow. The employees were ultimately fired for what their supervisor called "gross insubordination." Company officials admitted at the trial that these were good employees and they should have been given written guidelines before the trip.

When these employees tried to find new jobs, their prospective employers asked why they left Equitable. They said they had been terminated for "gross insubordination." When these prospective employers called Equitable to find out more, they were told only the dates these employees had been employed and their final job title. Needless to say, these employees did not find work. When they sued for defamation, the employer argued that the defamation had not been published. The jury found that the employer had published the defamatory statements by telling the employees who in turn were forced to tell other people. This is called "compelled self-publication." The Minnesota Supreme Court ruled that an employee could sue even if the employer made the defamatory statement to no one other than the employee if the employee is later put in a position where he or she must repeat the defamatory statement.

Because of this case attorneys tell employers and supervisors not to tell anyone, even the employee, why an employee is being fired. What is to be gained by saying anything to anyone? While it might help other employers to give out this kind of information, you do not get anything out of it. Even if you win a defamation lawsuit, lawsuits are expensive. An attorney once told a room full of personnel directors that they should tell only dates of employment and job title "officially" but they could meet the other managers informally, perhaps at a bar, and tell them the real story. That is very foolish advice. First of all, the conditional privilege would probably not apply to statements made off the record at a bar. Second, responding in writing to a formal request for information from another employer is a defense in some states to the criminal offenses we are about to discuss. Making oral statements in a bar is not.

Now to the criminal charges. A century ago defamation was a crime in every state. That is no longer true, but criminal-defamation statutes are still on the books in half the states. That means a supervisor risks criminal prosecution as well as a lawsuit by the former employee (see Table 16–1).

On top of that almost half the states have statutes that make it a crime to **blacklist** a former employee (see Table 16–1). Many of these laws were passed early in the twentieth century in response to union blacklists. These were lists of suspected union members. However, most of these statutes apply to more than just written lists of suspected union members. The Arizona statute defines blacklist to mean "any understanding or agreement whereby the names of any person or persons . . . or other means of identification shall be spoken, written, printed or implied for the purpose of being communicated or transmitted between two or more employers of labor, their bosses, foremen, superintendents, managers, officers or other agents, whereby the laborer is prevented or prohib-

TABLE 16–1. Criminal Defamation and Blacklisting Statutes*

Alabama	Defamation is a crime.	13A-11-160 to 164
	Blacklisting is a crime.	13A-11-123
Alaska	None	
Arizona	Blacklisting is prohibited.	Const. Art. 18, sec. 9
	Blacklisting is defined.	23-1361, 1362
Arkansas	Defamation is a crime.	41-3454 to 3462
	Blacklisting is a crime.	81-211
California	Defamation is a crime.	Penal Code 258 to 260
	Blacklisting is a crime.	Labor Code 1050
Colorado	Defamation is a crime.	18-13-105
	Blacklisting is a crime.	8-2-110 to 115
Connecticut	Blacklisting is a crime.	31-51
Delaware	None	
District of Columbia	None	
Florida	Defamation is a crime.	836.1 to 11
Georgia	Defamation is a crime.	16-11-40
Hawaii	None	
Idaho	Defamation is a crime.	18-4801 to 4809
Illinois	None	
Indiana	Blacklisting is a crime.	22-5-3-1,2
Iowa	Blacklisting is a crime.	730.1 to .3
Kansas	Defamation is a crime.	21-4004
	Blacklisting is a crime.	44-117 to 119
Kentucky	None	
Louisiana	Defamation is a crime.	14:47 to 50.1
Maine	Blacklisting is a crime.	17-401
Maryland	None	
Massachusetts	None	
Michigan	Defamation is a crime.	750.370, .371
Minnesota	Defamation is a crime.	609.765
	Blacklisting is a crime.	179.60
Mississippi	Blacklisting of telegraph operators forbidden.	77-9-725 to 729
Missouri	None	
Montana	Defamation is a crime.	45-8-212
	Blacklisting—punative damages allowed.	39-2-801 to 804
Nebraska	None	
Nevada	Defamation is a crime.	200.510 to 560
	Blacklisting is a crime.	613.210
New Hampshire	Defamation is a crime.	644:11
New Jersey	None	
New Mexico	Defamation is a crime.	30-11-1
	Blacklisting is a crime.	30-13-3
New York	None	

*The law is always changing. Consult an attorney about your situation.

TABLE 16–1. (Cont.)

North Carolina	Defamation is a crime.	14-47
	Blacklisting is a crime.	14-355, 356
North Dakota	Defamation is a crime.	12.1-15-01
Ohio	None	
Oklahoma	Defamation is a crime.	Title 21, sec. 771 to 781
	Blacklisting is a crime.	Title 40, sec. 172, 173
Oregon	Blacklisting is prohibited.	659.230
Pennsylvania	None	
Rhode Island	None	
South Carolina	Defamation is a crime.	16-7-150
South Dakota	None	
Tennessee	Defamation is a crime.	39-2-401 to 404
Texas	Blacklisting is a crime.	Art. 5196, 5197
Utah	Defamation is a crime.	76-9-404
	Blacklisting is prohibited.	34-24-1,2
		Const. Art. 12, sec. 19
		Const. Art. 16, sec. 4
Vermont	None	
Virginia	Blacklisting is a crime.	40.1-27
Washington	Defamation is a crime.	9.58
	Blacklisting is a crime.	49.44.010
West Virginia	None	
Wisconsin	Defamation is a crime.	942.01
	Blacklisting is a crime.	134.02
Wyoming	None	

ited from engaging in a useful occupation" (Ariz. 23-1361). The North Carolina statute says blacklisting is preventing or attempting to prevent a "discharged employee" by "word or writing of any kind" from "obtaining employment" (N.C. 14-355).

Given the problems inherent in the concepts of "conditional privilege" and "compelled self-publication," the expensive nature of defamation lawsuits, and the vague wording of criminal-defamation and blacklisting statutes, the best advice any attorney can give to any employer or supervisor is to keep quiet.

The advice to any employee who has been discharged is: try to find out why you were fired. If the supervisor will not tell you in writing, then get the information orally. Write down what is said as soon as possible, when it was said, and who said it. You may want to use that information later in a lawsuit or in an unemployment-compensation hearing.

At least three states have passed statutes in response to the fact that employers will not tell employees why they have been fired. The Missouri statute requires corporations to give former employees a letter "setting forth the nature and character of service rendered by such employee to such corporation and the duration thereof, and truly stating for what cause, if any, such employee was discharged or voluntarily quit such service" (Mo. 290.140). The employee has one year from the time of termination to ask for the letter and can sue the former employer if the letter turns out to be untrue. However, to win such a lawsuit employees must prove that the absence or inadequacy of this letter (called a service letter in Missouri) caused them not to be hired by prospective employers (*Kling*). The Minnesota statute says that an employee has five days after termination to request a written statement concerning the reasons for termination (Minn. 181.933). The request must be in writing. The statute prevents the employee from suing the former employer for defamation as a result of this statement. In Montana the employer must tell the employee the reason for discharge if the employee requests it (Mont. 39-2-801). Without similar statutes in other states, more and more employers and supervisors are not going to tell anyone, especially the employee, the reasons for termination.

INTENTIONAL INFLICTION OF EMOTIONAL DISTRESS

Many employees would like to sue their employers and supervisors for driving them crazy. However, the courts will not allow this unless the employer or supervisor behaved in an outrageous way. Just being harassed at work or fired from a job is usually not enough.

In 1987 the supreme courts of California and Massachusetts ruled that employees in those states cannot sue their employers for intentional infliction of emotional distress and are stuck with worker's compensation (*Fair Oaks, Foley*). These decisions are confusing because they seem to go against the general principle that employees can sue their employers for intentional injuries.

The Arizona Supreme Court does not agree that worker's compensation preempts a lawsuit for intentional infliction of emotional distress. Leta Fay Ford began work for Revlon as a secretary in 1973. After several years she had worked her way up to buyer. Revlon then hired Karl Braun to be her supervisor. On April 3, 1980, Braun invited her to dinner, at the end of which he announced that he "planned to spend the night with her." When she refused, he told her she would "regret" it. On May 3, 1980, at the company picnic Braun walked up to her in front of witnesses and said, "I want to fuck you, Leta." Later that day, as she was leaving the ladies' room accompanied by a friend, he grabbed her and put her in a choke hold. He ran his hands over her body and told her he wanted to fuck her.

She complained to higher executives at Revlon, who discussed her case for six months without doing anything. Meanwhile the harassment continued and she developed high blood pressure, a nervous tic in one eye, and other symptoms of emotional stress. On May 28, 1981, Revlon gave Braun an official letter of censure. In October 1981, Ford tried to kill herself. On October 5, 1981, Revlon fired Braun. In April 1982 Ford sued Revlon and Braun for assault, battery, and intentional infliction of emotional distress. The jury found Braun guilty of assault and battery but not intentional infliction of emotional distress. The jury found Revlon guilty of intentional infliction of emotional distress and awarded $10,000 in compensatory damages and $100,000 in punitive damages against the company. Revlon felt that it should not be liable for intentional infliction of emotional distress if Braun was not liable for intentional infliction of emotional distress. The Arizona Supreme Court disagreed. In this case Revlon, acting through its higher executives, was guilty of inflicting emotional distress because it failed to take action to stop the sexual harassment. The Arizona Supreme Court had no trouble finding the behavior of Revlon's executives to be "outrageous," the first requirement of the tort of intentional infliction of emotional distress. Second, the court said Revlon either intended to cause the emotional distress or "recklessly disregarded the near certainty that such distress" would result. Finally, severe emotional distress did result. What about worker's compensation as an exclusive remedy in this case? The Arizona Supreme Court held that because the acts of Braun and the Revlon executives were intentional, not "accidents," worker's compensation did not prevent this lawsuit (Ford).

INTENTIONAL INFLICTION OF PHYSICAL INJURY

Finally, employees can sue their employers for intentionally inflicting physical injury on them. These cases are difficult because it is often hard to draw the line between "accidents" on the one hand and "intentional" conduct on the other. As the Arizona Supreme Court said in the Ford case, it is intentional conduct if the employer consciously intends to cause harm, or "recklessly disregards the near certainty that such" harm is going to result. It is easy to call the conduct intentional when the target is known to everyone. For example, if an employer walks up to a particular worker with a stick of lighted dynamite and throws it at him, no court would have trouble finding that to be intentional conduct. The employer intended to harm a particular worker, and harm was certainly going to result.

What if the employer leaves a stick of lighted dynamite where workers frequently come and it kills one of them? Is that intentional behavior? It was no accident that the dynamite went off. It was highly certain that someone would be hurt, but the employer was not trying to kill a particular worker. During the past few years several state supreme courts have become so disgusted with the actions of some companies that they have allowed the workers or widow(er)s to sue in situations like this. Let's look at cases from Ohio, Michigan, and West Virginia.

In 1984 the Ohio Supreme Court allowed two workers to sue for intentional conduct that caused physical injury even though it was not a "certain harm to a particular worker" case. In one case the employer had cut off the safety cover on the conveyor belt with a blow torch. Eventually a worker was caught in the conveyor belt and crushed to death. In another case the employer took the labels off the toxic chemicals and told the workers there was no danger. The Ohio Supreme Court held in both cases there was no "accident" because there was a "substantial certainty" that some worker would be injured. The workers and widow(er)s were allowed to sue for intentional infliction of physical injury and to collect punitive damages (*VIP Development*).

In 1986 a research chemist at Dow charged that Dow failed to tell him he was being exposed to "agent orange." He sued for (1) intentional misrepresentation; (2) fraudulent concealment of potential danger; (3) intentional infliction of physical injury; and (4) intentional infliction of emotional distress. The Michigan Supreme Court allowed him to sue for all four things, saying that "if the injury is substantially certain to occur as a consequence of actions the employer intended, the employer is deemed to have intended the injuries as well" even if he did not have a particular worker in mind when he did what he did (*Beauchamp*).

Just as an employee can sue for fraud if the employer acted intentionally or was reckless, the same is true in intentional-injury cases. As the Supreme Court of West Virginia said, workers can sue if the employer was "willful, wanton, or reckless" (*Jumacris*).

SPECIAL LEGAL PROVISIONS

More and more states have passed special statutes or amended their worker's compensation statute to deal with employers who violate safety regulations. In 1978 Connecticut amended its statute to require higher worker's-compensation benefits in cases where a safety regulation has been violated. The statute calls for an increase in benefits from 66 percent to 75 percent of average weekly wages (*Mingachos*). Several states have provisions like this, including Arkansas, Missouri, New Mexico, North Carolina, Ohio, South Carolina, Utah, and Wisconsin. In California the compensation amount is increased by 50 percent. In Massachusetts it is increased by 100 percent.

The Texas Constitution has a provision that allows the widow(er) to sue the employer for punitive damages. Section 26 of Article XVI of the Texas Constitution says:

> Every person, corporation, or company, that may commit a homicide, through willful act, or omission, or gross neglect, shall be responsible, in exemplary damages, to the surviving husband, widow, heirs of his or her body, or such of them as there may be, without regard to any criminal proceeding that may or may not be had in relation to the homicide.

In a recent Texas case the jury awarded $450,000 in exemplary (punitive) damages. The trial judge decided for the employer anyway, ruling that the jury could not award exemplary damages because they had not awarded actual damages. This is a nice catch-22. The constitution does not allow them to award actual damages in a case controlled by worker's compensation. It allows them to award only exemplary damages. The Texas Supreme Court said it would be useless for the jury to make an award for actual damages in one of these cases and reinstated the jury's verdict (*Gifford-Hill*).

In some cases the employer tries to have it both ways, arguing that the worker's injury is not covered by worker's compensation but that the worker cannot sue in court because of the worker's compensation statute. Helen Mc-Carthy worked for 10 years in an office where she was regularly exposed to "cigarette and other kinds of tobacco smoke." She sued her employer, arguing that he failed to live up to his duty to provide her with a safe place to work. Usually, when someone sues for breach of this duty, we call it a negligence lawsuit and say it is barred by worker's compensation. In this case the state department of labor denied her worker's-compensation claim because they said her injury was not the result of a work-related injury or occupational disease. The Washington Appeals Court ruled that they cannot have it both ways. If this is not a case covered by worker's compensation, then McCarthy can sue in court under the common law (*McCarthy*).

CIGARETTES

This Washington case illustrates a problem with the present system. In thousands of cases the consumers of other products are made to bear the cost of injuries that are really caused by cigarettes. The 1979 changes in the New Jersey worker's-compensation statute require that worker's-compensation benefits be reduced by the amount of loss "attributed to cigarette smoking" (*Field #2*). The Pennsylvania Supreme Court decided in 1987 to do the same thing without a special provision in the worker's-compensation statute (*Martin #1*). What the New Jersey Legislature and the Pennsylvania Supreme Court have not done is require the makers of cigarettes to pay for the damages their products cause.

A decade ago a New Jersey Appeals Court handed down a landmark decision in the fight for smoke-free air. A nonsmoking employee sued to get an injunction to stop the smoking at her place of employment. She had a severe allergy to cigarette smoke and seven of the thirteen employees in her department smoked heavily. When the employer refused to make them stop, the employee sued for violation of the duty to provide a safe place to work. The court held that she could not sue and collect money for a violation of this duty (that was preempted by the worker's-compensation statute) but she could sue and ask for an injunction to stop an ongoing threat to her safety and health (*Shrimp*).

Many people are killed or disabled in this country by cigarettes. All of us pay for these costs through higher insurance premiums and taxes, whether we smoke or not. As long as the 25 percent of the population who smoke are able to stick the rest of the population with the costs involved in this habit, the cigarette companies will continue to be the most profitable in the world and our insurance premiums and taxes will continue to go up.

OTHER INTENTIONAL INJURIES

Fraud, defamation, intentional infliction of emotional distress, and intentional infliction of physical injury are the most common things employees sue employers for. This does not mean they are the only things employees can sue employers for. Anytime the employer or supervisor acts intentionally or recklessly and injures an employee, there is potential liability.

In one case a jury awarded $80,000 in damages because an employer brought theft charges against the employee that were unfounded (*Eggleston*). The law calls that malicious prosecution.

In another case the jury awarded $1.5 million for malicious prosecution, $1 million for defamation, and $500,00 for false imprisonment (being kept from leaving a room) (*Foley*).

The judges have said that these lawsuits by employees do not have to fit into one of the old categories such as false imprisonment or fraud. In one case the employee alleged that the company lied to him about his physical condition and kept giving him pain-killing drugs until he became a drug addict. The court found this to be an intentional injury for which the company could be sued by the employee (*Sterry*).

Any worker who thinks he or she has been intentionally injured at work should talk to an attorney immediately, before filing a claim for worker's compensation and before talking to the employer's attorney or insurance agent. Employers should investigate situations that might involve intentional injury and act quickly to end the outrageous conduct.

17

Social Security

THE PAST

The Social Security Act of 1935 created several new programs. The part most of us associate with the phrase "Social Security" is currently called the Federal Old Age, Survivors, Disability, and Hospital Insurance Program (OASDHI) (42 U.S.C.). It is funded by the Federal Insurance Contribution Act (FICA) (26 U.S.C. sec. 3101). That is why your Social Security deduction is called FICA on your paycheck stub. The national unemployment insurance system was also created by the 1935 Act (see Chapter 5). The 1935 Act also created the welfare system that has evolved into the system we have today. The original act set up federal grants to states to help fund local welfare programs. Part of this welfare system became a strictly federal program called the Supplemental Security Income program (SSI) (42 U.S.C. sec. 1381). This program helps old, disabled, and blind people who are too poor to help themselves. The rest of our welfare system is still a state-run system, with money coming from the federal government for things such as food stamps and Aid to Families with Dependent Children.

During the Presidential campaign of 1936 Social Security was a major issue. Alf Landon campaigned against it. Many pay envelopes just before election day contained a flyer that said: "You're sentenced to a weekly pay reduction for all your working life. You'll have to serve the sentence unless you help reverse it on November 3." On November 3, 1936, Franklin D. Roosevelt won by a landslide. In 1937 Justice Cardozo wrote the Supreme Court decision finding the Social Security Act of 1935 to be constitutional (*Helvering*). (This tactic of putting campaign literature in pay envelopes caused half the states to make it a crime for employers to influence how their employees vote. See Chapter 10.)

The Republicans were afraid of the large trust fund a true pension system would create. It is estimated that if Social Security had created a true pension system and used the money to buy common stock, the Social Security Administration (SSA) would be the majority stockholder of every major corporation in America today. That did not happen. The act was modified to provide a pay-as-you-go system. There is no real Social Security trust fund. When money is paid into the system, it goes to pay benefits to people presently drawing out of the system. During the next two decades the Social Security system will take in significantly more than it pays out for the first time in history in an effort to provide pensions for the post-World War II baby-boom generation.

THE SOCIAL SECURITY SYSTEM

The present Social Security system consists of five basic parts: a retirement system, a life-insurance system, a disability system, a medical-insurance system, and a welfare system called SSI. In 1988 and 1989 employees and employers will each pay 7.51 percent, and in 1990 and beyond each will pay 7.65 percent for a total of 15.30 percent. Self-employed people pay the whole amount themselves, but they receive a tax credit that reduces the effective rate in 1988 and 1989 from 15.02 percent to 13.02 percent. They are scheduled to receive a special income-tax deduction beginning in 1990.

While most people pay Social Security taxes on all their wages, there is a point beyond which Social Security taxes do not apply. In 1988 a wage earner did not have to pay Social Security taxes on income over $45,000. That figure increases each year as average wages increase. Also, Social Security taxes are a tax on wages, not on a person's entire income. Dividends and interest are exempt from Social Security taxes. Payments from pension funds and most rental income are also exempt.

For some people Social Security retirement benefits are subject to income taxes. Up to half of Social Security retirement benefits are taxable if adjusted gross income plus half of Social Security benefits plus nontaxable interest income is over $25,000 ($32,000 for a couple filing jointly; zero for a married couple filing separately). In a simple example, a single person with $25,000 of other income and $5,000 of Social Security retirement benefits would pay income taxes on $2,500 of the Social Security retirement benefits. If you think this might apply to you, get the Social Security pamphlet, "Part of Your Benefits May Be Taxable." Many people have suggested making all of the Social Security retirement benefits taxable as a way to balance the federal budget.

The 1983 changes to the Social Security system added millions of people, including all newly hired federal civil service employees and the employees of nonprofit corporations, to the system. Also, state and local governments will no longer be able to get out of the system. If they are in now or ever join, they cannot get out as they used to be able to do. The retirement age will start to rise above 65 in the year 2005. The retirement age will increase two months a year until it reaches 66 in 2010. It will do the same thing from 2022 to 2027 so that a person will have to be 67 to retire by 2027. The new law also changed the percent of retirement benefits people will get if they take early retirement (see Table 17—1).

Eligibility

The Social Security system works on quarters. Before 1978 a worker had to earn $50 or more in a quarter to earn a quarter's worth of credit in the Social Security system. After 1978 a worker earns a quarter's worth of credit for every so-many dollars earned during a year. He or she can only earn a maximum of four quarters of credit in any one year. In 1978, a worker earned a quarter's worth of credit for every $250 earned up to four quarters' worth of credit if he or she earned $1000 or more during the year. In 1988 a worker earned a quarter of credit for every $470 earned during the year up to four quarters' worth of credit for a yearly income of $1,880. This amount goes up as average wages go up.

Retirement Eligibility A worker is "fully insured" and eligible to retire when he or she is old enough and has 40 quarters of credit in the system (10 years). Starting in 1991 someone without 40 quarters cannot get Social Security retirement benefits. A worker reaching 62 in 1989 needs 38 quarters while someone reaching 62 in 1990 needs 39 quarters.

Disability Eligibility Workers who become disabled before age 24 need six quarters of credit during the last three years to be eligible for disability benefits. Between ages 24 and 31 they need credit for half the time between their 21st birthday and the time of the disability (a 25-year-old would need eight quarters). Between ages 31 and 42 a person needs 20 quarters over the last 10 years. Workers over 42 must meet two tests. First, they must have 20 quarters of credit during the last 10 years. Second, a person over 42 must meet a "Total of Quarters" test (see Table 17—2). For example, a person disabled at age 54 must have

TABLE 17—1. Percent of Retirement Benefits Received if the Worker Takes Early Retirement

Age	Currently You Get (%)	In 2010 You Will Get (%)	In 2027 You Will Get (%)
62	80	75	70
63	86.7	80	75
64	93.3	86.7	80
65	100	93.3	86.7
66	103	100	93.3
67	106	108	100

**TABLE 17–2. Total Quarters Test
for Disability Benefits**

Age	Lifetime Quarters Needed
42	20
44	22
46	24
48	26
50	28
52	30
54	32
56	34
58	36
60	38
62	40

20 quarters over the 10 years just prior to disability, and a total of at least 32 quarters over his or her lifetime. Special rules apply to blind people.

Of course, in addition to the required number of quarters of credit, the worker must be *disabled*. Disability is different under Social Security than it is under worker's compensation. First of all, Social Security does not care if the disability is work-related. Second, there is no such thing as "partial" disability under Social Security. If persons are still physically able to get a job, Social Security does not care that they can no longer get the high-paying job they had before becoming disabled.

The Social Security Administration defines disability as:

> inability to engage in any substantial gainful activity by reason of a medically determinable physical impairment, which can be expected to result in death or has lasted, or can be expected to last for a continuous period of not less than 12 months.

In other words Social Security covers long-term disability. The SSA does take age, education, and work experience into account, but the primary concern is physical impairment. To decide on eligibility, the SSA goes down a list of questions.

1. Are the persons currently engaged in "substantial gainful activity" (do they have a job)? If they have a job, they do not get disability payments. If they do not have a job the question is:

2. Do the persons have a severe impairment? If they do not have a severe impairment, they do not get disability payments. If they do have a severe impairment the question is:

3. Is the impairment in the Listings? If the impairment is in the Listings, they get disability benefits. If the impairment is not in the Listings, the question is:

4. Does the impairment prevent the persons from getting work? If the impairment does not prevent the persons from getting work, they do not get disability payments. If the impairment does prevent the persons from getting work, they get disability payments. The U.S. Supreme Court has approved this method of processing claims (*Bowan #2*).

The **Listings** are simply a list of impairments that are so severe the person is automatically qualified for disability benefits and the SSA does not need to go further. This list contains things such as loss of both feet, loss of both hands, cerebral palsy, and Parkinson's disease. If the impairment meets the requirements of the Listings, then the process is over and the person gets disability benefits. If the impairment does not meet these requirements, then the SSA looks at the physical impairment, along with the age, education, and work experience of the worker, and makes a determination whether he or she is too disabled to get a job.

In making the determination whether or not the person can get a job, the SSA uses the **grids.** The grids are simply charts that list age, education, and work experience along with level of impairment to help the SSA decide if the person is disabled or not.

There are people who do qualify for Social Security disability benefits not on their own but because their parent is covered by Social Security. A "disabled adult child" is a child of an insured worker who is over 18 and is disabled because of a condition that developed before the child reached 22. The "disabled adult child" is not entitled to benefits until the parent dies, retires, or becomes disabled.

Death

Surviving dependents of a deceased worker are eligible to receive benefits if the worker was eligible for (or receiving) retirement or disability benefits at the time of death. They are also eligible if the worker was "fully insured" (40 quarters) at the time of death. They are also eligible if the worker was "currently insured" (had six quarters of credit during the last 13 quarters) at the time of death. In addition, even if the worker was not receiving or was not qualified for either retirement or disability benefits, dependents may still qualify under a special rule. If the worker was 28 or younger and had a total of six quarters of credit, dependents are still eligible. If the worker was over 28, see Table 17–3.

If the worker is disabled and has enough quarters to qualify for death benefits, but not disability benefits, and then dies, his or her dependents get death benefits. For example, suppose a worker is disabled at age 36 with 14 quarters. Since he needed 20 quarters over the last 10 years to qualify for disability benefits, he did not qualify. But if he dies, his surviving dependents would qualify for death benefits.

Generally, dependent children or dependent parents qualify for death benefits. A widow(er) of an insured worker can receive benefits if he or she has

TABLE 17–3. Total Quarters Test for Death Benefits

Age	Lifetime Quarters Needed
28	6
30	8
32	10
34	12
36	14
38	16
40	18
42 and over (see Table 17–2)	

minor children at home, has reached 60 years of age, or has reached 50 years of age and is disabled.

Of course, the children and parents of the deceased worker must be dependent on the worker at the time of death. All of this is far more complicated than it needs to be. If someone dies, the dependents should go down to the Social Security office and find out what benefits they qualify for. Even a divorced spouse may qualify if he or she meets the "test."

Quarters Count

This system is based on quarters. A person would be smart to start earning quarters of credit as soon as possible, and to earn enough in "wages" each year to collect four quarters of credit every year.

Retirement Benefits

The amount of a Social Security retirement check depends on how much persons earned in **wages** over their working life. If persons retire early, their check is reduced as shown in Table 17–1. If they wait until after 65 to retire (or 66 after 2005), their check will be increased. Before the 1983 changes the check increased 3 percent for every year retirement was postponed. That percentage will gradually go up between 1990 and 2008. It will hit a high of 8 percent in 2008. For example, if persons could retire at age 66 in 2010 but wait three years, they will get 24 percent more per month than if they had retired at age 66. They cannot keep doing this forever. They do not get any more if they wait past age 70 to retire.

Social Security will allow retirees to earn a certain amount in wages and still receive retirement benefits (they can earn as much as they want from investments). If wages exceed the limit, the Social Security check will be reduced by one dollar for every two dollars earned over the limit. Beginning in 1990 a person will lose one dollar for every three dollars earned over the limit. Once someone is 70, today and in the future, they can earn as much as they want in wages and still get benefits.

The general principle is that retired persons should get from 26 percent to 60 percent of their preretirement income. The lower the preretirement income, the higher the percentage until those who earned the minimum wage all their life receive 60 percent. Social Security is not set up to support retired workers in the style to which they may have become accustomed. Those who have paid off the mortgage and the car and have no debts should be able to get by on Social Security.

There used to be a minimum amount people could get from the retirement system. That is no longer true, except for members of religious orders who take a vow of poverty. These people will be eligible for a minimum amount if they first become eligible for retirement benefits before 1992.

Unmarried children under 18 (19 if still in high school), severely disabled children, a spouse over 61, or a spouse caring for a child under 16 (or a disabled child) may also be eligible for benefits when the worker retires.

The SSA has a pamphlet called "Estimating Your Social Security Retirement Check" that will take you through the calculations needed to estimate what your check will be.

Disability Benefits

Disability benefits are based on wages earned prior to disability. The actual calculation is too complicated to go into here. In 1988 the average monthly payment to a disabled worker was $508 a month, and the average payment to a disabled worker with dependents was $919 a month.

The Social Security law says that the total of worker's-compensation benefits plus Social Security disability benefits cannot be more than 80 percent of the predisability earnings. There are several ways to calculate predisability earnings, and the worker is entitled to use the method that results in the highest amount.

A disabled person may be referred to the state vocational rehabilitation agency for help and retraining. After a person has been disabled for two consecutive years, he or she is entitled to Medicare.

Supplemental Security Income

Supplemental Security Income (SSI) is a type of welfare paid out of general revenue, not Social Security taxes, but it is administered by the Social Security Administration. To qualify people must be poor enough and be either 65 or older, blind, disabled, or retarded. To be poor enough the person must meet both the asset test and the income test.

Asset Test In 1990 and beyond (unless Congress changes the statute) a single person must have less than $2,000 in assets (property, savings, stocks, bonds).

A couple must have less than $3,000 in assets. Some things do not count as assets for this purpose:

1. The home a person lives in and the land it is on do not count.
2. Some personal and household goods and insurance policies may not count depending on value.
3. A car does not count if it is worth less than $4,500.
4. Burial plots do not count, nor do up to $1,500 in burial funds.

The biggest mistake some people make is to think that they have to sell their home to qualify. They do not.

Income Test Income includes wages, pensions, interest, and so on. Income also includes gifts in kind like food, shelter, or clothing. Some things do not count as income:

1. The first $20 of any kind of income received in a month does not count.
2. The first $65 of wages earned in a month does not count. If the person earns over $65 a month in wages, half of everything over $65 does not count.
3. Food stamps do not count.
4. Some food, clothing, and shelter received from private nonprofit organizations may not count.
5. Earnings used to pay for expenses that result directly from the person's disability do not count, such as the cost of a wheelchair.
6. For blind people, earnings used to pay expenses caused by working do not count, such as special transportation costs.

Given these rules, there is a maximum amount of income a person can have and still qualify for SSI. In 1988 a single person could have income up to $353 a month and still receive payments. A couple could have income up to $551 a month and still receive payments. The maximum changes every year. The general rule is that a person living in a public institution cannot get SSI, but there are many exceptions to that rule. Check with the Social Security Administration to find out the current exceptions. People cannot receive Aid to Families with Dependent Children and get SSI, but they can get food stamps and still receive SSI.

Medicaid

Medicaid is a joint federal-state program to provide poor people with medical care. If people are poor enough (meet asset and income tests), they can receive

Medicaid even if they are not old or disabled. Because it is a joint federal-state program, the asset and income tests are different in every state.

Medicare

People who are eligible to receive Social Security benefits either on their own wage record or as a dependent or survivor are eligible for Medicare at age 65. Anyone who has been entitled to Social Security disability for two consecutive years is also eligible for Medicare. People who need dialysis or kidney transplants are also covered.

Medicare has two parts: hospital insurance (Part A) and medical insurance (Part B). The hospital insurance helps pay the cost of inpatient hospital care and some kinds of follow-up care. The medical insurance helps pay doctor bills and other medical expenses. The medical insurance (Part B) is paid for every month, usually by having the premium withheld from the monthly Social Security retirement check. The cost of medical insurance in 1988 was $24.80 a month. This premium goes up every year so that the elderly pay 25 percent of the cost of this program.

On July 1, 1988, President Reagan signed into law the catastrophic health-insurance act, which will mean major changes in Medicare. Part A used to require Medicare recipients to pay part of the cost of a hospital stay after 60 days. That will no longer be true. Now, Medicare will pay the entire cost of hospitalization after the recipient pays a once-a-year deductible of $580. Under Part B, the recipient will pay a yearly deductible of $75 for doctor bills and 20 percent after that, but the recipient will never have to pay more than $1370 a year for "allowable" doctor bills. However, doctors will still be able to charge more than the "allowable" charges, and recipients will have to pick up that extra cost. After January 1, 1991, Medicare will also pay part of the cost of drugs. The premium for Part B is expected to be $31.10 a month in 1989 and rise to $42.60 a month by 1993. The higher cost for Part A will be paid by an income-tax surcharge on people over 64. The more income taxes elderly persons pay, the more they will pay in surcharges. Elderly people will pay an extra $22.50 of income taxes for every $150 of income-tax liability. It is estimated that 60 percent of the elderly pay less than $150 a year in income taxes and will not have to pay any surcharge. The maximum surcharge will go from $800 in 1989 to $1050 in 1993. Elderly people with a high income will be paying significantly more than they used to pay private insurance companies for this kind of coverage. Elderly people with a low income will be paying significantly less.

Appeals Procedure

When it comes time to file a claim call the Social Security Administration. They will tell you what documents you need to take when you go to the Social Security office. Most people do not need a lawyer at the initial claim stage. Once you have been turned down for benefits, it is time to see a lawyer. The SSA denies benefits to over a million people each year. Less than 30 percent of those people appeal the decision. Over half of those who appeal win. Most attorneys will take the case on a contingency basis; this means they do not get any fee unless they help you get something. Their fee is limited to 25 percent of the lump-sum amount you get when the case is finally over (your back-due payments). Also, their fee has to be approved by the SSA before they can collect. Once your initial claim has been turned down, there are several stages of appeal. Generally, at each stage, you have 60 days to appeal to the next level. The 60 days runs from the time you receive the letter, but the SSA assumes you got the letter five days after they mailed it.

Reconsideration After your initial claim has been turned down, you have 60 days to ask for reconsideration. You do not get a hearing yet, but your attorney can help you submit additional information that may convince the SSA you are entitled to the benefits after all.

Administrative Hearing After reconsideration, you have 60 days to ask for a hearing. The SSA's form requesting appeal has two boxes. Check the box that says you want a hearing. An administrative law judge will preside over the hearing, look at the medical records, and listen to testimony from witnesses. This is where you are most likely to reverse the SSA and get the benefits you seek.

Appeals Council After you receive a notice that you lost at the hearing, you have 60 days to appeal to the Appeals Council in Washington D.C. This is just a formality in most cases, but occasionally the council actually does overturn the administrative law judge.

The Federal Courts After the appeals council turns you down, you have 60 days to appeal to a federal court. The judges will overturn the SSA's decision only if they decide the SSA incorrectly interpreted the law or lacked substantial evidence to support their decision. People do win in federal court. In one recent case all the doctors and vocational experts testified that the worker was totally disabled by back pain that would prevent any kind of employment. The SSA and the administrative law judge denied benefits because they did not believe these experts. The Eleventh Circuit Court overturned this decision because there was no substantial evidence to support it. The SSA does not have the option of deciding that everyone is a liar and denying benefits on that basis alone (*Hale*).

Reopen Even if you have been turned down, you may be able to reopen your case later if you gain additional evidence. You will have to discuss this possibility with your attorney. Appeals from SSI, Medicaid, and Medicare are handled differently. Call the SSA to find out the details.

Common Misconceptions

The Social Security Administration used to talk about "contributions" to a "trust fund." There really was no trust fund, and the SSA does not talk like that anymore. The money paid into the system goes to pay benefits to people drawing out of the system. When you retire at some point in the future, the taxes paid by people working then will pay your benefits. During the next two decades the SSA will actually take in more than it pays out, and there will be a surplus, which will be used in the next century to pay retirement benefits to the post-World War II baby-boom generation.

Another misconception is that Social Security retirement is a good deal. It is a good deal for people drawing benefits today. In most cases people drawing benefits today receive more than they would have received if they had put that money into a private pension plan. For retirees in the next century the opposite will be true. They will probably receive a much lower payment than they would have received if they had put 15 percent of their income into a private retirement fund every year. Some people estimate that the average worker who put 15 percent into a private pension every year would have a million-dollar fund from which to receive payments upon retirement. Also, he or she would have a million dollars to leave to descendants. It is estimated that in the year 2025 the ratio of retirees to workers will be half what it is today (for every worker there will be twice as many retirees). If that is true, then either retirement benefits will have to go down in real terms, or those workers will have to be willing to pay more of their wages in Social Security taxes.

PRIVATE PENSIONS

Those who want to retire in the twenty-first century and live above the poverty level had better have more going for them than Social Security. Yet many people who tried to supplement Social Security in the past ended up empty-handed because their private pension plans went broke. The United States learned in the 1930s that financial institutions work well if the federal government regulates them enough. In the 1930s Congress put in place insurance and regulatory systems to protect the banking system. It took Congress another four decades to get around to regulating private pension funds.

Individual Retirement Accounts

Individual Retirement Accounts (IRAs) were born in 1974, expanded to allow even those with company pension funds to set them up, and then greatly curtailed in the Tax Reform Act of 1986. Why? Only upper-income people were taking advantage of IRAs. Today, if your income is below a certain level, the money put into an IRA is tax deductible. The latest IRS regulations should be consulted. If your income is too high, the contributions to the IRA are not tax deductible, but the income derived is not taxed as long as it stays in the IRA.

Keogh Plans

The law allows self-employed people and some people who are not covered by company pension plans to set up their own tax-free pension plans called Keogh plans. If you think you might be eligible, you should contact the IRS for information.

ERISA

The Employee Retirement Income Security Act (ERISA) of 1974 regulates private pension funds and employer benefit programs (29 U.S.C. sec. 1001). The act does not require employers to set up private pension plans or give employees any benefits whatsoever. It simply regulates these plans if employers set them up.

ERISA requires the plan administrator to file a plan description and an annual financial report with the U.S. Department of Labor and the IRS. The plan administrator must provide workers with a summary of these reports and must make the full reports available for inspection. The plan administrator must also provide workers with a summary of their individual account.

A plan must allow a worker to participate when the worker is over 25 and has worked for the company for one year. ERISA controls vesting. In most pension plans, part of a worker's income is deducted (before taxes) and invested in the plan. The employer matches this in some way. Vesting is when the employer's contributions become locked in and cannot be withdrawn. In other words, when the money the employer has put into the plan belongs to the employee, we say the money is vested.

Under present law the employer's contributions must vest at least 50 percent after 10 years and 100 percent after 15 years. The employer has three choices:

1. 10-year rule—full vesting after 10 years;
2. 5–15-year rule—25 percent vesting after 5 years, progressing steadily to 100 percent vesting after 15 years;
3. 45-year rule—if the employee has been employed for 5 years, when his or her age and years of employment add up to 45, he or she is 50 percent vested, with that percentage rising to 100 percent over the next 5 years.

Employers can be more liberal than this. It is not uncommon for an employee to vest 20 percent a year over the first five years of employment. Some Congressmen have proposed changing the statute to require full vesting after five years.

When an employee stops working for an employer, the IRS must be notified about the employee's pension status. The IRS gives that information to the SSA. The SSA is supposed to have a record of all private pension funds.

PBGC

PBGC stands for the Pension Benefit Guaranty Corporation. ERISA created PBGC to collect premiums from all the pension funds it insures to pay benefits for plans that go bankrupt. PBGC is to pension funds what the FDIC and FSLIC are to banks and savings and loans.

Many people have wondered why, in 1935, Congress did not just pass a statute such as ERISA instead of creating Social Security. The reason was that people at the time did not have any faith in private pension funds. Too many of them went broke during the Great Depression. The funds that owned stocks lost too much in the crash. Also, many of these funds were pay-as-you-go funds. There was no trust fund to pay retirees. The company planned to pay benefits out of the profits it would make in the future. When the company went bankrupt, it could not pay retirees. While ERISA has put an end to these pay-as-you-go plans, many of our pension funds are not yet solvent. ERISA calls for a gradual changeover from pay-as-you-go to fully funded pension plans, but the changeover will take decades.

Wrongful Discharge

What if an employer fires a worker to keep his retirement from vesting or because her son's medical bills were costing the group medical plan too much money? The worker cannot sue in state court. The U.S. Supreme Court has decided that with ERISA Congress intended to preempt this field of law (*Mass. Mutual, Pilot Life, Met. Life #1*). The states can still regulate the content of insurance policies and can still control the collection of wages, but they can no longer control employee retirement and benefit plans (*Met. Life #2, Ft. Halifax*).

While workers cannot sue in state court, they can sue in federal court. ERISA makes it unlawful to discharge an employee in order to interfere with "the attainment of any right to which such participant may become entitled" (29 U.S.C. sec. 1140). The act allows the worker to sue for reinstatement, attorney's fees, and more. In one case the judge found that Bethlehem Mines had fired William Ursic just to deprive him of his pension. He had worked 29 and a half years for the company and needed only six months to qualify for a substantial pension. The company said it fired him because he borrowed some tools without permission. The judge found this to be a pretext and awarded William Ursic his pension (*Ursic*).

In another case the judge found Marriott Corporation had discharged John Folz soon after he informed Marriott he had multiple sclerosis in order to deprive him of his benefits under the group medical and disability insurance plan. Because of the extreme hostility between Folz and the company the judge did not order reinstatement (he could have ordered it). Instead he ordered

Marriott to pay back pay from the time of discharge to the time of trial. The judge also ordered front pay, which means Marriott had to pay John Folz the salary he would have earned if Marriott had rehired him and he had worked until retirement. Marriott also had to reinstate Folz into the medical, disability, and life-insurance plans and pay him any pension, profitsharing, and stock-option benefits to which he would have been entitled as a lifetime employee (*Folz*).

Should Private Pension Plans be Mandatory?

ERISA will, over the years, make existing private pensions financially sound. Without private pension funds to supplement Social Security in the next century, retirement is not going to be very happy for most people. If half the present work force is covered by financially sound private pensions, should we require the other half to participate also? Switzerland and the Netherlands have passed compulsory private pension laws rather than expand their existing social-security retirement systems.

PUBLIC SECTOR PENSIONS

State and local governments were pioneers in the pension business. New York City policemen had a retirement system by 1878. In 1911 Massachusetts set up a retirement system for state workers. Today, almost every state and local government worker is covered by a government pension system. Some of these public pension systems are pay-as-you-go, some have an invested trust fund, and some are a combination of both.

The federal government set up the Civil Service Retirement System in 1920. In theory employee contributions were matched by the federal government and put into a trust fund to pay benefits. In practice, the fund has never been large enough to pay out the ever-increasing benefits.

The military retirement system is strictly pay-as-you-go. There is no trust fund. Military employees can retire after 20 years at half their basic pay. This large, unfunded, military trust fund means that much of the cost of today's military buildup will be borne by future taxpayers.

DEFINED-CONTRIBUTION VERSUS DEFINED-BENEFIT PLANS

Whether public or private, there are two basic types of plans. A **defined-benefit plan** works the way Social Security does. Workers put in whatever is required each year, and when they retire, they get a percentage of preretirement salary until death (possibly adjusted for inflation). The amount of the benefit is defined.

A **defined-contribution plan** means the individual worker puts in money (possibly matched by the employer). This money is in an individual account with the worker's name on it. The income from investments goes into this individual account. When the person retires, there is a large pool of money available to pay retirement benefits. The amount of the retirement payments each month will depend on how much money is in the individual's account. IRAs and KEOGHs work like this as do many private pension plans.

During the last four decades, a person would usually have been better off with a defined-contribution plan. This is going to be true as long as interest rates are reasonable and inflation is stable. If inflation goes way up, a government defined-benefit plan can be modified to increase benefits accordingly. That is what happens with cost-of-living adjustments in the Social Security retirement system. A private defined-benefit plan that cannot adjust for inflation would be the worst of all possible worlds.

The ideal world might be two plans: a defined-benefit plan set up and guaranteed by government with cost-of-living adjustments (that is what Social Security is) and a private defined-contribution plan invested in stocks and bonds and allowed to grow as the economy grows. That is exactly what millions of Americans have.

THE FUTURE

While many people like to point out that in the year 2025 there will be twice as many retired people per working person as there are today, there is some good news in the future. Imagine a household at the beginning of this century: six children, a grandparent living at home, a stay-at-home wife, and one wage earner. The ratio of dependents to workers was 8 to 1, or 800 percent more dependents than workers. A ratio of 100 percent means that for every worker there is, on average, only one other person who is not working. This ratio has been at or below 100 percent for a decade now. If predictions hold true, it will hit an all-time low of 66 percent in 2010. It will go up to 79 percent by 2050, but over the course of the next century it should never go above 100 percent. The big difference will be the dependents. As the twentieth century began, the vast majority of dependents were children. The majority of dependents in the next century will be elderly. This will require a tremendous shift in national resources away from things such as education and toward care for the elderly. Coping with this change will be a major task of government in the twenty-first century.

18

OSHA and Fining the Boss

The law has two functions: to provide an incentive not to hurt people and to provide funds to compensate victims. At the beginning of the twentieth century the law of the workplace fulfilled neither of these functions. Worker's compensation and Social Security have tried to provide the victim with some compensation. Neither law provides any real incentive to prevent injuries.

By 1970 everyone agreed something had to be done. Work injuries had risen steadily in the 1960s, and Congress created the Occupational Safety and Health Administration (OSHA). The basic idea was that OSHA would write safety standards and OSHA inspectors would fine employers who violated the standards.

The act also created the National Institute for Occupational Safety and Health (NIOSH), which conducts research into ways to make the workplace safe.

STATE OSHA

The act allows states to set up their own state OSHA. The state program must be "at least as effective" as the federal program. Big business lobbied against state OSHAs. It is much easier for a large corporation with facilities in several states to comply with one set of safety rules instead of many. Big labor lobbied against state OSHAs because they felt the state agencies would not be as effective as the federal OSHA. Given these efforts, most states did not set up state OSHAs.

FEDERAL OSHA

The Employer's Duties

Employers have two main duties under the act: a general duty and specific duties. The **general duty** is to furnish to each employee a place of employment that is free from **recognized hazards** that are "causing or likely to cause death or serious physical injury."

The hazard must be "recognized," that is, the employer knew it was a hazard or it is generally known in the industry to be a hazard. It is also "recognized" if safety experts familiar with the industry consider it to be a hazard (*Brennan #1*). The Eighth Circuit Court ruled that a hazard is "recognized" even if it takes special instruments to detect its presence (*American Smelting*). A hazard can be both the presence of something dangerous such as poison gas or the absence of something that would make the workplace safer, such as handles on valves (*Champlin Petroleum*).

If a hazard is "recognized" and "causing or likely to cause death or serious physical injury," the employer can be fined and ordered to correct the problem even though no safety standard deals with this special hazard. The employer is fined for violating the general duty to provide a safe place to work.

Because the general duty is so vague, Congress intended the Secretary of Labor to write specific safety standards for each industry so that employers would know exactly what was expected of them. The first step in writing these standards is for the secretary to publish proposed standards in the federal register. This is followed by a 30-day comment period. If anyone asks for a hearing, the secretary must hold one. Then the standard is made official and published again in the federal register. For the next 60 days the standard may be challenged in a federal circuit court. Employers can ask for a variance if for some reason they feel they should be exempt from the standard.

Record Keeping

Like all federal regulatory schemes, this one includes a heavy record-keeping burden. Employers must record injuries, illnesses, and deaths. They must also keep records concerning exposure to toxic materials. The employer must report to OSHA within 48 hours any accident that kills one worker or hospitalizes more than four workers. The penalty for not following these requirements is a fine. In 1987 OSHA fined several employers more than a million dollars for violations of the record-keeping rules.

Posting

The act requires employers to post an OSHA poster telling employees they are protected by OSHA and a variety of other notices depending on what OSHA thinks is important.

Inspections

The purpose of OSHA is to *prevent* injuries and illness. After standards are promulgated, OSHA inspectors are supposed to go out, find violations, and fine employers who do not comply with the safety standards. The U.S. Supreme Court has held that if the employer does not consent to a search, OSHA must get a search warrant (*Marshall*). OSHA has an inspection priority list.

1. Situations involving imminent danger are the first priority.
2. Worksites where deaths or major accidents have occurred are the next priority.
3. Next are investigations of complaints by employees, and inspections of industries with high accident rates.
4. Last on the list are routine inspections to find safety violations.

Enforcement

OSHA is allowed by the statute to fine employers who "willfully" or "repeatedly" violate the act not more than $10,000 for each violation. The maximum fine for other violations is $1,000.

Usually a violation is cited, a small fine is imposed, and the employer is given time to fix the problem. An employer who fails to comply can be fined a maximum of $1,000 a day for each day the citation is not complied with.

The act also contains criminal penalties. An employer who willfully violates a standard and causes a death of a worker can be fined up to $10,000 and imprisoned for up to six months. If he does it again, he can be fined up to $20,000 and imprisoned for up to one year. Anyone who warns an employer that an OSHA inspection is about to take place can be fined up to $1,000 and imprisoned for up to six months. Anyone who makes a false statement to OSHA can be fined up to $10,000 and imprisoned for up to six months. There are also special penalties for anyone who assaults or kills an OSHA inspector.

Employer Appeals Procedure

If an employer wants to fight a citation, he or she first has an informal conference with the OSHA area director. Fines are usually negotiated down at this point. An employer must ask for this conference within 15 days of receiving the citation.

If an employer has received a citation for safety violations, a notice will be posted on the employee bulletin board. If he or she is contesting the citation, a notice to that effect will appear next to the citation notice. This gives employees a chance to get involved in the process. Even if the employer is not going to contest the citation, the employees can contest the length of time given to the employer to correct the problem. They must do this within 15 days of the day the notice is posted.

If the employer contests the citation beyond the area director, the complaint goes next to the Occupational Safety and Health Review Commission. This is an independent commission with three members appointed by the President for overlapping six-year terms. The employer will be given a hearing before an administrative law judge. Anyone who participates in the hearing—the employer, OSHA, or the employees—can ask the commission to review the judge's decision. They have 20 days to ask for this review from the day the decision is mailed out, but the commission does not have to review the decision. Then either the employer or OSHA can appeal the decision to a federal circuit court.

Wrongful Discharge

What if a worker files a complaint with OSHA or testifies at a hearing and gets fired or mistreated because of it? The act protects these workers, but they cannot sue for themselves. They must go to the Secretary of Labor within 30 days of being fired or mistreated and ask for help. The secretary can sue the employer asking for reinstatement and back pay.

Secretary of Labor Ray Marshall wrote a regulation that prohibits an employer from taking action against any worker who "refuses in good faith to expose himself to dangerous conditions" (29 C.F.R. 1977.12(b)(2)). The U.S. Supreme Court upheld this regulation (*Whirlpool*).

In Chapter 14 we learned that workers can take "concerted action" to protect their safety and complain to the National Labor Relations Board if they are made to suffer because of it. Between OSHA and the National Labor Relations Board, workers who refuse to work for safety reasons should be protected from discharge.

THE PROBLEM WITH OSHA

Two decades ago Congress dreamed of an agency that would forge a consensus on what had to be done to create a safe workplace and write safety standards that would guarantee everyone a safe place to work. The reality has been very different. For the first few years OSHA inspectors spent a great deal of time "nitpicking" employers about minor problems that were not really likely to cause serious injury. When OSHA insisted that every small appliance in every place of business be "grounded," this caused a high cost to employers with very little increase in safety.

While the act talks about fines of $1,000 and $10,000, in reality the fines imposed by OSHA have been trivial. It took the agency until the spring of 1988 to write a comprehensive regulation for toxic substances.

Throughout almost two decades, OSHA has seldom gotten more than a thousand inspectors into the field. From 1980 to 1986 the number of inspectors decreased from 1,328 to 1,044 and the number of injuries and illnesses on the job increased from 7.6 per hundred workers in 1983 to 8 per hundred workers in 1985.

The absence of an incentive for safety is exemplified by Victor Nazario's death in Austin, Texas. OSHA files showed that the construction company had been inspected several times, and almost every time OSHA inspectors found workers deep in trenches that were not shored up or sloped to protect workers from cave-ins. Each time the company paid the modest fine, never more than $2,000, and continued working. Victor Nazario died when a trench collapsed. The OSHA fine for the violation that killed Victor Nazario was $1,260 (*The New York Times*, August 2, 1987).

CRIMINAL CHARGES AGAINST THE EMPLOYER

Prosecutors in a number of states have begun to file criminal charges against employers. The county attorney in Austin, Texas, charged several employers in 1987 with criminally negligent homicide in cases where workers were buried alive in collapsing trenches. In Illinois an employer was charged with aggravated battery and reckless conduct when he knowingly exposed workers to toxic substances beyond safe levels. However, Illinois and Texas appeals courts threw out these indictments because they felt these cases were preempted by the Occupational Safety and Health Act (*Chicago Magnet*). In their view, only OSHA can punish these employers.

Four thousand years ago the city of Eshnunna flourished in the region east of today's Baghdad. The records they left behind suggest a civilized and fair people. One of their laws says: "If a wall is threatening to fall and the authorities have brought the fact to the knowledge of its owner, and he does not strengthen his wall, and the wall collapses and causes a free man's death, it is a capital offense." In an age when very few crimes justified the death penalty, causing the death of someone when it could have been prevented was considered a terrible crime. At the end of the twentieth century, in America, the average fine is less than $1,000.

19

Conclusion: Suing and Being Sued

Employers and supervisors have read about lawsuits throughout this book. It is only natural that some might think that anything they do might land them in court. But if you will recall most of the cases, you will realize that many of the supervisors and employers in this book deserved to be sued. Managers who follow generally accepted principles of management, and keep in mind the general dictates of the law, do not get sued.

There are some general rules that everyone—employer, supervisor, and employee—should follow:

1. **Keep a record of everything.** Many employers lose in court or at the unemployment-compensation office because they do not have the proper documentation. The same rule applies to employees. Every employee should keep a daily logbook or diary noting who ordered them to do what, along with a record of accomplishments and complaints.

2. **Keep your mouth shut.** In this book we have seen supervisors sued for defamation and employees fired for having a foul mouth. Add to that the fact that everything people say really can be used against them in a court of law and you have a very good reason to keep quiet.

3. **Talk to an attorney early.** Many lawsuits could be prevented if supervisors would talk to an attorney *before* taking action. Many employees could avoid throwing their cases away if they would talk to an attorney *before* doing something stupid, like resigning or admitting guilt.

4. **Keep pay records.** Employees have seen throughout this book that there are many times when they will have to prove what they are earning. A special box for paycheck stubs would be a good idea for everyone.

5. **Ask questions.** The law is constantly changing, and no one should think definitive answers to all questions are in this book. However, both supervisors and employees should now have a better idea of the questions they need to ask when the time comes to talk to an attorney.

6. **Keep up with deadlines.** You have seen that the law loves deadlines. An employer may have only a few days to decide whether to challenge an application for unemployment. An injured employee may have only a few days to notify his or her employer of a work-related injury. Appeals in worker's-compensation and unemployment-compensation cases must be filed in days, not months, while civil rights complaints must be filed in months, not years. The major cause for malpractice lawsuits against lawyers is that they waited past the deadline to file a lawsuit. You, as the client, should take enough interest in your own case to ask the attorney when the deadline is and make sure the lawsuit is filed on time.

7. **Do not accept legal advice from anyone other than your own attorney.** Many supervisors and co-workers mean well when they give free legal advice, but this kind of advice is not dependable.

8. **Tell your attorney everything that might be relevant.** You should now have a better idea of the kinds of things your attorney would like to know. If you are going to sue, your attorney will want to sue for everything that is reasonable under the law. The legal system wants you to do that. Once the system goes to the time and expense of a trial, the system would like you to get everything taken care of. Employers who are being sued should keep in mind that supervisors may not want to tell it all to the employer's attorney for their own personal reasons. An internal investigation may be called for and may pay off in the end.

9. **A little kindness goes a long way.** Many of the cases in this book came about because the supervisor could not resist being mean. Some employers have the idea that they must back up their supervisors no matter what. While that may be a good general rule, there are times when exceptions are called for. Too many lawsuits come about because a supervisor has been totally unreasonable, and higher management has failed to act. Firing people who have every right to complain about the way their supervisor has treated them is a sure way to end up in court.

Here is a scene that repeats itself all too often in American business. Mary, the employee, is doing a wonderful job, so wonderful that everyone in the company respects her and calls on her for help and advice concerning her area of expertise. They do not call on her supervisor, John. John feels jealous and left out. He imposes a series of work rules on Mary that cause her more and more difficulty until she finally breaks one of the rules and John fires her. Everyone in the company is upset. Mary is very distressed because her infraction is trivial compared to the amount and quality of work she was doing. Mary is going to sue for something because she does not feel she was treated fairly by either John or the company. In most cases she sues for either race or sex discrimination. Of course, higher management will support John, blindly and without question. When Mary files for unemployment compensation, the company will fight it. After all, isn't Mary guilty of misconduct? The company law firm explains that such a battle will be expensive and will force the company to expose much of its case to Mary's attorney, which will make it easier for him or her to prepare for the forthcoming discrimination battle. The law firm also explains that their legal fees for an all-out battle will be much higher than the increased cost to the company in unemployment taxes. If the state is New York, they will also explain that any facts decided in the unemployment hearing will be set in concrete and that the unemployment hearing is biased in favor of the worker in these kinds of cases. It is biased in that the worker is presumed not to have engaged in misconduct and the burden to prove misconduct is on the employer. Company executives say they do not care; it is the principle of the thing. Since most of the other employees feel Mary got a raw deal, company morale sinks to an all-time low. Most of them refuse to testify for Mary unless forced by subpoena, but when subpoenaed they sound like Mary supporters, and this makes company executives even more angry. Mary's lawyer is overjoyed. He or she gets to hear all the testimony of the other side. Even in a state that does not agree with New York and does not give the facts found by the unemployment hearing officer collateral estopple effect, these people are on record and cannot change their story later in the discrimination lawsuit. In many cases Mary gets her unemployment compensation and goes on to win her discrimination lawsuit.

Higher management should think twice about this story. While the decisions of line supervisors should be supported most of the time, blind allegiance is very costly. When you add the cost in lower company productivity because of the loss of Mary's excellent work and the reduction of morale to the cost in legal fees and bad publicity, it is just not worth it. It also costs every other employer because judges are so outraged by the company's behavior that they twist legal doctrines to allow Mary to win. While no state requires employers to treat their employees "fairly," every employer should consider doing just that. The long-term rewards could be very great.

References

The reader should go back to page 3 for an explanation of how to use these references.

Aasmundstad—337 N.W.2d 792 (N.D. 1983)

ABC—438 N.Y.S.2d 482 (N.Y. 1981)

Action for Boston—525 N.E.2d 411 (Mass. 1988)

Adler—432 A.2d 464 (Md. 1981)

Aebisher—622 F.2d 651 (2d Cir. 1980)

Aetna—724 S.W.2d 770 (Tex. 1987)

Aetna-Standard—493 A.2d 1375 (Pa. App. 1985)

AFSCME—770 F.2d 1401 (9th Cir. 1985)

Aiello—818 F.2d 1196 (5th Cir. 1987)

Airline Stewards—573 F.2d 960 (7th Cir. 1978)

Alaska Airlines—217 F.2d 295 (9th Cir. 1954)

Albuquerque—545 F.2d 110 (10th Cir. 1976)

Allegri—684 P.2d 1031 (Kan. App. 1984)

Allen #1—601 F. Supp. 482 (N.D. Ga. 1985)

Allen #2—501 A.2d 1169 (Pa. App. 1985)

Allen #3—494 N.E.2d 978 (Ind. App. 1986)

Alva—750 P.2d 28 (Ariz. 1988)

Ambroz—416 N.W.2d 510 (Neb. 1987)

American Can—424 F.2d 356 (8th Cir. 1970)

American Newspaper—345 U.S. 100 (1953)

American Smelting—501 F.2d 504 (8th Cir. 1974)

Amos—107 S. Ct. 2862 (1987)

Anchor Motor—424 U.S. 554 (1976)

Anco—693 P.2d 1183 (Kan. 1985)

Anderson—401 N.W.2d 75 (Minn. App. 1987)

Andracki—508 A.2d 624 (Pa. App. 1986)

Angelo—555 F.2d 1164 (3d Cir. 1977)

Ansonia—107 S. Ct. 367 (1986)

Aranda—748 S.W.2d 210 (Tex. 1988)

ARCO—515 A.2d 1095 (D.C. 1986)

Arline—107 S. Ct. 1123 (1987)

Armstrong—725 S.W.2d 953 (Tenn. App. 1986)

Arnett—416 U.S. 134 (1974)

Arnold—614 F. Supp. 853 (D.C. Okla. 1985)

Atascadero—662 F. Supp. 376 (C.D. Cal. 1987)

Atchley—729 S.W.2d 428 (Ark. App. 1987)

A.T. Hudson—524 A.2d 412 (N.J. App. 1987)

Attisano—531 A.2d 72 (Pa. App. 1987)

Auddino—507 A.2d 913 (Pa. App. 1986)

Ayala—831 F.2d 1314 (7th Cir. 1987)

Babcock & Wilcox—351 U.S 105 (1987)

Bader—505 A.2d 1162 (R.I. 1986)

Baker—394 N.W.2d 564 (Minn. App. 1986)

Bakke—438 U.S. 265 (1978)

Ball—731 S.W.2d 536 (Tenn. App. 1987)

Ballard—581 F. Supp. 160 (N.D. Ga. 1983)

Baltimore—504 A.2d 657 (Md. App. 1986)

Bama Tran.—732 P.2d 483 (Okla. App. 1986)

Barnes #1—561 F.2d 983 (D.C. Cir. 1977)

Barnes #2—745 F.2d 501 (8th Cir. 1984)

Barrentine—450 U.S. 728 (1981)

Barrett—649 F.2d 1193 (5th Cir., Unit A, 1981)

Bauman—475 So. 2d 1322 (Fla. App. 1985)

Beauchamp—398 N.W.2d 882 (Mich. 1986)

Beazer—440 U.S. 568 (1979)

Belasco—510 A.2d 337 (Pa. 1986)

Bello—504 A.2d 1015 (R.I. 1986)

Belwood Nursing—505 N.E.2d 1026 (Ill. 1987)

Bender Ship—379 So. 2d 594 (Ala. 1980)

Benoir—514 A.2d 716 (Vt. 1986)

Bergman—734 S.W.2d 673 (Tex. 1987)

Bergstedt—499 N.E.2d 902 (Ohio App. 1985)

Bernasconi—548 F.2d 857 (9th Cir. 1977)

Bernoudy—828 F.2d 1316 (8th Cir. 1987)

Berutti—496 N.E.2d 350 (Ill. App. 1986)

Bethlehem Mines—529 A.2d 610 (Pa. App. 1987)

Bever—724 F.2d 1083 (4th Cir. 1984)

Bhandari—829 F.2d 1343 (5th Cir. 1987)

Bird—740 P.2d 243 (Or. App. 1987)

Bishopp—788 F.2d 781 (D.C. Cir. 1986)

Black—354 S.E.2d 696 (Ga. App. 1987)

Blackwell—726 S.W.2d 760 (Mo. App. 1987)

Blake—595 F.2d 1367 (9th Cir. 1979)

Blanchard—499 A.2d 1345 (N.H. 1985)

Blue Mountain—503 A.2d 1073 (Pa. App. 1986)

BMY—504 A.2d 946 (Pa. App. 1986)

Boeing Vertol—528 A.2d 1020 (Pa. App. 1987)

Bohen—799 F.2d 1180 (7th Cir. 1986)

Boles—353 S.E.2d 286 (S.C. 1987)

Bostic—359 S.E.2d 614 (W. Va. 1987)

Bouchet—730 F.2d 799 (D.C. Cir. 1984)

Boudar—742 P.2d 491 (N.M. 1987)

Boundy—514 N.E.2d 931 (Ohio App. 1986)

Bouselli—402 A.2d 729 (Pa. App. 1979)

Bowan #1—724 P.2d 223 (N.M. 1986)

Bowan #2—107 S. Ct. 2287 (1987)

Bowers—402 A.2d 308 (Pa. App. 1979)

Bowman—331 S.E.2d 797 (Va. 1985)

Bradley—405 N.W.2d 243 (Minn. 1987)

Branti—445 U.S. 507 (1980)

Brazinski—513 N.E.2d 76 (Ill. App. 1987)

Brennan #1—494 F.2d 460 (8th Cir. 1974)

Brennan #2—504 A.2d 432 (Pa. App. 1986)

Brevik—416 N.W.2d 714 (Minn. 1987)

Broadrick—413 U.S. 601 (1973)

Brown County—369 N.W.2d 735 (Wis. 1985)

Browning-Ferris—501 A.2d 711 (Pa. App. 1985)

Bryant—722 P.2d 579 (Kan. 1986)

Buddle—613 F. Supp. 491 (S.D.N.Y. 1985)

Bundy—641 F.2d 934 (D.C. Cir. 1981)

Bunkers—521 F.2d 1217 (9th Cir. 1975)

Bunnell—741 P.2d 887 (Or. 1987)

Burlington—349 S.E.2d 842 (N.C. 1962)

Buscemi—736 F.2d 1348 (9th Cir. 1984)

Bussell—498 A.2d 787 (N.J. App. 1985)

Cagle—726 P.2d 434 (Wash. 1986)

Cahoon—499 N.E.2d 522 (Ill. App. 1986)

Cal. Fed.—107 S. Ct. 683 (1987)

Caldor—105 S. Ct. 2914 (1985)

Califano—430 U.S. 199 (1977)

Callaway—832 F.2d 414 (7th Cir. 1987)

Candelaria—730 P.2d 470 (N.M. App. 1986)

Capua—643 F. Supp. 1507 (D.N.J. 1986)

Carey—505 N.E.2d 111 (Ind. App. 1987)

Carpenter—401 N.W.2d 242 (Iowa 1986)

Caruso—506 N.Y.S.2d 789 (N.Y. Dist. 1986)

Castiglione—517 A.2d 786 (Md. App. 1986)

Castro—459 F.2d 725 (1st Cir. 1972)

Catlett—828 F.2d 1260 (8th Cir. 1987)

Central Point—554 F. Supp. 600 (D. Or. 1982)

Central Telephone—738 P.2d 510 (Nev. 1987)

Cert. Question—399 N.W.2d 320 (S.D. 1987)

Chaline—693 F.2d 477 (5th Cir. 1982)

Champlin Petroleum—593 F.2d 637 (5th Cir. 1979)

Chelsea—425 So. 2d 1090 (Ala. 1983)

Chevron—745 S.W.2d 314 (Tex. 1987)

Chicago Magnet—510 N.E.2d 1173 (Ill. App. 1987)

Chicago Teachers—106 S. Ct. 1066 (1986)

Childers—676 F.2d 1338 (10th Cir. 1982)

Chrisman—751 P.2d 140 (Kan. 1988)

Christensen—563 F.2d 353 (8th Cir. 1977)

Cilley—514 A.2d 818 (N.H. 1986)

City Stores—479 F.2d 235 (5th Cir. 1973)

Civil Service—413 U.S. 548 (1973)

Clanton—677 S.W.2d 441 (Tenn. 1984)

Cleary—168 Cal. Rptr. 722 (Cal. App. 1980)

Clifford—353 N.W.2d 469 (Mich. 1984)

Cline—352 S.E.2d 291 (S.C. App. 1986)

Cloutier—436 A.2d 1140 (N.H. 1981)

Codd—429 U.S. 624 (1977)

Coleman—520 A.2d 1341 (N.J. 1986)

Coley—561 F. Supp. 645 (E.D. Mich. 1982)

College-Town—508 N.E.2d 587 (Mass. 1987)

Collins #1—203 N.W.2d 594 (Iowa 1973)

Collins #2—349 F.2d 863 (2d Cir. 1965)

Colonial Taxi—521 A.2d 536 (Pa. App. 1987)

Columbus Ed. Assoc.—623 F.2d 1155 (6th Cir. 1980)

Colvig—42 Cal. Rptr. 473 (Cal. App. 1965)

Columbia—568 F.2d 953 (2d Cir. 1977)

Com. Bankers—516 N.E.2d 110 (Ind. App. 1987)

Com. Edison—494 N.E.2d 1186 (Ill. App. 1986)

Com. Office Prod.—108 S. Ct. 1666 (1988)

Conder—739 P.2d 634 (Utah App. 1987)

Connick—103 S. Ct. 1684 (1983)

Cook #1—488 A.2d 1295 (Conn. App. 1985)

Cook #2—501 N.E.2d 615 (Ohio 1986)

Cooper—723 P.2d 298 (Or. 1986)

Cordle—325 S.E.2d 111 (W. Va. 1984)

Corley—566 F.2d 994 (5th Cir. 1978)

Cornelio—243 F. Supp. 126 (E.D. Pa. 1985)

Corp. 613—510 A.2d 103 (N.J. App. 1986)

Coston—831 F.2d 1321 (7th Cir. 1987)

Cottrell—743 P.2d 716 (Or. 1987)

Coursey—234 N.E.2d 339 (Ill. App. 1967)

Craig—721 F.2d 77 (3d Cir. 1983)

Crawford—511 A.2d 1079 (Md. 1986)

Crenshaw—693 P.2d 487 (Mont. 1984)

Cuevas—500 N.E.2d 1047 (Ill. App. 1986)

Curran—498 A.2d 51 (Pa. App. 1985)

Curry—348 S.E.2d 465 (Ga. App. 1986)

Curtis—490 A.2d 178 (D.C. 1985)

Daniel Adams—519 A.2d 997 (Pa. App. 1987)

Danielson—742 P.2d 717 (Wash. 1987)

Danielson Mobil—394 N.W.2d 251 (Minn. App. 1986)

Darby—312 U.S. 100 (1941)

Darneille—744 P.2d 1091 (Wash. App. 1987)

Darrone—465 U.S. 624 (1984)

DaSilva—402 A.2d 755 (Conn. 1978)

Davis—35 FEP cases 975 (6th Cir. 1984)

Dean Van Horn—395 N.W.2d 405 (Minn. App. 1986)

Deauville—756 F.2d 1183 (5th Cir. 1985)

DeBartolo—108 S. Ct. 1392 (1988)

DeFosse—510 N.E.2d 141 (Ill. App. 1987)

Del Borrello—508 A.2d 368 (Pa. App. 1986)

Delaney—681 P.2d 114 (Or. 1984)

Demech—400 A.2d 502 (N.J. App. 1979)

Denver—756 P.2d 373 (Colo. 1988)

DeRose—496 N.E.2d 428 (Mass. 1986)

Derosia—519 A.2d 601 (Vt. 1986)

Desai—510 A.2d 662 (N.J. 1986)

Diaz—442 F.2d 385 (5th Cir. 1971)

Dillingham—348 S.E.2d 143 (N.C. App. 1986)

Dist. 709—412 N.W.2d 320 (Minn. App. 1987)

Doering—496 A.2d 720 (N.J. 1985)

Donahue—471 F.2d 475 (7th Cir. 1972)

Donaldson—496 A.2d 1370 (Pa. App. 1985)

Donato—379 F.2d 288 (3d Cir. 1967)

Dothard—433 U.S. 321 (1977)

Downes—775 F.2d 288 (Fed. Cir. 1985)

Downslope—676 F.2d 1114 (6th Cir. 1982)

Dred Scott—60 U.S. 393 (1857)

Drews—727 P.2d 1121 (Colo. App. 1986)

Duldulao—505 N.E.2d 314 (Ill. 1987)

D'Ulisse-Cupo—520 A.2d 217 (Conn. 1987)

Dunkle—496 A.2d 880 (Pa. App. 1985)

Duran—742 P.2d 1197 (Or. App. 1987)

Durango—614 P.2d 880 (Colo. 1980)

Durepos—516 A.2d 565 (Me. 1986)

Dye—781 S.W.2d 826 (Ky. App. 1987)

East Point—359 S.E.2d 672 (Ga. App. 1987)

Easter Seal Society—815 F.2d 323 (5th Cir. 1987)

Eavenson—730 P.2d 464 (N.M. 1986)

Eckles—548 F.2d 905 (10th Cir. 1977)

Eddings—496 N.E.2d 1167 (Ill. App. 1986)

EEOC—829 F.2d 392 (3d Cir. 1987)

Eggleston—724 S.W.2d 462 (Ark. 1987)

Eib—633 S.W.2d 432 (Mo. App. 1982)

Eide—397 N.W.2d 532 (Mich. App. 1986)

Eldridge—417 N.W.2d 797 (N.D. 1987)

Ellett—505 A.2d 888 (Md. App. 1986)

Elliott—106 S.Ct. 3220 (1986)

Elrod—427 U.S. 347 (1976)

Enstar—737 S.W.2d 890 (Tex. App. 1987)

Equitable—389 N.W.2d 876 (Minn. 1986)

Espinoza—414 U.S. 86 (1973)

Exxon #1—508 A.2d 142 (Md. App. 1986)

Exxon #2—491 A.2d 318 (Pa. App. 1985)

Fairmont—454 F.2d 490 (4th Cir. 1972)

Fair—542 A.2d 1118 (Conn. 1988)

Fair Oaks—729 P.2d 743 (Cal. 1987)

Fansteel—306 U.S. 240 (1939)

Farley—529 S.W.2d 751 (Tex. 1975)

Farmers Ins.—713 P.2d 1027 (Olka. 1985)

Farwell—4 Metc. 49 (Mass. 1842)

Favors—367 S.E.2d 328 (Ga. App. 1988)

Ferraro—368 N.W.2d 666 (Wis. 1985)

Fichera—32 Cal. Rptr. 159 (Cal. App. 1963)

Field #1—503 N.E.2d 627 (Ind. App. 1987)

Field #2—507 A.2d 1209 (N.J. App. 1986)

Figgie—502 N.E.2d 797 (Ill. App. 1986)

Finley—520 A.2d 208 (Conn. 1987)

Firefighters—549 F.2d 506 (8th Cir. 1977)

Firestone Textile—666 S.W.2d 730 (Ky. 1983)

First Victoria—420 F.2d 648 (5th Cir. 1969)

Fisher—14 Wend. 10 (N.Y. 1836)

Flowers—552 F.2d 1277 (7th Cir. 1977)

Foley—508 N.E.2d 72 (Mass. 1987)

Folz—594 F. Supp. 1007 (W.D. Mo. 1984)

Ford—734 P.2d 580 (Ariz. 1987)

Ford Motor Co.—345 U.S. 330 (1953)

Fore—727 S.W.2d 840 (Ark. 1987)

Fortner—357 S.E.2d 167 (N.C. 1987)

Fortune—364 N.E.2d 1251 (Mass. 1977)

Frampton—297 N.E.2d 425 (Ind. 1973)

Francis—726 P.2d 852 (N.M. 1986)

Franks—424 U.S. 747 (1976)

Frazee—512 N.E.2d 789 (Ill. App. 1987)

Freidrichs—410 N.W.2d 62 (Minn. App. 1987)

French—526 A.2d 861 (Conn. 1987)

Frontiero—411 U.S. 677 (1973)

Ft. Halifax—107 S. Ct. 2211 (1987)

Furno—522 A.2d 746 (Vt. 1986)

Gamble—345 U.S. 117 (1953)

Gannon—561 F. Supp. 1377 (N.D. Ill. 1983)

Garber—552 F.2d 1032 (4th Cir. 1977)

Garcia—105 S. Ct. 1005 (1985)

Gardner—752 F.2d 1271 (8th Cir. 1985)

Gardner-Denver—415 U.S. 36 (1974)

Gates—668 P.2d 213 (Mont. 1983)

Gathering—495 N.E.2d 207 (Ind. App. 1986)

Gatins—349 S.E. 2d 818 (Ga. App. 1986)

Gee—139 F. 582 (S.D. Iowa 1905)

Geiser—722 S.W.2d 122 (Mo. App. 1986)

General Motors—373 U.S. 734 (1963)

Georgia Power—250 S.E.2d 442 (Ga. 1978)

Gibson—358 S.E.2d 320 (Ga. App. 1987)

Gifford-Hill—725 S.W.2d 712 (Tex. 1987)

Gilbert—429 U.S. 125 (1976)

Gilbertson—403 F. Supp. 1 (D. Conn. 1975)

Givhan—99 S. Ct. 693 (1979)

Gladden—728 S.W.2d 501 (Ark. 1987)

Glanville—637 S.W.2d 328 (Mo. App. 1982)

Globe Sec.—520 A.2d 545 (Pa. App. 1987)

Golden Bear—494 N.E.2d 581 (Ill. App. 1986)

Gompers—221 U.S. 418 (1911)

Goettler—508 A.2d 630 (Pa. App. 1986)

Goose Creek—519 F.2d 53 (5th Cir. 1975)

Gov. Employees—651 F. Supp. 726 (S.D. Ga. 1986)

Grace—395 N.W.2d 576 (N.D. 1986)

Grand Rapids Die—831 F.2d 112 (6th Cir. 1987)

Grant—490 A.2d 1115 (D.C. App. 1985)

Great Plains—407 N.W.2d 166 (Neb. 1987)

Green #1—526 A.2d 1192 (Pa. App. 1987)

Green #2—499 A.2d 870 (D.C. 1986)

Green Hills—514 N.E.2d 1227 (Ill. App. 1987)

Greenfield—500 N.E.2d 1083 (Ill. App. 1986)

Greenwood—108 S. Ct. 1625 (1988)

Griggs—401 U.S. 424 (1971)

Grossart—758 F.2d 1221 (7th Cir. 1985)

Grove City—465 U.S. 555 (1984)

Guffey—727 S.W.2d 826 (Ark. 1987)

Guimarales—503 N.E.2d 113 (N.Y. 1986)

Gunther—452 U.S. 161 (1981)

Hale—831 F.2d 1007 (11th Cir. 1987)

Hamm—708 F.2d 647 (11th Cir. 1983)

Hammer—247 U.S. 251 (1918)

Hammond—498 N.E.2d 48 (Ind. App. 1986)

Hanley—506 A.2d 994 (Pa. App. 1986)

Hansen—507 N.E.2d 573 (Ind. 1987)

Hardison—432 U.S. 63 (1977)

Hardy—145 Cal. Rptr. 176 (Cal. 1978)

Harless—246 S.E.2d 270 (W. Va. 1978)

Harper—383 U.S. 663 (1966)

Hartford—492 A.2d 1270 (Md. 1985)

Hayes—505 N.E.2d 408 (Ill. App. 1987)

Hazlett—496 N.E.2d 478 (Ohio 1986)

Heck's—342 S.E.2d 453 (W. Va. 1986)

Hedrick—454 N.E.2d 1343 (Ohio App. 1982)

Heideck—446 A.2d 1095 (Del. 1982)

Hellwig—538 A.2d 1243 (N.J. 1988)

Helvering—301 U.S. 619 (1937)

Henry—221 N.W.2d 174 (Mich. App. 1974)

Henson—682 F.2d 897 (11th Cir. 1982)

Hentzel—188 Cal. Rptr. 159 (Cal. App. 1982)

Hepp—150 Cal. Rptr. 408 (Cal. App. 1978)

Herbert—A.C. 209, 111 (1930)

Hercules—356 S.E.2d 453 (Va. App. 1987)

Hercules Powder—53 S.E.2d 804 (Va. 1949)

Herley—490 A.2d 979 (R.I. 1985)

Hicklin—437 U.S. 518 (1978)

Higgins—578 F.2d 281 (10th Cir. 1978)

Hill—421 U.S. 289 (1975)

Hines—531 F.2d 726 (5th Cir. 1976)

Hinson—742 P.2d 549 (Okla. 1987)

Hinthorn—519 N.E.2d 909 (Ill. 1988)

Hobbie—107 S. Ct. 1046 (1987)

Hodge #1—778 F.2d 794 (D.C. Cir. 1985)

Hodge #2—707 F.2d 961 (7th Cir. 1983)

Hoffman—512 So. 2d 725 (Ala. 1987)

Hoffsetz—757 P.2d 155 (Colo. App. 1988)

Hogan—458 U.S. 718 (1982)

Holbrook—405 N.W.2d 537 (Minn. App. 1987)

Hooks—367 S.E.2d 647 (N.C. 1988)

Hopewell—528 A.2d 1082 (Pa. App. 1987)

Horn—796 F.2d 668 (3d Cir. 1986)

Howard—414 A.2d 1273 (N.H. 1980)

Howard U.—484 A.2d 958 (D.C. 1984)

Hughes—746 S.W.2d 796 (Tex. App. 1988)

Hunt—4 Metcalf 111 (Mass. 1842)

Hurst—724 P.2d 946 (Or. App. 1986)

HV—747 P.2d 55 (Idaho 1987)

IBP—727 P.2d 468 (Kan. 1986)

Ingersoll-Rand—542 A.2d 879 (N.J. 1988)

Inside Radio—498 A.2d 791 (N.J. App. 1985)

Ives—498 A.2d 297 (N.H. 1985)

Jackson—768 F.2d 1325 (Fed. Cir. 1985)

Jacksonville Terminal—451 F.2d 418 (5th Cir. 1971)

Jasany—755 F.2d 1244 (6th Cir. 1984)

Jeffcoat—732 P.2d 1073 (Alaska 1987)

Jenks—490 A.2d 912 (Pa. App. 1985)

Jett—798 F.2d 748 (5th Cir. 1986)

Johnson #1—498 N.E.2d 575 (Ill. App. 1986)

Johnson #2—107 S. Ct. 1442 (1987)

Johnson #3—408 N.W.2d 261 (Neb. 1987)

Johnson #4—490 A.2d 676 (Me. 1985)

Johnson #5—105 S. Ct. 2717 (1985)

Johnson #6—745 S.W.2d 661 (Mo. 1988)

Johnston—357 S.E.2d 450 (S.C. 1987)

Jones #1—392 U.S. 409 (1968)

Jones #2—508 N.E.2d 1322 (Ind. App. 1987)

Jones #3—746 S.W.2d 891 (Tex. App. 1988)

Jordan—620 F.2d 298 (5th Cir. 1980)

Jumacris—355 S.E.2d 378 (W. Va. 1987)

K Mart—732 P.2d 1364 (Nev. 1987)

Kachinski—532 A.2d 374 (Pa. 1987)

Kalman—443 A.2d 728 (N.J. App. 1982)

Kaluza—403 N.W. 2d 230 (Minn. 1987)

Kater—728 P.2d 746 (Colo. App. 1986)

Katz—709 F.2d 251 (4th Cir. 1983)

Kear—517A.2d 586 (Pa. App. 1986)

Kearney—492 A.2d 790 (Pa. App. 1985)

Keast—503 A.2d 507 (Pa. App. 1986)

Keenan—731 P.2d 708 (Colo. 1987)

Kelly—397 So. 2d 874 (Miss. 1981)

Kelsay—384 N.E.2d 353 (Ill. 1978)

Kem—355 S.E.2d 437 (Ga. App. 1987)

Kenall—504 N.E.2d 805 (Ill. App. (1987)

Kennedy—449 F. Supp. 1008 (D. Colo. 1978)

Kerr—733 P.2d 1292 (Mont. 1987)

KGB—164 Cal. Rptr. 571 (Cal. App. 1980)

Kiehl—535 A.2d 571 (Pa. 1987)

Kiepura—358 F. Supp. 987 (N.D. Ill. 1973)

Kinoshita—724 P.2d 110 (Hawaii 1986)

Kiriaka—509 A.2d 560 (Conn. App. 1986)

Kling—735 S.W.2d 168 (Mo. App. 1987)

Knight—714 P.2d 788 (Alaska 1986)

Koellmer—527 A.2d 1210 (Conn. App. 1987)

Kolman—412 N.W.2d 109 (S.D. 1987)

Kostaras—650 F. Supp. 576 (S.D.N.Y. 1986)

Kowal—512 A.2d 812 (Pa. App. 1986)

Krein—415 N.W.2d 793 (N.D. 1987)

Kreinz—406 N.W.2d 164 (Wis. App. 1987)

Krolick—308 N.Y.S.2d 879 (N.Y. 1970)

Kuebler—473 F.2d 359 (6th Cir. 1973)

Kuna—512 A.2d 772 (Pa. App. 1986)

LaBlanc—501 N.E.2d 503 (Mass. 1986)

La Crosse—407 N.W.2d 510 (Wis. 1987)

LaFalce—712 F.2d 292 (7th Cir. 1983)

Laffey—567 F.2d 429 (D.C. Cir. 1976)

Lapare—742 P.2d 819 (Ariz. App. 1987)

Lapham—519 A.2d 1101 (Pa. App. 1987)

Larimer County—727 P.2d 401 (Colo. App. 1986)

Larose—508 A.2d 1364 (Vt. 1986)

Lavey—502 A.2d 344 (R.I. 1985)

Lauritzen—835 F.2d 1529 (7th Cir. 1987)

Ledbetter—350 S.E.2d 299 (Ga. App. 1986)

Lee—401 A.2d 12 (Pa. App. 1979)

Lee Way—431 F.2d 245 (10th Cir. 1970)

Lehman—651 F.2d 520 (7th Cir. 1981)

Leikvold—688 P.2d 170 (Ariz. 1984)

Leithead—721 P.2d 1059 (Wyo. 1986)

Lemons—620 F.2d 228 (10th Cir. 1980)

Lessley—727 P.2d 440 (Kan. 1986)

Leveck—498 N.E.2d 529 (Ill. App. 1986)

Lewis—500 N.E.2d 47 (Ill. App. 1986)

Lilly—797 F.2d 191 (4th Cir. 1986)

Lindsey—754 P.2d 1152 (Ariz. App. 1987)

Lingle—108 S. Ct. 1877 (1988)

Livas—711 F.2d 798 (7th Cir. 1983)

Local 28—106 S. Ct. 3019 (1986)

Local 93—106 S. Ct. 3063 (1986)

Lochner—198 U.S. 45 (1905)

Locricchio—833 F.2d 1352 (9th Cir. 1987)

Loeb—600 F.2d 1003 (1st Cir. 1979)

Loffa—738 P.2d 1146 (Ariz. App. 1987)

Lopata—493 A.2d 657 (Pa. 1985)

Loudermill—105 S. Ct. 1487 (1985)

Loughry—494 N.E.2d 70 (N.Y. 1986)

Lovato—742 P.2d 499 (N.M. 1987)

Lovely—347 N.W.2d 752 (Mich. App. 1984)

Lovvorn—647 F. Supp. 875 (E.D. Tenn. 1986)

Lowe—207 S.E.2d 620 (Ga. App. 1974)

Lucas—736 F.2d 1202 (8th Cir. 1984)

Luddie—497 A.2d 435 (Conn. App. 1985)

Ludwick—337 S.E.2d 213 (S.C. 1985)

Lukoski—748 P.2d 507 (N.M. 1988)

Lutheran—340 N.W.2d 388 (Neb. 1983)

Lynn—564 F.2d 1282 (9th Cir. 1977)

Lyon—400 A.2d 1010 (Vt. 1979)

MacKay Radio—304 U.S. 333 (1938)

Mahaffey—562 F. Supp. 887 (D. Kan. 1983)

Mailhiot—510 N.E.2d 773 (Mass. App. 1987)

Mallory—165 S.E.2d 913 (Ga. App. 1968)

Manatawny Manor—401 A.2d 424 (Pa. App. 1979)

Mantech—347 S.E.2d 548 (Va. App. 1986)

Mantolete—767 F.2d 1416 (9th Cir. 1985)

Marine—391 U.S. 418 (1964)

Marshall—436 U.S. 307 (1978)

Martin #1—528 A.2d 947 (Pa. 1987)

Martin #2—447 A.2d 1290 (N.J. 1982)

Martinez—710 F.2d 1102 (5th Cir. 1983)

Mason—832 F.2d 383 (7th Cir. 1987)

Mass. Mutual—105 S. Ct. 3085 (1985)

Mastro Plastics—350 U.S. 270 (1956)

Matson—510 A.2d 819 (Pa. App. 1986)

Mays—775 F.2d 258 (8th Cir. 1985)

MCA Records—153 Cal. Rptr. 153 (Cal. App. 1979)

McCarthy—730 P.2d 681 (Wash. App. 1986)

McCartney—508 A.2d 1254 (Pa. App. 1986)

McClanahan—517 N.E.2d 390 (Ind. 1988)

McClung—360 S.E.2d 221 (W. Va. 1987)

McCluskey—484 So. 2d 398 (Ala. 1986)

McCoy—412 N.W.2d 24 (Minn. App. 1987)

McCray—205 S.E.2d 674 (Va. 1974)

McDaniel—350 S.E.2d 225 (Va. App. 1986)

McDonald—427 U.S. 273 (1976)

McDonell—809 F.2d 1302 (8th Cir. 1987)

McDonnell Douglas—411 U.S. 792 (1973)

McGill—724 P.2d 905 (Or. App. 1986)

McGraw—352 S.E.2d 435 (N.C. App. 1987)

McIntosh—469 P.2d 177 (Hawaii 1970)

McKenzie—833 F.2d 335 (D.C. Cir. 1987)

McMullan—65 N.W. 661 (Minn. 1896)

McQuary—684 P.2d 21 (Or. App. 1985)

Medrano—416 U.S. 802 (1974)

Meeks—779 F.2d 417 (7th Cir. 1985)

Mendez #1—516 A.2d 806 (Pa. App. 1986)

Mendez #2—725 P.2d 584 (N.M. App. 1986)

Mennor—829 F.2d 553 (5th Cir. 1987)

Mercer—361 N.E.2d 492 (Ohio App. 1977)

Meritor—106 S. Ct. 2399 (1986)
Mers—483 N.E.2d 150 (Ohio 1985)
Met. Life #1—107 S. Ct. 1542 (1987)
Met. Life #2—471 U.S. 724 (1985)
Metz—828 F.2d 1202 (7th Cir. 1987)
MGM—728 P.2d 821 (Nev. 1986)
Michels—497 N.E.2d 586 (Ind. App. 1986)
Michelson—808 F.2d 1005 (3d Cir. 1987)
Mignowe—525 A.2d 1297 (Pa. App. 1987)
Miller—513 A.2d 597 (R.I. 1987)
Millison—501 A.2d 505 (N.J. 1985)
Mingachos—491 A.2d 368 (Conn. 1985)
Miranda—384 U.S. 436 (1966)
Misco—108 S. Ct. 364 (1987)
Mobile Auto Trim—725 S.W.2d 168 (Tex. 1987)
Mobile Coal—704 P.2d 702 (Wyo. 1985)
Monge—316 A.2d 549 (N.H. 1974)
Moniodis—494 A.2d 212 (Md. App. 1985)
Moore—452 F.2d 726 (5th Cir. 1971)
Morris—513 A.2d 66 (Conn. 1986)
Morriss—738 P.2d 841 (Kan. 1987)
Mouradian—503 N.E.2d 1318 (Mass. App. 1987)
Mt. Healthy—429 U.S. 274 (1977)
Mudd—543 A.2d 1094 (Pa. App. 1988)
Mulei—739 P.2d 889 (Colo. App. 1987)
Mummau—687 F.2d 9 (3rd Cir. 1982)
Murphree—449 So. 2d 1218 (Ala. 1984)
Murphy—461 N.Y.S.2d 232 (N.Y. 1983)
Myrtle Springs—705 S.W.2d 707 (Tex. App. 1985)
National Settlement—349 S.E.2d 177 (Ga. 1987)
Nees—536 P.2d 512 (Or. 1975)
Nelson—655 P.2d 242 (Wash. 1982)
Ness—660 F.2d 517 (3d Cir. 1981)
Newark—524 A.2d 430 (N.J. App. 1987)
Newport—462 U.S. 669 (1983)
Nichols—729 P.2d 13 (Or. App. 1986)
Northwest Foods—731 P.2d 470 (Utah 1986)
Norton—728 P.2d 1025 (Utah 1986)
Novosel—721 F.2d 894 (3d Cir. 1983)
Numed—724 S.W.2d 432 (Tex. App. 1987)

O'Connor—107 S. Ct. 1492 (1987)
Odgers—525 A.2d 359 (Pa. 1987)
O'Hollaren—730 P.2d 616 (Or. App. 1986)
Ohio Council 8—499 N.E.2d 1276 (Ohio App. 1985)
Oliver—466 U.S. 170 (1984)
Opp Cotton—459 So. 2d 814 (Ala. 1984)
Oregon—400 U.S. 112 (1970)
Oregon Beauty—733 P.2d 430 (Or. 1987)
Ortwein—511 F.2d 696 (5th Cir. 1975)
Osterkamp—332 N.W.2d 275 (S.D. 1983)
Owen—445 U.S. 622 (1980)
Owensboro—750 S.W.2d 422 (Ky. 1988)
Oxford—743 S.W.2d 380 (Ark. 1988)
Pa. Labor—502 A.2d 771 (Pa. App. 1986)
Palmateer—421 N.E.2d 876 (Ill. 1981)
Palmer—752 P.2d 685 (Kan. 1988)
Panhandle—637 P.2d 1020 (Wyo. 1981)
Paradise—107 S. Ct. 1053 (1987)
Parker—89 Cal. Rptr. 737 (Cal. App. 1979)
Parnar—652 P.2d 625 (Hawaii 1982)
Patchogue-Medford—505 N.Y.S.2d 888 (N.Y. App. 1986)
Patsy—457 U.S. 496 (1982)
Pattern Makers—105 S. Ct. 3064 (1985)
Patton—741 P.2d 301 (Ariz. App. 1987)
Paul's Auto—409 N.W.2d 506 (Minn. 1987)
Payne—520 A.2d 586 (Vt. 1986)
Paynter—491 A.2d 1186 (Md. 1985)
Peeples—522 A.2d 680 (Pa. App. 1987)
Pemberton—502 A.2d 1101 (Md. App. 1986)
Percival—539 F.2d 1126 (8th Cir. 1976)
Perry—408 U.S. 593 (1972)
Petermann—344 P.2d 25 (Cal. App. 1959)
Pfenning—522 A.2d 743 (Vt. 1986)
Phillips—711 F.2d 1524 (11th Cir. 1983)
Phipps—408 N.W.2d 569 (Minn. 1987)
Phung—491 N.E.2d 1114 (Ohio 1986)
Pickering—391 U.S. 563 (1968)
Pickles—492 A.2d 90 (Pa. App. 1985)
Pierce—417 A.2d 505 (N.J. 1980)
Pilot Freight—351 S.E.2d 560 (N.C. App. 1987)
Pilot Life—107 S. Ct. 1549 (1987)

Pine River—333 N.W.2d 622 (Minn. 1983)

Piscopo—521 A.2d 846 (N.J. App. 1986)

Pistner—499 N.E.2d 566 (Ill. App. 1986)

Poll—498 A.2d 142 (Conn. App. 1985)

Pollock—322 U.S. 4 (1944)

Polly—407 N.W.2d 751 (Neb. 1987)

Ponderosa Villa—399 N.W.2d 813 (Neb. 1987)

Poole—750 P.2d 1000 (Kan. 1988)

Pope—500 N.E.2d 209 (Ind. App. 1986)

Powell—514 A.2d 241 (Pa. App. 1986)

Pranzo—521 So. 2d 983 (Ala. 1988)

Priest—634 F. Supp. 571 (N.D. Cal. 1986)

Priestly—3 M & W 1 (1837)

Puckett—725 S.W.2d 674 (Tenn. 1987)

Pugh—171 Cal. Rptr. 917 (Cal. App. 1981)

Quinn—711 P.2d 139 (Or. 1985)

Rabidue—584 F. Supp. 419 (E.D. Mich. 1984)

Radcliffe—508 N.E.2d 953 (Ohio 1987)

Ragland—724 P.2d 519 (Alaska 1986)

Railway Express—421 U.S. 454 (1975)

Rancourt—526 A.2d 1385 (Me. 1987)

Rankin—107 S. Ct. 2891 (1987)

Redgrave—502 N.E.2d 1375 (Mass. 1987)

Reed—404 U.S. 71 (1971)

Reich—454 So. 2d 982 (Ala. 1984)

Reichman—536 F. Supp. 1149 (M.D. Pa. 1982)

Renfroe—722 F.2d 714 (11th Cir. 1984)

Renny—398 N.W.2d 327 (Mich. 1986)

Rent-A-Mom—727 P.2d 403 (Colo. App. 1986)

Republic Aviation—324 U.S. 793 (1945)

Reynolds #1—235 U.S. 133 (1914)

Reynolds #2—377 U.S. 533 (1964)

Richland Shoe—108 S. Ct. 1677 (1988)

Richmond Memorial—349 S.E.2d 419 (Va. App. 1986)

Rieger—521 A.2d 84 (Pa. App. 1987)

Riffert—530 A.2d 906 (Pa. App. 1987)

Rivera—504 N.E.2d 381 (N.Y. 1986)

Roadway Express—830 F.2d 179 (11th Cir. 1987)

Roberson—722 S.W.2d 380 (Tenn. 1986)

Robinson's Case—198 N.E. 760 (Mass. 1935)

Rocke—503 A.2d 1103 (Pa. App. 1986)

Rodeen—733 P.2d 544 (Wash. App. 1987)

Rodriquez—569 F.2d 1231 (3d Cir. 1977)

Rogers—454 F.2d 234 (5th Cir. 1971)

Romack—511 N.E.2d 1024 (Ind. 1987)

Rosenfield—827 F.2d 1493 (11th Cir. 1987)

Roth—408 U.S. 564 (1972)

Rowlett—832 F.2d 194 (1st Cir. 1987)

Rudman—330 N.Y.S.2d 33 (N.Y. 1972)

Ruffiner—506 N.E.2d 581 (Ill. 1987)

Russ—680 F.2d 97 (8th Cir. 1982)

Sabetay—506 N.E.2d 919 (N.Y. 1987)

Sabine—687 S.W.2d 733 (Tex. 1985)

Sadler—409 N.W.2d 87 (N.D. 1987)

Safety Med.—724 P.2d 468 (Wyo. 1986)

Sage Realty—507 F. Supp. 599 (S.D.N.Y. 1981)

Salida Sch.—732 P.2d 1160 (Colo. 1987)

Salisbury—615 F. Supp. 1433 (D.C. Ky. 1985)

Salzhandler—316 F.2d 445 (2d Cir. 1963)

Sanchez—733 P.2d 1234 (Idaho 1986)

Sarzillo—501 A.2d 135 (N.J. 1985)

Savich—501 N.E.2d 464 (Ind. App. 1986)

Schafer—728 P.2d 394 (Idaho 1986)

Schechter—491 A.2d 938 (Pa. App. 1985)

Scheduling Corp.—503 N.E.2d 806 (Ill. App. 1987)

Schmerber—384 U.S. 757 (1966)

Schuermann—351 S.E.2d 339 (S.C. 1986)

Scott—409 So. 2d 791 (Ala. 1982)

Scovile—338 F.2d 678 (7th Cir. 1964)

Seaboard—347 S.E.2d 627 (Ga. App. 1986)

Security—460 F.2d 57 (8th Cir. 1972)

Seeger—380 U.S. 163 (1965)

Seeley—505 A.2d 95 (Me. 1986)

Seibel—752 P.2d 291 (Or. 1988)

Seiler—507 N.E.2d 628 (Ind. App. 1987)

Selcraig—705 F.2d 789 (5th Cir. 1983)

Semancik—466 F.2d 144 (3d Cir. 1972)

Setser—657 F.2d 962 (8th Cir. 1981)

Shakman—722 F.2d 1307 (7th Cir. 1983)

Shannon—425 N.W.2d 165 (Mich. App. 1988)

Shaw #1—328 N.E.2d 775 (Ind. App. 1975)

Shaw #2—539 A.2d 1383 (Pa. App. 1988)

Shebar—544 A.2d 377 (N.J. 1988)

Sheet Metal Workers—416 F.2d 123 (8th Cir. 1969)

Sheets—427 A.2d 385 (Conn. 1980)

Shelby Memorial—726 F.2d 1542 (11th Cir. 1984)

Shepherd—506 N.E.2d 874 (Mass. 1987)

Sherman—500 A.2d 230 (Vt. 1985)

Shingles—513 A.2d 575 (Pa. App. 1986)

Shoemaker—795 F.2d 1136 (3d Cir. 1986)

Shrimp—368 A.2d 408 (N.J. App. 1976)

Shultz—421 F.2d 259 (3d Cir. 1970)

Sides—328 S.E.2d 818 (N.C. App. 1985)

Simpson #1—643 P.2d 1276 (Or. 1982)

Simpson #2—522 A.2d 110 (Pa. App. 1987)

Sinai Hosp.—522 A.2d 382 (Md. 1987)

Sindermann—408 U.S. 564 (1972)

Siteman—511 S.W.2d 436 (Mo. App. 1974)

Slochower—350 U.S. 551 (1956)

Small—357 S.E.2d 452 (S.C. 1987)

Snarr—504 N.E.2d 1168 (Ohio App. 1985)

Soliman—531 A.2d 819 (Pa. App. 1987)

South Wind—494 N.E.2d 1158 (Ohio App. 1985)

Southeastern—442 U.S. 397 (1979)

Southern Pacific—729 S.W.2d 946 (Tex. App. 1987)

Southside—827 F.2d 270 (8th Cir. 1987)

Southwest Gas—668 P.2d 261 (Nev. 1983)

Specialty Cabinet—734 P.2d 437 (Utah 1986)

Speckman—508 N.E.2d 1336 (Ind. App. 1987)

Spencer—501 A.2d 1159 (Pa. App. 1985)

Sprogis—444 F.2d 1194 (7th Cir. 1971)

St. Barnabas—525 A.2d 885 (Pa. App. 1987)

St. Francis—107 S. Ct. 2022 (1987)

Staggs—486 A.2d 798 (Md. App. 1986)

Steamfitters—542 F.2d 579 (2d Cir. 1976)

Stebbins—442 F.2d 843 (D.C. Cir. 1971)

Steele—323 U.S. 192 (1944)

Steelworkers #1—443 U.S. 193 (1979)

Steelworkers #2—429 U.S. 305 (1977)

Steelworkers Trilogy—363 U.S. 564, 574, 593 (1960)

Sterry—494 A.2d 748 (Md. App. 1985)

Stewart—504 N.E.2d 84 (Ill. 1987)

Stone—522 A.2d 211 (R.I. 1987)

Stotts—104 S. Ct. 2576 (1984)

Stover—366 S.E.2d 670 (Ga. 1988)

Stowe Spinning—336 U.S. 226 (1941)

Suchodolski—316 N.W.2d 710 (Mich. 1982)

Sullivan—491 A.2d 1096 (Conn. 1985)

Sun Ship—447 U.S. 715 (1980)

Suscy—538 F.2d 1264 (7th Cir. 1976)

Swan—521 N.E.2d 787 (Ohio 1988)

Sweeney #1—439 U.S. 24 (1978)

Sweeney #2—669 F.2d 542 (8th Cir. 1982)

Swift—504 N.E.2d 621 (Mass. 1987)

Swilley—629 F.2d 1018 (5th Cir. 1980)

Swing—312 U.S. 321 (1941)

Synthetic Rubber—655 S.W.2d 489 (Ky. 1983)

Syverson—406 N.W.2d 688 (N.D. 1987)

Tameny—610 P.2d 1330 (Cal. 1980)

Tate—403 N.W.2d 666 (Minn. App. 1987)

Tattrie—521 A.2d 970 (Pa. App. 1987)

Taylor—413 N.W.2d 736 (Mich. App. 1987)

Teamsters—431 U.S. 324 (1977)

Terry—392 U.S. 1 (1968)

Texaco—729 S.W.2d 768 (Tex. App. 1987)

Theriault—495 F.2d 390 (5th Cir. 1974)

Thomas—107 S. Ct. 2520 (1987)

Thompson #1—685 P.2d 1081 (Wash. 1984)

Thompson #2—490 A.2d 219 (Me. 1985)

Thornhill—310 U.S. 88 (1940)

Tomczak—765 F.2d 633 (7th Cir. 1985)

Tomkins—568 F.2d 1044 (3d Cir. 1977)

Torres—781 F.2d 1134 (5th Cir. 1986)

Total Health—502 N.E.2d 1240 (Ill. App. 1986)

Tourville—508 A.2d 1263 (Pa. App. 1986)

Toussaint—292 N.W.2d 880 (Mich. 1980)

Tree Fruits—377 U.S. 58 (1964)

Trigg—766 F.2d 299 (7th Cir. 1985)

Trombetta—265 N.W.2d 385 (Mich. App. 1978)

Tron—517 A.2d 113 (Md. App. 1986)

Trotman—635 F.2d 216 (3d Cir. 1980)

Trotti—677 S.W.2d 632 (Tex. App. 1984)

True—513 A.2d 257 (Me. 1986)

TSEU—746 S.W.2d 203 (Tex. 1987)

TWA—525 F.2d 409 (8th Cir. 1975)

Tyler—517 F.2d 1089 (5th Cir. 1975)

United Public—330 U.S. 75 (1947)

United Steelworkers—830 F.2d 924 (8th Cir. 1987)

Unitel Corp—731 S.W.2d 636 (Tex. App. 1987)

Ursic—719 F.2d 670 (3d Cir. 1983)

Usery—544 F.2d 148 (3d Cir. 1976)

Va. Electric—703 F.2d 79 (4th Cir. 1983)

Vaca—386 U.S. 171 (1967)

Vagelahn—167 Mass. 92 (Mass. 1896)

Valdes—501 A.2d 166 (N.J. App. 1985)

Valentine—654 F.2d 503 (8th Cir. 1981)

Vann—494 A.2d 1081 (Pa. 1985)

Velantzas—536 A.2d 237 (N.J. 1988)

Vermont Camping—497 A.2d 353 (Vt. 1985)

Vernon—731 P.2d 480 (Utah 1986)

Vigil—687 P.2d 1038 (N.M. 1984)

VIP Development—472 N.E.2d 1046 (Ohio 1984)

Visser—530 F. Supp. 1165 (N.D.N.Y. 1982)

Volk—638 F. Supp. 1555 (C.D. Ill. 1986)

Wachsman—704 F.2d 160 (5th Cir. 1983)

Wade—741 P.2d 634 (Alaska 1987)

Wagenseller—710 P.2d 1025 (Ariz. 1985)

Wagner—722 P.2d 250 (Ariz. 1986)

Wainwright's Travel—500 A.2d 476 (Pa. App. 1985)

Walker—185 Cal. Rptr. 617 (Cal. App. 1982)

Wallace—393 A.2d 43 (Pa. App. 1978)

Walters—803 F.2d 1135 (11th cir. 1986)

Wandry—384 N.W.2d 325 (Wis. 1986)

Wang—501 N.E.2d 1163 (Mass. 1986)

Warsocki—726 F.2d 1358 (8th Cir. 1984)

Wash. Metro.—506 A.2d 1127 (D.C. 1986)

Washburn—831 F.2d 1404 (8th Cir. 1987)

Washington Aluminum—370 U.S. 9 (1962)

Wassenaar—331 N.W.2d 357 (Wis. 1983)

Watson #1—720 P.2d 632 (Idaho 1986)

Watson #2—108 S. Ct. 2777 (1988)

Weahkee—587 F.2d 1256 (D.C. Cir. 1978)

Webster #1—118 S.W.2d 1082 (Tex. App. 1938)

Webster #2—499 A.2d 1117 (Pa. App. 1985)

Weinberger—420 U.S. 636 (1975)

Weiner—443 N.E.2d 441 (N.Y. 1982)

Weingarten—420 U.S. 251 (1975)

Weisman—519 A.2d 795 (Md. App. 1987)

Welch—727 P.2d 140 (Or. App. 1986)

West Coast Hotel—300 U.S. 379 (1937)

Western Airlines—105 S. Ct. 2743 (1985)

Western Media—727 P.2d 547 (Mont. 1987)

Westport—517 A.2d 1050 (Conn. App. 1985)

Wheeler—496 A.2d 613 (D.C. 1985)

Whirlpool—435 U.S. 1 (1980)

White—660 F.2d 680 (5th Cir. 1981)

Whitlock—715 P.2d 1017 (Idaho App. 1986)

Whittlesey—35 FEP Cases 1089 (2d Cir. 1984)

Wiersma—401 N.W.2d 265 (Mich. App. 1986)

Wiggins—357 S.E.2d 745 (W. Va. 1987)

Williams #1—734 P.2d 854 (Okla. App. 1987)

Williams #2—406 N.W.2d 222 (Mich. App. 1987)

Willis—376 P.2d 568 (Cal. 1962)

Wimberly—107 S. Ct. 821 (1987)

Winston—105 S. Ct. 1611 (1985)
Wirtz—391 U.S. 492 (1968)
Woods #1—579 F.2d 43 (4th Cir. 1978)
Woods #2—525 A.2d 1262 (Pa. App. 1987)
Woolley—491 A.2d 1257 (N.J. 1986)
Wygant—106 S. Ct. 1842 (1986)
Wyndham—354 S.E.2d 399 (S.C. App. 1987)
Xerox—480 N.E.2d 695 (N.Y. 1985)

Yaindl—422 A.2d 611 (Pa. App. 1980)
Yamavchi—638 P.2d 1253 (Wash. 1982)
Ybarra—444 U.S. 85 (1979)
Young—509 F.2d 140 (5th Cir. 1978)
Zabkowicz—589 F. Supp. 780 (E.D. Wis. 1984)
Zadworny—404 N.W.2d 7 (Minn. App. 1987)
Zelenka—324 A.2d 35 (N.J. App. 1974)

Index